CONTENTS

Helion & Company Limited
Unit 8 Amherst Business Centre
Budbrooke Road
Warwick
CV34 5WE
England
Tel. 01926 499 619
Email: info@helion.co.uk
Website: www.helion.co.uk
Twitter: @helionbooks
https://helionbooks.wordpress.com/

Published by Helion & Company 2026
Text and maps © Kevin Wright 2026
Artworks by Renato Dalmaso and Jean-Marie Guillou © Helion & Company 2026

Cover image: A wartime member of the Royal Observer Corps scans the skies over central London, searching for enemy aircraft. (Crown Copyright)

Designed and typeset by Mach 3 Solutions (www.mach3solutions.co.uk)
Cover design Paul Hewitt, Battlefield Design (www.battlefield-design.co.uk)

Every reasonable effort has been made to trace copyright holders and to obtain their permission for the use of copyright material. The author and publisher apologise for any errors or omissions in this work, and would be grateful if notified of any corrections that should be incorporated in future reprints or editions of this book.

ISBN: 978-1-806722-88-4

British Library Cataloguing-in-Publication Data
A catalogue record for this book is available from the British Library

All rights reserved. No part of this publication may be reproduced, stored in a retrieval system, or transmitted, in any form, or by any means, electronic, mechanical, photocopying, recording or otherwise, without the express written consent of Helion & Company Limited.

We always welcome receiving book proposals from prospective authors.

Note: In order to simplify the use of this book, all names, locations and geographic designations are as provided in *The Times World Atlas*, or other traditionally accepted major sources of reference, as of the time of described events.

ABBREVIATIONS AND ACRONYMS

ACM	Air Chief Marshal
ADGB	Air Defence Great Britain
Air Cde	Air Commodore
AM	Air Ministry
AOC	Air Officer Commanding
ARP	Air Raid Precautions
CAI	*Corpo Aereo Italiano* (Italian Air Force)
CAS	Chief of the Air Staff
CROC	Commandant Royal Observer Corps
DEMS	Defensively Equipped Merchant Ship
Flt Lt	Flight Lieutenant
FO	Flying Officer
GPO	General Post Office
LCVP	Landing Craft Vehicle Personnel
LDV	Local Defence Volunteers
MoHS	Ministry of Home Security
Obs Lt	Observer Lieutenant
Obs Off	Observer Officer
OC	Observer Corps
OCLO	Observer Corps Liaison Officer
ORB	Operational Record Book
PDU	Photographic Development Unit
PO	Pilot Officer
RAF	Royal Air Force
RDF	Radio Direction Finding
ROC	Royal Observer Corps
ROCC	Royal Observer Corps Club
ROCLO	Royal Observer Corps Liaison Officer
RSS	Radio Security Service ('Y' Service)
SASO	Senior Air Staff Officer
TNA	The National Archive
USAAF	United States Army Air Force
WAAF	Women's Auxiliary Air Force

INTRODUCTION

In this volume, I concentrate entirely on the Observer Corps during the Second World War. Researching this book has been fascinating; my regret is that it is not possible to include far more material than space allows.

We go from the very first days of mobilisation through to the last days of the war. I have tried to capture as many aspects of the topic as possible, ranging from the high politics of the Cabinet and Royal Air Force (RAF) Fighter Command to the stories of individual Observers and their wartime experiences.

Bear in mind that some of the individual incidents I have detailed here are just a microscopic proportion of many thousands more that went unnoticed or unrecorded. They are intended just to give a flavour of the events that happened every day across the country to men and women Observers.

During the writing of this book, a few remarkable things became clear about the men and women of the Corps who served during the war. First, they came from every social background and every possible occupation. From those who took on the task full-time to those who did regular part-time shifts, at all hours of the day and night. These thousands of men and women volunteered for a wide variety of reasons, from liking aircraft, feeling they 'should do their bit', to some looking for excitement. The tenacity required to turn up for shifts after a hard day's work, and the Post members who watched outside in all weathers throughout the war, should never be underestimated.

Then there was the extraordinary. From reporting events at Posts set on roofs high above British cities amid bombs falling all around, helping aircrews escape from crashed aircraft, working in Centres with incendiary bombs striking the building, being beneath a V-1 'flying bomb' and hoping its engine did not cut out, to being a volunteer on a merchant ship anchored off the coast of Normandy during the D-Day invasion. And doing these things not just once, but repeatedly.

Being British, there were sometimes grumbles, but when it counted, Observers were there and often did more than 'their bit' in all weathers and at all times and with great modesty and not a little humour. However, most of what they did went unnoticed, and the importance of their task was not often appreciated outside the circle in which they worked.

I have drawn heavily on National Archive files and the Royal Observer Corps (ROC) Archive now held by Hampshire County Council. My thanks especially to Alistair McCann for lots of help, but especially for copying his collection of ROC Operating Instructions, Ed Combes and the Mersea Island Museum for their help with materials and images. Inaccuracies and omissions are entirely down to me.

1
THE LAST DAYS OF PEACE

The Observer Corps had consisted of just two Groups when it was first formed in 1925. It numbered 10 Groups a decade later, in 1935, by the eve of war in 1939, had ballooned to 33 Groups that now covered England's and Scotland's eastern coastlines. In 1940, coverage would reach the south-west of England, Wales and the rest of Scotland.

The 1938 Munich crisis had seen the Observer Corps mobilised for the first time. While it proved that the Observer Corps could be quickly activated, the short period of mobilisation did not test its operational procedures or the organisation's resilience to operate for a prolonged period. The crisis showed many shortcomings that needed immediate attention, leaving the armed forces and civil defence organisations scrambling to address multiple deficiencies.

As the Danzig crisis unfolded during 1939, the RAF and Observer Corps both underwent a marked increase in the number of training exercises and in their size and complexity. In most earlier Observer Corps exercises, a variety of civilian light aircraft were 'hired' to take part and reported by Posts to their respective Centres. Aircraft recognition was considered unimportant because Posts were required only to report aircraft as 'friendlies' or 'hostiles'. This made reporting the many different aircraft types unnecessary, but could have been useful. During 1939, RAF aircraft were employed more systematically in much larger exercises in which the Corps participated.

Serious Training

A whole series of 'minor' air exercises was planned each month from February to June 1939.[1] In July, there were two 'Fighter Group' 24-hour exercises, one each for 11 and 12 Groups of Fighter Command. These also involved the Observer Corps Groups linked to each Fighter Group and some adjoining Groups. The RAF 11 Group exercise was scheduled for 8–9 July, and the 12 Group exercise for 13–14 July, 1939.

For the 11 Group exercise, the aim was 'to test the operational efficiency of No 11(F) Group and the air defence system in the South East of England'. That area was to cover the coast of south-east England, from Great Yarmouth to Bridport and inland south of a line from Bridgewater to Newport to Saffron Walden to Great Yarmouth. RAF Bomber Command's 1, 2, 3, 4, 5, and 6 Groups were to provide 'hostile' aircraft. These aircraft were to fly out to sea, in minimum-sized groups of three aircraft, to 100 miles out from the coast (60 miles for the Fairey Battle aircraft), then turn back towards land at no less than 2,000 feet. On reaching the coast, they could descend below 2,000 feet if they wished. There was also limited participation by anti-aircraft gun and searchlight units.[2]

In preparation for these exercises, the General Post Office (GPO) had to switch over the necessary telephone circuits to the appropriate Fighter Command and Observer Corps units, including Horsham, Maidstone, Winchester, Oxford, Bury St Edmunds, Watford, Colchester, Bromley, Yeovil, Bristol and Gloucester. The only raids to be tracked were those reported and numbered by Radio Direction Finding (RDF) stations, which required special linkages to the coastal Groups (Bury St Edmunds, Colchester, Bromley, Maidstone, Horsham and Winchester). The RAF was keen to get as many RAF and RAF Volunteer Reserve personnel, whose war duty stations were the Groups and Sector Operations Rooms, to take part as possible. Participating RAF stations were also expected to put their 'station schemes' against air attack into effect and test their gas warning systems.

Table 1: Observer Corps Groups direct lines to nearby RAF 11 Group Sector Stations

1 Group, Maidstone	RAF Hornchurch and RAF Kenley
2 Group, Horsham	RAF Tangmere and RAF Kenley
3 Group, Winchester	RAF Northolt and RAF Tangmere
4 Group, Oxford	RAF Northolt
14 Group, Bury St Edmunds	RAF Debden
17 Group, Watford	RAF Northolt, RAF North Weald, RAF Hornchurch, RAF Kenley, RAF Debden
18 Group, Colchester	RAF North Weald and RAF Hornchurch
19 Group, Bromley	RAF Hornchurch, RAF Biggin Hill, RAF Kenley, RAF North Weald and RAF Northolt

MANUFACTURER OF PORTABLE BUILDINGS GARAGES. GREENHOUSES POULTRY HOUSES AND APPLIANCES

CONTRACTOR TO THE AIR MINISTRY

TELEPHONE . ROCK 204

April 5th.1939.

Dear Sir,

You have, no doubt, been informed that I have to supply and erect the necessary GUARD HUT and FENCE for your Observer Post. As there are 65 to be erected in Scotland in three weeks I should be very grateful to have your kind co-operation in this work. During the last three weeks we have been doing the East Coast of England and there the Head Specials have assisted me considerably and I have no doubt that the Scotland gentlemen will be just as considerate.

It is difficult for me to tell you exactly when the Hut will arrive at your Post but it will give you some idea when I say that your number on the delivery list is 14. and that we are commencing on Thursday of this week to load at the rate of four Huts per day.

Men will follow to erect and they will commence at the beginning of next week.

My men will probably call at your address for directions and the erecting men will have a Certificate to be signed by you. Will you also please see that they leave you the key.

Thanking you in anticipation of your kind co-operation,

To Head Specials,
Observer Corps,
Scotland Groups, No.31, 34, 36.

Yours faithfully,

W A Pound.

During the 'Munich Crisis' mobilisation in September 1938, the Corps' individual Posts were suddenly authorised to erect small huts to provide shelter for their Observers. During 1939, as expansion continued in northern England and Scotland, things became more organised. Contractors WA Pound from near Kidderminster in the West Midlands were employed to construct a large number of 'Guard Huts' at Observer Corps Posts. (Alistair McCann)

In a sequence titled "Air 'Invasion' of Britain", *Gaumont British News* filmed a brief news report of the July 1939 RAF air exercises for cinemagoers in those last weeks of peace. Large numbers of RAF Hampdens, Wellingtons, Battles, and Blenheims acted as hostile raiders.[3] (Crown Copyright)

Post-Exercise Conference

A major post-exercise debrief took place at HQ RAF Fighter Command on 24 July 1939 to discuss the experiences of 11 and 12 Group in the two July exercises.[4] In his opening remarks, the chairman, Air Chief Marshal (ACM) Hugh Dowding, expressed satisfaction with the newly introduced procedures that relied on RDF as the primary means to identify incoming enemy raids. He stated that he had high confidence that:

> When the RDF system is complete, it should be possible to rely on RDF getting 100% of the raids identified and numbered. At the present time, low raids cannot easily be detected, but the scientific developments now being carried out at Bawdsey should soon enable all the low raids to be detected with the same accuracy as the high raids.

Of the Observer Corps' reporting, Air Commodore (Air Cde) Keith Park said that the new reporting system had actually increased the reporting lag from the report at the Post to reaching 'the user' from between one and two minutes to between two and three-and-a-half minutes. This was believed to be attributable to the Observers wanting to ensure their reports were accurate before passing on the information to their Centre.

Both Fighter Groups expressed a general dissatisfaction with the number of 'enemy' bomber missions committed to the exercise, which was reiterated by the Observer Corps Commandant Air Cde Warrington-Morris, saying that 'Many of the Observer Posts had telephoned to the Centres to find out if the Exercises had been cancelled, as they had not seen or reported any aircraft for considerable periods'. Other exercise participants criticised Bomber Command for not providing enough aircraft. Civil aircraft movements also presented difficulties, as they were often classified as raids by RDF operators and were therefore unnecessarily plotted. The reality, as everyone would soon discover, was that although these difficulties were not always good for training, they were a much closer reflection of wartime experience.

Before the 'mass debrief' conference, both the RAF's 11 and 12 Groups had prepared their own exercise reports that had a little more detail on the Observer Corps' performance. 11 Group considered that, allowing for the prevalence of cloud during the exercise, 'the information supplied by the Observer Corps was of a high standard'. Working with, and indeed becoming reliant on, RDF was a growing feature of operations. Within coastal Groups, the procedure was applied where RDF detected raids out at sea; they numbered them. The RAF passed the details to the Observer Corps, which passed the essentials to the coastal Posts likely to see the incoming aircraft. The information came directly from Fighter Command to the 'Sea Plotter' in Observer Corps Centres, a semi-covert term used to disguise the use of RDF. As raids disappeared from RDF coverage, when they passed over the coast, or were too close to an RDF station, the Observer Corps Post could ensure an accurate continuity of track, so avoiding confusion or the false alerting to 'new' raids. However, RDF was not the complete panacea it was sometimes believed to be. During the exercise, one RDF station suffered a defect that caused it to generate fictitious raids, which the Observer Corps was then blamed for failing to detect. In other instances, thick clouds or low-flying raiders operating beneath RDF coverage meant that RDF could not detect some raids. There was also a complete procedural reliance on RDF to identify enemy raids. In some situations, where the Observer Corps occasionally picked up something RDF missed, the Observer's report was not believed and so went untracked. This was particularly the case for low-flying raids, where the 'Low Raid Urgent' priority message that could be passed by Posts and Centres was simply ignored, and so the raid went unreported. Such was the problem, that the importance of reporting and recording of a low-flying enemy aircraft below 1,000 feet had to be reinforced through the issuing of HQROC Operating Instruction No. 53 reminding everyone how important it was to track even individual enemy aircraft movements.

Coastal Groups needed to be given the facility to originate details of raids on their own initiative. This procedure could also be adopted when RDF stations become inoperable for whatever reason. For exercises, the Fighter Groups utilised the concept of 'Lost Property Offices' in their Operations Rooms, where small cells of individuals reconciled differences between RDF information and that from the Observer Posts, to eliminate duplication or confusion.[5]

RAF Sector stations connected to Observer Corps Groups would sometimes pass information to them on outgoing friendly aircraft, with approximate departure and return timings. This enabled the Centres to monitor the movements of some friendly aircraft and so avoid mis-labelling and misidentifications that would have been reported back up to the RAF as enemy raids.[6] From RAF 12 Group monitoring of Observer Corps personnel, there were also criticisms that some personnel used 'irregular' speech when passing information. They felt this meant time was wasted clarifying details if the correct telling procedures were not precisely adhered to.[7]

Full-Scale Home Defence Exercise

The largest exercise scheduled for 1939 was the annual 'Home Defence Exercise' from 9 to 11 August, to involve Horsham, Maidstone, Winchester, Oxford, Coventry, Derby, Lincoln, Bedford, Bury St Edmunds, Cambridge, Norwich, Watford, Colchester, Bromley and part of East Riding and North Lincolnshire Observer Corps Groups. In addition to RAF and Observer Corps participation, blackout exercises were scheduled for selected local authority areas.

The exercise was described by TE Winslow as the 'first full-scale practice for the defences that had taken place, and involved a large number of bomber and fighter squadrons, Anti-Aircraft Divisions, the Observer Corps and Air Raid Warning organisation'. As he described it.[8]

The RAF employed large numbers of Wellingtons, Hampdens, Battles, Blenheims, Hurricanes and Spitfires. However, the difficulty in differentiating between 'enemy' and 'friendly' aircraft was becoming increasingly apparent. Not prepared to employ any aircraft recognition skills, resort was made to ensuring that friendly bomber formations flew in line astern and that fighters had their undersurfaces painted half white and half black to assist identification. After the early communication problems, the main difficulty was the prevalence of low cloud during the exercise. It enabled small bomber formations of three to six aircraft to evade detection by both RDF and the Observer Corps with relative ease.[9]

Throughout the reports, there is no mention of RDF's role in detecting raids approaching from the sea. That is perhaps unsurprising given the secrecy surrounding the system at the time; instead, the raid detections out over the sea were credited to the Observer Corps.

214 Squadron Wellingtons took part in the 1939 as Eastland Forces attacking Westland, defended by friendly fighter forces supported by the RAF and the Observer Corps. To help the Observer Corps and RDF identify Eastland bomber formations, they were required to work in formations of three aircraft to simulate large raid formations. (Crown Copyright)

Made after the Munich Crisis, 'The Warning' was a 30 minute official film, restored by the British Film Institute, gives an idealised view of all the elements civil and home defence preparations in Britain during 1939. Perhaps the most chilling part was the expected widespread use of gas attacks. (BFI)

THE AUGUST 1939 AIR EXERCISES WERE NEWS AROUND THE WORLD

The British Official Wireless Service was funded by the Foreign Office and broadcast from the General Post Office high-power wireless station at Rugby. News agencies and newspapers around the world used the information it broadcast. Some of the best details about the August 1939 exercises available today come from New Zealand newspapers, which utilised information broadcast by the British Official Wireless Service.

These newspaper articles provide an official account of the day's main activities, reflecting the British Official Wireless Service's role in broadcasting news overseas. In New Zealand, the *Auckland Star* reported on 9 August 1939

BOMBERS DIVE ON CITY OF LONDON. HEAVY OFFENSIVE. Battles Between Raiders And Defenders.

MIMIC WARFARE
BRITISH AIR FORCES
EFFICIENT OBSERVATION
RAIDERS DETECTED
(British Official Wireless.)
(Received August 9, 1.30 p.m.)
RUGBY, August 8.

Air "warfare" broke out at 8 o'clock tonight for "Westland"—an imaginary state comprising over twenty counties to the east of the southern half of England, and including London.

"Westland" fighter squadrons and their ground organisations were anxiously on watch, as the time and objectives of the first attacks by the "Eastland" bombers were unknown. "Eastland," with 500 of the most modern bombers, was expected to launch wave after wave of its planes across "Westland's" frontier, which was defended by 800 aeroplanes, including the world's fastest fighters, reconnaissance machines, and bombers ready to retaliate on the "Eastland" bases. "Westland" also had 15,000 Territorials to man the anti-aircraft guns and searchlights, ten squadrons of the London balloon barrage, and fifteen groups of observer corps equipped with secret apparatus stretching invisible feelers into the night sky to seek out high-flying raiders.

This is the greatest mimic war in the history of the Royal Air Force.

Despite low visibility and intensive activity by the air raiders, the observer system worked perfectly, detecting and reporting all aircraft crossing the coast. Many squadrons of "Westland" bombers made counter raids against "Eastland."

SOUTH-EASTERN ENGLAND
ATTACKS FROM SEA
STURDY DEFENCE

OBSERVER SYSTEM WORKED PERFECTLY
MIMIC WARFARE
BRITISH AIR FORCES
EFFICIENT OBSERVATION
RAIDERS DETECTED

This year's exercises of the Royal Air Force - from next Tuesday until the following Friday - will be on a larger scale than ever before. In the manoeuvres, which will include important night operations, there will be engaged more than 1,000 aeroplanes of different types - bombers, fighters and scouting machines - and a ground staff of 20,000 men. The latest methods of attack and defence will be tested in operations of a magnitude never before possible. Coinciding as they will with the Territorial Army camp season, the exercises will enable members of the anti-aircraft and Observer Corps to co-operate.

A blackout over 27 counties, including London, in the early hours of August will he incidental to the manoeuvres. Approximately 1300 'planes will participate in the exercise which will commence on Tuesday next. They will test air and ground defences of Britain and the efficiency of the Air Force.[10]

From 11 August 1939, the *Auckland Star* provided a further report with more details of the activities.

BOMBERS DIVE ON CITY OF LONDON.
HEAVY OFFENSIVE. Battles Between Raiders And Defenders.
RAF WAR GAMES CONTINUE.

British Official Wireless. (Received 10.30 a.m.) RUGBY, August 10.

Eastland conducted a heavy offensive against Westland during the hours of darkness, says the official report of the progress of the RAF exercises up to 1 am. The enemy had concentrated on targets around the Thames Estuary, while Kent, Surrey, Sussex and South London were also heavily attacked.

In the northern area Eastland made 60 raids during the early morning and about 40 fighter patrols went up to meet them. A number of these raids were intercepted and Westland bomber squadrons continued a counter-offensive during the night. The Observer Corps continued to work smoothly in spite of heavy activity and low clouds.

A small flight of Battle 'planes was intercepted over Southampton Water soon after 8am. A large force of bombers again attacked Southampton half an hour later, but was intercepted by fighters.

Eastland bombers then began to attack on a wider front. Raiders were intercepted two miles north of Skegness. Twelve enemy bombers were intercepted by defending fighters five miles northwest of Maidstone. Three battle 'planes were intercepted near Tollbridge. Eleven battle 'planes were met by fighter squadrons over Southend-on-Sea.

Soon after 9am a number of raiders began to converge on London. Eight formations moved up the Thames Estuary and some swept up the front of the south-east counties, where they met sturdy defence by fighters and anti-aircraft batteries. Some of the raiders succeeded in circling round London to the west, where they had a hot reception in the neighbourhood of Uxbridge and Surbiton.

In the northern area of Westland a lull continued until 9.30am when bomber movements were detected by the Observer Corps some miles from the coast. Between 10 and 11am raiders came over Chelmsford, and others over points east of Cambridge. An enemy squadron, making for the north-east of London, was beaten off by fighter aircraft and anti-aircraft batteries.

Action over the east coast near the Wash began again between 10 and 11am. Two raids converged on a point near Lincoln, and another penetrated as far as Burton-on-Trent. Interception fighters were active throughout the operation.

GOOD TRAINING, BUT AT A COST

Both Fighter Command and Bomber Command were markedly increasing their crew training efforts; however, these efforts had a human cost. East Anglia housed many RAF bomber units at the time, among them was 149 (East India) Squadron. Based at RAF Mildenhall in Suffolk, part of 3 Group, it had swapped its old Heyford bombers for Wellington Mk1s in January 1939. The squadron took part in the many exercises that year. On 9 August 1939 Wellington L4258 took off from Mildenhall to practice a night bombing raid during the first evening of the RAF's largest pre-war air defence exercise. The general weather was poor, with limited visibility due to low cloud and drizzle. It is believed that the aircraft came down in the sea somewhere off the Norfolk coast, near Happisburgh, probably on its run out or in, from the coast. All five crew members were lost, and the aircraft has never been recovered.

The briefest of reports was carried in *Flight Magazine* on 17 August 1939:[11]

> With reference to the disappearance on August 9 of an aircraft of 149 Squadron, the Air Ministry announces with regret that, as extensive searches have failed to find the aircraft and the occupants, it must now be accepted that the following personnel lost their lives on that date[.]

The same issue of *Flight Magazine* carried details of two more aircraft lost during the same exercise in a further Air Ministry announcement. During the night of 10/11 August, taking part in the same exercise, two RAF Hurricane pilots from RAF Biggin Hill. Flying Officer (FO) Arthur Robin Buchanan-Wollaston and Pilot Officer Harold Stewart Olding were killed when they crashed into hills at Tatsfield, near Biggin Hill, in two separate incidents. P/O Olding volunteered for blackout patrol on a night of poor visibility. The Merlin engine of his Hurricane L1567 cut out, and he crashed into the hill at Tatsfield. Minutes later, F/O Buchanan-Woolaston was ordered to drop a flare by Olding's crash site. He, too, flew into the side of the hill less than 100 yards from the first wreck. Both men were killed.

The New Zealand Evening Post reported a further loss on 12 August 1939: 'A RAF bomber participating in a raiding test struck a high-tension cable at Cranfield and caught fire. Two occupants were killed, including an Australian, Flying Officer William Kinane'.[12]

At the end of the day on 10 August 1939, Sir Kingsley Wood, then Secretary of State for Air, passed a message of thanks to members of the Corps via Group Centres for the day's activities. Noting also the poor weather, he said, 'This is one more indication of the keenness and enthusiasm of the Corps as a whole, which continued undampened in spite of the weather'.[13]

That keenness and enthusiasm would soon be put to the biggest test of all. With the August event over, Posts and Centres stood down from the exercise. At that stage, they were unaware that just 14 days after its end, they would be mobilised for real and remain on duty until May 1945.

2
THE CORPS READIES FOR WAR

The failure of Britain and France to guarantee Czech security in 1938 saw Nazi expansion plans unchecked. During 1939, the storm clouds gathered and eventually broke. Hitler began increasing pressure on Poland to pass the Free City of Danzig over to the Reich. In his need for oil to sustain German industry and the military, Hitler became even more bellicose towards Romania, making more impossible demands on the oil and resource-rich country. The war of words and diplomatic action grew ever more heated, with a level of fervour that made opportunities for a peaceful solution, other than capitulation to German demands, unlikely.

In Britain, by March 1939, Prime Minister Neville Chamberlain had become resigned to the fact that war with Nazi Germany was inevitable. Making a public statement on 17 March 1939, the following day he sought to explain to his Cabinet the policy change, saying that 'Up till a week ago we had proceeded on the assumption that we should be able to continue with our policy of getting on to better terms with the Dictator Powers, and that although those powers had aims, those aims were limited ... he had now come definitely to the conclusion that Herr Hitler's attitude made it impossible to continue to negotiate on the old basis... No reliance could be placed on any of the assurances given by the Nazi leaders'.[1]

On 31 March 1939, the Prime Minister announced to the House of Commons that Britain would go to war with Germany if there were an attempt to end Polish independence. From May 1939, German planning for the invasion of Poland intensified with the Danzig 'crisis' continually stoked to become the Nazi pretext for invasion. During the summer of 1939, in an increasingly febrile atmosphere, Britain's preparation for war became overt as events around Danzig and Poland reached boiling point.

Mobilisation

Much had been learned from the 1938 Munich crisis, when the Observer Corps was mobilised and initial steps taken to put it on a war footing. However, much remained to be resolved if the Observer Corps was to be made ready for the reality of war.

The experiences of the German Condor Legion bombers in the Spanish Civil War, and the rapidly expanding Luftwaffe, had fed a public perception and British military planning assumption that the first stage of any future war with Germany would likely see an immediate and massive air attack on Britain. As a result, British war plans built in the necessity of mobilising the Observer Corps at a very early stage.

At a Cabinet meeting on 21 August 1939, discussing preparatory war and mobilisation measures, the Air Ministry was relatively satisfied with the arrangements for the activation of the 'Air Defence Intelligence Scheme', of which the Observer Corps was a part, recording that it 'Can be put into operation in 24 hours and the Air Ministry do not consider it necessary that it is required at this stage'.[2]

On the evening of 23 August, developments had moved on, with orders being sent to police force Chief Constables to mobilise the Observer Corps the following day, 24 August 1939. Because of the longer time frame necessary for the mobilisation of anti-aircraft and coastal defence unit reservists, a preliminary warning to those 'key parties' had already been issued on 21 August. The orders for their full mobilisation were also passed to them on 23 August.[3]

The 18 Group Colchester Centre log records that by 20.30hrs on 24 August 1939, it was fully manned. In the following hours, the circuits to the many Posts in the Group were switched through, faults were resolved by GPO engineers, and the Group was readied for action. The same process was replicated in all the other Observer Corps Groups across the country.

Mobilisation Brings Change

At that stage, the terms of service for the Observer Corps, which had been inconclusively debated for so many years, were now rapidly put into place. This had to be done quickly, especially for those whose primary income would now become their Observer Corps service. Chief Constables were well aware that their administrative systems would not be able to cope with the huge expansion in administrative work this required. New mechanisms had to rapidly be put in place. It was accomplished through an expanded number of staff at Observer Corps Area HQs.

On 25 August 1939, the identical message was recorded in the Centre Logs of both 18 and 19 Group (Watford) as being passed to all their Posts, indeed across the whole organisation, that:

> In the event of War, the administration of the Observer Corps will be transferred from the Police to the Air Ministry.[4]
>
> Members will be asked to undertake either,
>
> (1) A guaranteed 48 hours per week at such time as ordered, or
>
> (2) Part-time service for a period of at least 3 months from the outbreak of war.
>
> The rate of pay in such a case will be 1/3d an hour whilst on duty with a maximum of £3 per week. No other expenses will be payable.
>
> Head specials of Posts will receive £1 per week for supervising duties and may draw the hourly rate for duty up to £2 per week (= £3 per week)
>
> Every Observer will shortly receive a form of application.
>
> The Controller, Assistant Controller of the Centre will be paid on a salary basis, details of which are being issued separately.

With the full transfer to the Air Ministry, Observers relinquished their Special Constable status. Those making the commitment to work full-time would become known as 'Class A' Observers and the part-timers 'Class B' although their terms and conditions would be somewhat modified over time.

The arrival of payment was a surprise to many; though some rejected the idea and refused it throughout the war. However, for most, the extra few shillings that the watch hours brought were useful.

WE TURN OUT

We can get a tiny glimpse of mobilisation of events at a more human level from some surviving documents. In an immediate post-war history compiled by an unnamed writer from 16 Group at Norwich, he outlined their mobilisation in a little more detail.

> The Home Defence Exercise was held from 19.00 August 9th till 19.00 August 12th.
>
> Exactly twelve days later, on August 24th, 1939, we were called out again, and this time it was not a false alarm.
>
> The police warned all Centre members to report for duty forthwith. There were now six crews, a provisional rota was devised, and each crew was informed of its watch periods. 'A' Crew, under WH Cleland, was the first on duty.
>
> The Posts members sorted themselves out into pairs and made their own rough rotas.
>
> It was an evening full of foreboding, and throughout the night, the elements made protest, giving us an augury of the fury that was to come. Those of us who were on duty will never forget that first wild night of the storm.
>
> At 11 o'clock, on September 3, 1939, Mr Chamberlain told us we were at war.
>
> THE PHONEY WAR
>
> War, but not the sort of war we had expected.
>
> A golden day of autumn, and we thought the bombing would start immediately. The Posts anticipated the worst, whilst the two on duty searched the skies for the first hostile planes, the rest set to work constructing makeshift shelters and digging slit trenches. A lot of hard work was put in on that Sunday.
>
> We felt surprised, and slightly hurt, when nothing happened. Admittedly, the first Air Raid Warning was sounded during the night, 'G' crew were on duty for this historic occasion - but it proved to be a false alarm.
>
> Actually, this period of inactivity was a blessing in more ways than one. It gave us the opportunity to organise ourselves.

The Observers' Lot

Following mobilisation in 1939, many issues surfaced that required attention, as routine patterns of operation and practice began to evolve. For most, the urgency of mobilisation and the outbreak of war gave way to anti-climax. Much of it became dull routine for Observers at Posts and Centres. Listening and watching for aircraft at the Posts in long shifts with just one other person as company, when there was no flying and in bad, wet, or cold weather, often unprotected, would naturally dampen anybody's enthusiasm and give rise to boredom. In Centres, although there were lots more people, long periods of inactivity again dampened crew members' interests.

Whilst the period of the 'Phoney War' created the space to address the shortcomings, it would take combat operations to fully shape the organisation. The continual manning of Posts and Centres allowed many 'wrinkles' in the observation and reporting system to be identified. With so many part-time Observers who had a primary employment elsewhere, this meant putting together duty rosters that did not create ruinously long shifts or severely interfere with the individuals' civilian working hours. It was often a challenging task for Head Observers and Centre Controllers. There were issues of equipment supply and Centre and Post protection to be resolved, so that Observers were at least not totally exposed to the machinations of the enemy and the vagaries of the weather.

Before the war, training was often rudimentary, with few opportunities for everyone to practise aircraft detection and use the approved reporting and telling sequences, even during major exercises. Most pre-war air exercises were conducted for the RAF's needs, with those of the Observer Corps understandably secondary at best. It meant that, for long periods, even while on duty, Observers might have nothing to do or report. Then there were questions about the individuals' capabilities. Those who might be best at seeing or hearing approaching aircraft might not have the best 'telephone voice' to report the sighting quickly, accurately, and clearly to the Centre's tellers. So creating pairs at Posts who could complement each other and work well together was an essential consideration for Head Observers preparing the duty rosters.

The Corps' social mix was always interesting throughout its existence. The Norwich Group wartime historian captures some of this in his description:

> There was nothing snobbish about the Observer Corps. Each member was as good as his neighbour, whatever their

Every Post was different. In addition to the working area, each Post put together an area where Observers could prepare and eat a meal and most had a sleeping area. They varied hugely in structure and comfort, from the most basic to the more comfortable. (Picryl)

The sleeping area at another Post. (Picryl)

A very basic Post and exposed working area, with an image most likely taken during the winter of 1939-40, the period of the Phoney War. The domestic area was probably sited some distance away. (Picryl)

> respective civilian occupations. Do you remember that paraphrase which some wag chalked up at the Centre – 'Abandon rank all ye who enter here?' Nothing could illustrate better the democratic spirit of the Corps.[5]

The Corps drew members from all occupational groups and social classes with a wonderful mix of individuals. These included combinations of farm workers, bank officials, retired servicemen, shop workers, small business owners, mechanics, clerks, solicitors, accountants and so on.

Across the country, many different patterns of crew and Post organisation arose. In some locations, complete Centre or Post crews were provided by a single organisation, such as a factory or industrial plant. In Norwich, there was an early example of this dating from 1935:

> The choice of personnel was left entirely in the hands of the police, but the task of the Chief Constable of Norwich was considerably eased by the offer of the General Manager of the Norwich Union Fire office, Mr EF Williamson, who, in conjunction with the Manager of the Life Office, undertook to provide all the men required for the Centre. Thirty was the number, and they were sworn in as Special Constables in the Board Room of the Fire Office; Mr SC Spalding was chosen as Controller and Mr CF Hill, Assistant Controller.[6]

The extent to which such practices were a healthy approach to recruitment and manning has not been documented.

As in the early years of its history, official views varied on whether the Corps should be a civilian or military organisation. Members themselves often held different opinions on the nature of the organisation and their role in it. These ranged from many who regarded it as an entirely voluntary organisation, almost a 'club', in which outside views of officers and Group HQs were sometimes regarded with suspicion. Some were just keen on the task itself, with little regard for the administrative aspects. Others just wanted to 'do their bit'. Then some preferred the Corps' organised structure and civilian character. At the same time, others regarded it more as a military-style organisation and an adjunct to the RAF in particular. Those differences in attitude could vary between individual Posts and crews, and within them as well. It was to the credit of the organisation that it was such a broad 'church' able to accommodate and successfully operate with such a diverse composition, without resort to a rigid rule or discipline system.

Working Conditions

The working conditions for those at Posts and Centres could not have been more different. Posts in urban areas were often on the rooftops of public or private buildings, where access could sometimes be problematic. In rural areas, Posts could be close to human habitation, but were more often in isolated areas, situated in or next to open fields. Wind protection, weatherproof clothing, heavy boots, and somewhere to get warm were the bare essentials for the Post members to survive. Small sums were made available from public sources to enable Post crews to build some form of shelter for their Observers. However, many engaged their ingenuity and the skills of their members and friends to provide materials themselves and laboured to make their Posts as comfortable as possible.

Group Centres were often on floors within an appropriate local telephone exchange. They were frequently small, cramped and definitely not designed for the task they were now fulfilling. During operations, they could be very noisy, with lots of voices, the Group teleprinter, and telephones, and often hot as a result. Many accounts mention a fog of cigarette and pipe smoke in the room, as Norwich Group recorded:

> One ever-present problem during the hours of darkness in the Ops Room was the thick unhealthy atmosphere. Through the generosity of a Director of Boulton & Paul's, an Air Purifying Machine was installed, but its use was somewhat nullified by the fact that no instructions came with it, and no member ever solved how best to turn the knobs to bring it into proper operation. It was a frequent occurrence that, whilst members on duty were complaining of the heat, the internal parts of the machine were found to be coated with ice.[7]

During the Phoney War and, indeed, throughout the war, some Groups, including Norwich, moved from their original, often unsatisfactory pre-war accommodation to better, and later in some cases, purpose-built premises. For 16 Group, it was a move from Norwich's Dove Street to the much larger automatic telephone exchange a short distance away at St Andrews Street in May 1940. The new premises were viewed at the time by crews as 'great luxury' and 'the last word in comfort' compared to their old quarters.[8]

The original Watford Centre was in the town's GPO building. The conditions look decidedly cramped, and the furniture basic. Sitting, pencil in hand, at the highest vantage point is Centre Controller George R Bolton. (*Observers' Tale*, p.4)

From the 1920s, aviation captured the public's imagination, its achievements widely reported in the news and recorded on cigarette cards and other popular media. (Kevin Wright)

Aircraft Reporting

Mobilisation changed many things; among them was the introduction of twice-daily aircraft exercises, intended to improve aircraft detection, message-passing skills and test external communication links. These exercises were continued until August 1944, when they were discontinued, with some exceptions due to weather, enemy action, and major operations.[9] Such practice increased familiarity between individuals and quickly improved Post reporting.

One factor, which certainly seems peculiar today, was that at the time the Corps was not required to report the aircraft types that it saw and heard, merely that they could see or hear an aircraft, with some efforts to make distinctions between 'bombers' and 'fighters'. RAF Operations Rooms were expected to make the appropriate distinctions between 'friendlies' and 'hostiles'. It was an approach that undervalued the skills of many Observers and placed unfair expectations on RAF personnel to make accurate aircraft identifications in the frequent absence of complete information.

In the interwar years, the identification of aircraft by type had been accorded a low priority by the British military services. This practice continued with the new Observer Corps. After the First World War, the boundaries of aviation continued to be pushed ever further; Britain had become very much an 'air-minded' country. There was great public interest in aviation challenges and achievements, with new aircraft always under development. A large proportion of the population smoked, and cigarette packets contained cards with pictures and details of aircraft, new aviation successes, records, and were collected by adults and young people alike.

Frequent newspaper reporting created significant public interest in aviation, and some soon became experienced at aircraft recognition, certainly more than many members of the armed forces and the Observer Corps. Many schoolboys and adults soon became adept at recognising aircraft by type, well ahead of officially defined capabilities and requirements.

It was only in 1933 that the Air Ministry belatedly prepared an initially classified 'Restricted' publication, with the catchy title 'AP1480A'. This contained aircraft silhouettes to help authorised recipients learn to recognise them, and was eventually made available to the Observer Corps in 1935. Still, it was much criticised for its poor quality and lack of relevance with the silhouettes described as both 'limited and crude' because it did not include aircraft from potential adversary states.[10] The quality of AP1480 was said to be significantly improved after war was declared. However, it would be some time before the Observer Corps properly exploited the potential of aircraft recognition.

The 'Battle of Barking Creek'

The importance of accurate aircraft recognition was soon, tragically, brought home to the RAF by a mistake within just a few days of the start of the war that resulted in the death of a pilot. Inappropriately referred to as 'The Battle of Barking Creek', much of it is well known. Still, some recent research casts a slightly different light on events, calamitous as they were.

On 6 September 1939, at 06.15, a searchlight unit on the Essex coast detected a high-flying flight of aircraft over Mersea Island in Essex and reported it to RAF Sector Control at North Weald. The RAF's 11 and 12 Group HQs were also contacted. The RAF North Weald Sector Controller contacted 18 Group Observer Corps at Colchester to advise them of 'raiders' at 06.18. Neither RDF nor the Colchester Posts could confirm the raiders. At 06.30, RAF 11 Group scrambled six Hurricanes from 56 Squadron 'A' Flight and another eight from 'B' Flight, including the aircraft flown by Pilot Officer (PO) Rose and PO Hulton-Harrop, getting airborne between 06.40 and 06.50 to intercept the incoming raid.[11] Twelve aircraft from 151 Squadron also got airborne at 06.30.[12]

56 Squadron Hurricanes take off from RAF North Weald in 1939. (Crown Copyright)

The Sector Controller advised 18 Group Centre that fighters would be seen heading on an easterly course. By that time, 06.40, Observer Corps Posts were reporting unidentified aircraft at high altitude along the projected track of the raiders. Ten minutes later, the RDF station at Canewdon was reporting multiple contacts approaching the Thames Estuary. For the RAF's 11 Group, this was 'confirmation' to them of an enemy attack. They scrambled four flights of Spitfires from 54, 65 and 74 Squadrons, including 12 aircraft from 74 Squadron's 'A' and 'B' Flights from Hornchurch at 06.45.

In Greater London, air raid sirens were sounded as the formation was believed to be heading towards the metropolis. The popular account runs that two of 74 Squadron's Spitfires mistook the 56 Squadron Hurricanes ahead, silhouetted against the low morning sun, for enemy aircraft and attacked them. That the Hurricanes were shot at went against Fighter Command's standing instructions not to attack single-engined aircraft, as no German single-engine aeroplanes could yet reach Britain from their current German bases. Both Hurricanes were shot down as they were pursued towards Ipswich. The 56 Squadron Operational Record Book entry for the day records the simple fact of the loss and where the aircraft came down.

The airspace above which most of the action took place was monitored by the Observer Corps' Colchester Group, which recorded details of events that morning as they unfolded and later as the implications became more apparent. Messages go between the RAF's 12 Fighter Group at Hucknall, 11 Group at RAF Uxbridge, the RAF Sector Control at North Weald, and HQ 18 Group Observer Corps at Colchester. The log from Colchester Centre's 'A2' Watch records a message from North Weald:

06.18 Searchlight report aircraft flying very high over or near West Mersea – Posts informed.
06.26 Message from Uxbridge, Posts to keep a special lookout near Clacton.
06.27 North Weald reports six planes ordered to take off going East.
06.41 North Weald, six more planes taken off.
06.45 Air Raid Warning.
06.55 North Weald reports 12 planes taken off.

Nearly an hour-and-a-half later:

08.22 Hornchurch reports all our planes ordered to land.
08.30 Report of forced landing of plane in Ipswich area required by North Weald.

6.9.39.L.1990.	F/Lt. Soden.	"	0640	0745	" " " "
L.1992.	P/O Down.	"	0640	0745	" " " "
L.1983.	F/Sgt. Higginson.	"	0640	0745	" " " "
L.1985.	P/O Rose.	"	0640	0710	Shot down at Wherstead near Ipswich. Forced Landed.
L.1980.	P/O Hulton-Harrop.	"	0640	0710	Shot down near Ipswich. Killed.
L.1981.	P/O Illingworth.	"	0640	0745	Raid recognised as friendly. No Interception.
L.1986.	P/O EReminsky.	"	0640	0745	" " " "
L.1987.	F/O Coghlan.	"	0640	0745	" " " "
Magister. L.8277.	Sgt. Elliott.	"	0905	0945	To Martlesham Heath to collect P/O Rose.

The Hurricanes were shot down by pilots from 74 Squadron, and their Operational Record Book for the day contains some details about the day's events. (TNA AIR 27/527/2)

Appendix R.A.F. Form 541.

OPERATIONS RECORD BOOK.

DETAIL OF WORK CARRIED OUT.

From 1800hrs. 5 / 9 / 1939 to 1800hrs. 6 / 9 / 39. By "~~A" Flight~~ No.74 Squadron. No. of pages used for day 1

Aircraft Type and No.	Crew.	Duty.	Time Up.	Time Down.	Remarks.	References.
Spitfire.					A FLIGHT	
K.9932	F/L. Malan.	Patrol	0645	0725	To intercept enemy raid which turned out to be a	Form 765 of Summ…
K.9873	F/O. Measures.	"	"	"	friendly formation of Hurricanes of No.56 Squadron.	Dated 6.9.39
K.9870	Sgt. Hawken.	"	"	"	North Weald. F/O. Byrne and P/O.Freeborn opened fire	
K.9863	F/O. Byrne.	"	0645	0735	on two Hurricanes,thinking they were hostile Escort	
K.9865	P/O. Freeborn.	"	0645	0735	Fighters. Both Hurricanes were brought down. One pilot.	
K.9867	Sgt. Flinders.	"	0645	0735	P/O. Halton-Harrop, was killed. The other pilot was	
K.9953	F/O. Malan.	Training	1440	1535	uninjured. No enemy aircraft were sighted.	
K.9865	Sgt. Mould.	"	1440	1535		

Pilot Officer M L Hulton-Harrop was listed in the RAF Casualty List No 2, 25 September 1939, as 'Killed in Action, 6 September 1939'.[13] The event resulted in the arrest and, soon after, court-martial of Gp Capt Lucking, the Sector Controller, with F/Os Byrne and Freeborn from 74 Squadron also arrested. All were later cleared of wrongdoing. However, the whole event was a massive embarrassment for the RAF, which they kept as far as possible from public attention. (TNA AIR 27/641/1)

08.55 Report from Tattingstone Post – Hurricane [unreadable] reported by Mistley Police.

At 09:00, B1 Watch took over for the next shift.

08.58 Reported to Uxbridge that Post reported a plane down near Tattingstone and another one near M66.
09.02 All Clear given.
09.04 Hucknall asked for information regarding one Hurricane from Group 11. We are to report back if traced.
09.10 Reported to Hucknall, message received as 08.55 from Tattingstone.
09.18 J2 report Ipswich Police phone 2296 can give information about the missing plane.
09.19 Ipswich Police report plane to be a Hawker Hurricane piloted by PO Charles Rose from North Weald. Bullets in petrol tank and wings, Pilot uninjured.
09.20 Message received at 09.19 reported to Hucknall.
09.35 Hucknall ask for information about a plane marked L2080.
09.37 Ipswich Chief Constable refused to give us further information regarding crashes.
10.10 Hucknall asked for information re bombs dropped and enemy aircraft brought down – none could be given.
10.43 Hucknall asked if any enemy aircraft were plotted on our table. We were unable to give information of any.

As the day progresses and the calamity of what has happened sinks in, several messages are received from senior officers about what was seen, what was not, and what was recorded that day. At 11.30, the Group Controller (also the Colchester Borough Police Chief Constable), Col Herring, passed a report of events in response to the 10.10 message from Hucknall that hinted at issues with RDF reports:

11.30 Ref your phone message at 10.10hrs this morning.
1. Herewith recorder sheets for raid period 06.45 to 09.00.
2. Visibility throughout was poor owing to ground mist, audibility also seems to have been very bad. In several cases where the RDF gave position of a raid as immediately over a Post, the Post concerned could neither see nor hear anything.
3. Posts were unable to state with any certainty whether planes were friendly or hostile.

There are further enquiries later in the day from Group Captain Courtney, the Observer Corps Southern Area Commandant, trying to unearth more details, the final ones seeking to preserve any evidence.

15.05 Please keep in a safe place teleprinter report of air raids this morning, ready to be forwarded if requested.

It cannot be a coincidence that, in the following days, the Colchester Centre Log records far more detail from linked RAF Sector Controls, including times and aircraft launched from their airfields, as well as their training and operational activities.[14]

Recent research from Nick Black provides a very detailed account of the RAF's events that day, and attributes an early source of the confusion that developed to the RDF Chain Home Station at Canewdon. He suggests that a simple, but vital, technical failure in the RDF equipment at RAF Canewdon meant that a device designed to block extraneous radar returns outside of the Chain Home radar's field of view had failed, and this made it appear that the 151 Squadron Spitfires taking off were really approaching enemy aircraft. The over-reliance on the accuracy of RDF reports at the time likely led to the apparent attack escalating very quickly into the subsequent confusion.[15]

If the Observer Corps and RAF were poorly trained in aircraft recognition, the situation in the Navy was even worse. Naval gunners received no serious training in aircraft recognition. RAF pilots regularly accused them of shooting at any aircraft within sight of a ship or naval shore base. The Air Ministry adopted the view that failures in the RAF's plotting and telling systems caused the tragedy over North Essex, and procedures were subsequently modified.

The incident may perhaps have been avoided altogether if pilots had been better trained in aircraft recognition, or if Fighter Command and the Observer Corps had been better able to detect and record the movements of friendly aircraft, perhaps referring to them by type, rather than the imprecise reporting standards used at the time. It would be some time before the deficiencies in RAF and Observer Corps recognition training would be resolved.

Spy Fever

Was it the Observer Corps' still-close connection with local police forces, or just the general hysteria about enemy spies that led everyone to worry about enemy agents around every corner? In the early days after mobilisation, whilst waiting for the expected mass air attack, Posts were warned to keep a lookout for suspicious people and their activities and to report them to the local police.

The density of Observer Corps Posts created a near-nationwide network with a now-constant presence that no military organisation or even the police could rival. Its communications network enabled it to quickly pass information, via its Centres, on everything visible from the Posts. These included not just enemy and friendly air movements, but bombs and mines dropped, reporting lights and flares, major fires, destruction, plus anyone thought to be engaged in nefarious activities. After the initial post-mobilisation excitement calmed, it was a useful informal capability that often assisted British military and civil authorities for the rest of the war.

With the feverish atmosphere of mobilisation and the declaration of war, Observer Corps members were certainly on alert for enemy agents and saboteurs. Most, it would turn out, were legitimate individuals going about their own duties or, in the early days, the idly curious wondering why two men might be standing in a field all day. Centre logbooks contain many such reports of potentially suspicious activity; two give a taste of the type of events recorded.

In the Bromley Centre log for 26 September 1939, is a report from N2 Post (Cliffe in Kent):

> 17.30: N2 reported that four officers in Royal Engineers uniform came to the post in car No FLG 550 with a GB number plate. They enquired if it was an Observer Corps Post and also if there were any empty houses in the neighbourhood. They left hurriedly before the Post could detain them. The car was a large blue saloon. The driver was stout and of medium build age 40 – 50. The other three were about 35 – 40.

A margin note in the log records the action taken by the Centre:

> Cliffe Police rung but PC was out so Rochester Police were informed and are dealing with the matter. Liaison Officer also informed. Information passed to all posts.[16]

From Colchester (18 Group) on 7 November 1939:

> A1 (Bradwell) Post. At about 12.45, a car, DGU 535 with 2 occupants drew up at the telephone pole near the post. The occupants were looking at that and appeared to be intending to climb the pole. The Observer on duty approached and asked what they were doing and one man replied that they were connected with the electricity supply. They inquired if the electricity interfered with telephone reception. He also inquired how long Observers were on duty – whether for the whole 24 hours.
>
> The men then got in the car and drove off. One man was foreign looking about 35 to 40 5'8" ins in height, pale face, very dark blue suit, grey overcoat and trilby hat, black shoes. This man did not speak. There is no electricity within 5 miles. The man who spoke also inquired if any planes had been over. As the line was out of order the Post could not communicate with Centre and it did not occur to Observers to notify Police.
>
> Colchester Police informed of above.[17]

A lot of police time must have been spent dealing with such information from the public and Observers in those early months.

The First Raids

It was not until 16 October 1939, that the Luftwaffe put in a serious appearance with a raid on Rosyth in Scotland. The very secret British 'Y' Service had listened to Luftwaffe radio traffic. At 09.27, a German reconnaissance aircraft monitored the fleet. An attack by 12 Ju 88s followed in the afternoon, flying at 15,000ft. Their approach was initially detected by a Chain Home station, which soon went out of action due to a power failure. The Observer Corps 31 Group (Galashiels) and 36 Group (Dunfermline) Posts reported the raid's progress. Three ships were hit before defending fighters attacked two Ju 88s. The Germans returned the following day and struck the elderly battleship HMS *Iron Duke*.

ACM Dowding was pleased with the Observer Corps' actions that day, issuing the message:

> I am very pleased with the way in which the Observer Corps acquitted themselves in this, the first action of the war in which they are able to take part. The visibility conditions were difficult and the bomber formation split up into individual aircraft. In the circumstances I consider that the Observer Corps operated with great efficiency and I should like all concerned to be informed accordingly.[18]

In October 1939, with no mass Luftwaffe raids, there were soon efforts to try to save money. Whilst the coastal belt of Posts, up to a 30-mile depth, was to be maintained at Readiness (Posts and Centres fully manned), others more inland were to be at 'Available' level with one Observer at Posts and skeletal manning at Centres and other personnel to be available at 10 minutes' notice. The plan was poor, and the Groups would have been unable to quickly reach full manning in the event of a sudden attack.[19]

However, for most of the Corps, this period of the 'Phoney War' was a quiet one. Enemy action was generally low-key, which gave time for routines to develop and for across-the-board improvements and preparations to be made. Things would take a dramatic turn in spring 1940.

3
BEFORE THE AIR BATTLE

The period from the start of the war, through to the spring of 1940, was a comparatively quiet one for the Observer Corps. During this time the formation of Groups at Wrexham (26 Group), Lancaster (29 Group), Carlisle (32 Group), Glasgow (34 Group), Dundee (37 Group), Aberdeen (38 Group), Inverness (39 Group), Truro (20 Group), Exeter (21 Group), Carmarthen/Caernarvon (28 Group) and Oban (35 Group) were all completed. The Corps now covered most of the country, apart from Northern Ireland, the north-west of Scotland and some of the Scottish Islands.

The winter of 1939 was a bitterly cold one for everyone, but especially so for the men at the Posts standing in exposed fields or on top of high buildings. The most that was generally felt of the enemy presence was out to sea, where German reconnaissance aircraft could sometimes be heard, and occasionally seen by the coastal Posts. Overland, the watching mainly was of friendly aircraft movements and the daily training exercises, when the weather permitted. In the Centres, it was the hourly communication checks with the RAF Sector and Fighter Group Controls, the fog of cigarette and pipe smoke and efforts to keep boredom at bay.

That changed in spring 1940 with the Nazi invasion of Norway on 9 April 1940. The following month, 10 May, France and the Low Countries were invaded and the full force of Blitzkrieg quickly brought about military collapse across Western Europe.

Enemy activity gradually grew in the North Sea with raids on shipping and deeper probing reconnaissance missions. The coastal Posts, often in conjunction with the Coastguard, bore the brunt of the work, hearing explosions and aircraft engines, and sighting ships and lights out at sea.

Most likely filmed in the hard winter of 1939, *Eyes on the Skies!* was a segment of a British Pathe newsreel shown in 1940 praising the Observer Corps. (British Pathe)

Dunkirk Evacuation

As France collapsed, in the skies above it, the RAF lost nearly 1,000 aircraft to the Luftwaffe and German forces, heavily depleting the RAF's strength. However, the successful evacuation of large numbers of troops at Dunkirk was a significant achievement, even though they had lost all their equipment, in what was otherwise a disaster for the British Army.

Now Britain was in existential danger. During the Dunkirk beach evacuation, Operation Dynamo, the RAF's Photographic Development Unit (PDU), still a semi-clandestine unit not long moved from its original Secret Intelligence Service-led origins, played a significant role. Based at Heston aerodrome, it was regularly active at high altitude above the coasts of northern France and Belgium. Several of the very first Spitfires modified for photographic reconnaissance were seen by numbers of Posts up and down the British coastline, as they headed out on missions over Norway, the Netherlands, France, Belgium and Germany's North Sea coast.

During this period, the Colchester Centre Logs and other Groups regularly contain the details of scheduled PDU fighter movements. For the Observer Corps to be pre-warned in detail about these operationally critical flights was very unusual. The pilots of these early camera-equipped photographic reconnaissance Spitfires used the distinctive geographical coastal features, of the river estuary area around Southwold and Orfordness in Suffolk, to aid accurate navigation. An example of such a flight comes from the Colchester 5 June 1940 log, the day Hitler proclaimed that Dunkirk had fallen.

At 13.05hrs, RAF Uxbridge passed a message to Colchester about a forthcoming flight:

> From Uxbridge message F18
>
> PDU Spitfire No P9307 colour blue. Heston 14.30, Stradishall 14.50. Depart Stradishall 15.15, Southwold 15.30 at 15,000ft climbing. Return Southwold 17.45 at 25,000ft, arrive Heston 18.15.

Spitfire P9307 would have routed from Heston, refuelled at RAF Stradishall in Suffolk. Flown by Flying Officer SL Ring, its three hour mission was to cover airfields at Emden and Jever, close to the naval port at Wilhelmshaven, at 32,500 ft. On this early mark of the photographic reconnaissance Spitfire, the cameras were wing-mounted, but no images are available from that mission because of complete cloud covering the target. That same day, on a different sortie flown from Heston flown by Flt Lt Corbishley in Spitfire PR C, N3116 passed over the Bromley and Maidstone Group areas and collected some 116 images along the newly German occupied Belgian and French coastline to the north and south of Dunkirk, and a further 24 in an arc around just to the south of Antwerp.[1]

Timings for these photographic reconnaissance flights were regularly passed to Colchester, Bromley, Norwich and the other Observer Corps Centres by RAF Sector Controls throughout the summer of 1940 to prevent them from being misidentified as enemy aircraft. The number of Spitfire and soon Hudson sorties from RAF Heston PDU quickly ramped up as the RAF sought to gather intelligence over newly occupied Europe.

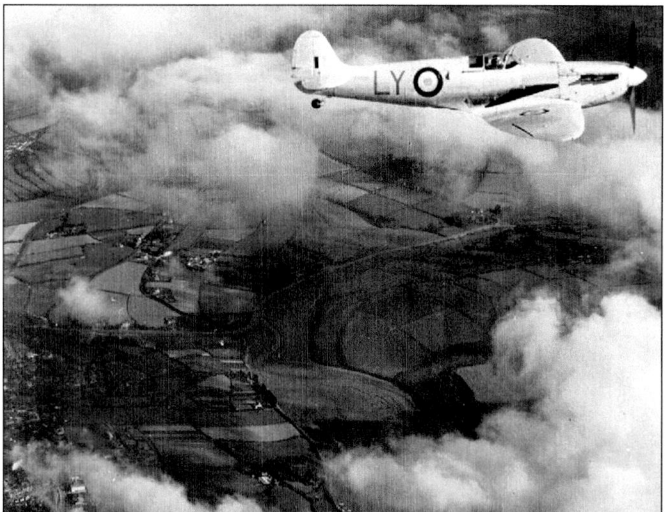
Early version Spitfire photographic reconnaissance aircraft engaged in low-level operations wore a very pale pink paint scheme at the start of the war. (Crown Copyright)

An image of the Dunkirk beach showing grounded vessels taken by Spitfire N3116 on 5 June 1940, the day after the beach had fallen into German hands. (NARA)

As well as the large number of RAF sorties to support the British Expeditionary Force and its retreat, there was also some civilian and 'non-British' air activity through May and June 1940. Aircraft from the Netherlands, Belgium and France brought fleeing government officials and some refugees to the east coast, watched and plotted by the local Posts. Some Royal Netherlands Navy aircraft evacuated to France before heading to England, with some 26 ending up at Calshot. Among them were eight Fokker T.VIII floatplanes that were eventually operated from the seaplane bases at Felixstowe and Pembroke for a while. Pressed into RAF service, they were operated by their Dutch crews and used for coastal patrols and some agent-related operations. Another Fokker T.VIII aircraft would join them in 1942, having escaped from the occupied Netherlands.[2]

Several Netherlands Air Force Fokker T8s escaped to Britain when it was occupied and soon pressed into service in RAF markings. (NIMH)

THE FLARE LINE

One of several additional tasks taken on by Observer Corps Posts was operating various flare systems to aid friendly aircraft attempting to return safely to their bases at night. The RAF requested the Observer Corps to use 'flares' at selected Posts. When lit, these created a pattern that returning bomber crews, equipped with a suitable map, could use to determine their position from the lights on the ground. The RAF provided these 'money flares'. They were kept at a large number of Posts, including five Posts in the Colchester Group. The Posts equipped with these flares stored them in a paraffin-filled bucket. When ordered to light them, they had to be hooked out of the bucket, placed on the ground, and lit with a match, all while taking a quick step back to avoid being burned. To put them out, they had to be hooked up again, put back into the paraffin, and a lid put on smartly to extinguish the flames![3]

Derek Wood described the whole process as 'messy, time-consuming and dangerous'. A description of the flare use at some coastal Posts in the Norwich Group illustrated some of the difficulties in a little more detail:

> Head Observer Bill Thurgur of P1 said "They made us as black as sweeps, and lugging five-gallon drums across a ploughed field at night was no joke, especially when some nights we used 30-40 gallons of oil…You should have heard the language when the order came to put them out as soon as we had lit them". Another Head Observer, Wilfred Southerland of N1, said, "The first time we lit them, we had Police, Army, RAF, ARP and everybody else up to see what was happening". Someone said, "They must be put out: didn't we know there was a blackout on? … The best show was when water got into the oil; it sent balls of fire about 20ft in the air". But the flares were used a lot, and they served their purpose.[4]

A further, small number of specially selected Posts along the edge of the RAF's nighttime 'Outer Patrol Line' were in coastal districts of the southeast. C2 Post, at West Mersea in Essex, was the only one in 18 Group and received sets of four flares to be lit on special instruction. When the heavy night raids began in 1940, it was felt that the flares just attracted enemy attention and confused the defences. Failures in communication, mainly because the appropriate RAF Sector Control did not inform the police, Home Guard and Air Raid Precautions (ARP) wardens, meant the flares were also often mistaken for signals to enemy aircraft and agents. This led to efforts to extinguish them and arrest the Post members. Sometimes these actions were near-fatal and later in the year they were withdrawn from use.

As the Luftwaffe settled into newly occupied airfields across Western Europe, the number of probing missions began to increase. From these new locations, the Luftwaffe could now reach virtually the whole of Britain. These started with reconnaissance flights, soon followed by attacks on shipping in the Channel and North Sea.

The fear of invasion was rapidly growing and creating a hysteria of its own. Even before the total collapse of France, the decision was taken to arm some Observer Corps Posts and Centres in likely invasion areas. On 18 May 1940, a message was received in Colchester, and at other Centres, from the Southern Area Commandant: 'The Commandant of the Observer Corps wishes to inform you that he is taking steps to have certain Posts armed with rifles'. Within three days, these had arrived at the Centre. The Observer Corps received its weapons even before the Local Defence Volunteers (later to become the Home Guard) was formed. In Norwich, the entrance to the Centre was already guarded by a policeman, and the Centre itself was now issued with six rifles and 300 rounds of ammunition. Each Post received two rifles and ammunition. Some officers were issued revolvers.[5] The Observer Corps and the police were the only two British civilian organisations to be armed during the war.

Soon, Post members were regularly reminded by Centres that they needed to wear their brassards and lapel badges when on duty, but this was not just about getting them to look somewhat more 'official' when about their work. This was much more about whether members would be regarded as 'combatants' or 'Non-combatants' if captured by the Germans following an invasion, and any subsequent protections that might, or might not, be afforded to them by the Geneva Convention as a result.

An Observer Corps armband and badge (sometimes worn with a beret), were believed by the Air Ministry to be an adequate uniform to afford Observers protection under the Geneva Conventions if captured by German invasion forces. (Via Picryl)

Civilian or Armed Service?

A significant body of correspondence tries to clarify the status of Observers going back to the mid-1930s. After the start of the war in 1939, thoughts became a little more focused.[6] A key point was that if the Observers wore their armband and lapel badge, which could be identified at 'gunshot distance' and were part of an organised body of men under orders, they might be regarded as combatants and thus receive the protections of the Geneva Convention. If they could not demonstrate this, they were unlikely to receive any such consideration. Instead, they risked being regarded as civilians 'performing military duties'.

One of the wonderful things about the Observer Corps was that it drew members from a vast range of occupations, many with very specialist expertise. In February 1940, the Observer Group Officer for 3 Group (Winchester) was a retired Major General Twiss. The Head Observer of his G3 (Freshwater) Post, himself a retired major, forwarded a letter to Twiss from one of the Post members asking for a ruling on whether service with the Observer Corps counted as 'Active Services with His Majesty's Forces in the United Kingdom'. The Observer asking the question was Mr Rigby Wason, a barrister. The Air Ministry informed Corps Headquarters, instead unconvincingly adhering to their original position, that the badge and beret afforded sufficient legal protection for Observers. By 19 May 1940, Commandant Warrington-Morris was instructing Area Commandants that Post members wear their 'uniform' items, as 'This has become more important now that landings by the enemy may take place'.[7]

The following day, 20 May, the situation changed again due to the decision to put the newly formed members of the Local Defence Volunteers (LDV) into uniform to ensure they received the protections under the Geneva Convention. This caused the uniform issue for the Observer Corps to be raised again, especially as they were now to be armed, whereas the Local Defence Volunteers, at that stage, was not.[8] By 4 June, the decision to issue blue 'combination suits' to Observers with badges led the Judge Advocate General to state that they now met the conditions for protection as combatants in war. However, Observers were regarded as civilian employees of the Air Ministry under English law.[9]

That same month, these overalls and berets began being issued as a priority along the coastal Groups. The overalls in particular were immediately despised by Post Observers.[10] The extent of derision with which they were regarded can be judged in a postwar account from 17 Group:

> There were boiler suits for men and a new style beret that might have been designed for a sailor on a water cart. The men looked like third rate plumbers [sic] assistants. There was no pretence at fitting; fat or thin, long or short, no one ever succeeded in looking presentable. But no outfit ever caused so much laughter. It was impossible to appear anything but comic in it, and when the new beret was added it was too, too much. When the spirit was jaded at an Observer Post became a place of melancholy the outfit could be produced and thereafter shrieks of uncontrollable laughter filled the air. The boiler suit and the beret were laughed out of existence and Observers continued to wear the strangely assorted garb which has so frequently inspired the cartoonist.[11]

It was only after the end of 1941 that a battledress pattern of uniform was issued for the Corps.

Fortunately, the wearing of a uniform was non-compulsory because of the practical difficulties it posed for some members who came straight to Observer Corps duty from their civilian occupations. There were also related issues about whether, as civilians, members of the Home Guard or the Observer Corps were required to hold valid firearms certificates to carry rifles. That situation was more easily resolved by stating that such certificates were not required if members carried weapons while engaged in official duties.[12]

The issues of uniforms, the status of Observers, the carrying of firearms, and comparisons with other war services, such as the Home Guard, ARP and Auxiliary Fire Service would rumble on well into 1941 and the further reorganisation of the Corps. Fortunately, the

Corps' status was never tested by enemy invasion. One wonders to what extent the average German paratrooper or infantryman would have devoted time to thinking about the legal status of a man he had captured in a raincoat, armband and lapel badge who perhaps had been shooting at him until a few minutes before.

The War Gets Warmer

As the fear of invasion grew, so did aircraft reporting activity during the fine summer of 1940. Secondary tasks expanded too. The Corps became a key element in the evolving invasion warning network. Observer Corps Posts, Coastguard positions and searchlight units were all expected to be among the first to see the beginning of any enemy invasion, whether from the sea or the air. Army Command and Home Guard formations developed links with appropriate Centres around the south-east coast. Had the German Operation 'Sea Lion' gone ahead, as the German High Command planned, Maidstone and Horsham Posts and Centres would have been vital in raising the alarm as the first German forces had landed.

The Observer Corps' extensive telephone communication system, with multiple links, made it an ideal mechanism to spread a general alert up the chain of command and across the country if the enemy landed. In case the Post communication system was disrupted during any enemy landing, they were issued with 'red star' distress flares to indicate enemy action on land in the hope that a neighbouring Post, still in communication, would be able to pass the warning. A green star flare indicated a seaborne assault and a white flare a submarine landing.[13]

The invasion of France and the Low Countries, on 10 May 1940, sparked an immediate scare, with warnings circulated among the Coastguard some of which also fed into the Observer Corps system: 'There is a possibility of enemy landing troops tonight or tomorrow morning by parachute from aircraft, or from small vessels. All Coastguards and Coast watchers are to be warned accordingly and keep a sharp lookout'.[14]

That warning caused significant disruption as it was subsequently passed to some of the RAF Sector Controls and other Observer Corps Centres in the south-east. What had started as a general warning passed around the Coastguard, sparked a much broader alarm. Unspecified 'measures' were taken subsequently to ensure such an incident was not repeated.

There was another regularly used selective early warning mechanism. For example, on many occasions, 18 Group Centre advised selected Posts along the coast in Essex, from the Thames Estuary to the Harwich naval port, were frequently instructed to adopt 'Special Vigilance'. This warning was passed to Posts at Southminster (M1), Foulness (M2), Bradwell-on-Sea (A1), West Mersea (C2), Brightlingsea (C3) and Clacton (D3). The same 'Special Vigilance' notifications for selected Posts are also recorded in the Norwich Group logs. The alerts applied to specially numbered areas that corresponded to grid squares on the Observer Corps' maps.[15] This warning required the Posts to be especially alert to the possibility of invasion or enemy incursion. The codeword 'Dull' was passed to the appropriate Posts to activate 'Special Vigilance', and it was terminated with the codeword 'Shining'.[16] On what basis the alert was raised remains uncertain; perhaps due to expected clear weather conditions, the moon cycle, or intelligence from other sources.[17]

Posts were instructed that in the case of a real invasion, and if they were forced to abandon their location, Observers were to cut telephone lines, take away, or destroy the Post Instrument and later. After their issue, the rifles and ammunition were to be taken away as well.[18]

Following RAF raids on the Ruhr on 17 May, a signal advising what response might be expected in the future from the Luftwaffe was passed from Fighter Command to Observer Corps Centres on 18 May 1940: 'German High Command threaten reprisals for our bombing in Germany last night, in which they say we attacked open towns. This is significant, and heavy attacks on this country must be expected in the immediate future'.[19]

That very evening, the German response came in the form of the heaviest raid on the country to date, a precursor to thousands more over the rest of the war. Over 100 aircraft attacked the country, the most serious publicly reported damage being to Vicarage Terrace in Cambridge, where a significant number of houses were destroyed and nine people were killed. However, the Germans did not get everything their own way.

The Heinkels of KG4 and KG27

Observer Corps Posts and Centres often witnessed air battles over their areas. One night in June would be a very busy one for the Observer Corps, RAF, and other home defences.

On 18 June 1940, Churchill delivered his prophetic speech to the House of Commons, warning that the Battle of Britain was about to begin as the air war was developing, and he ended with his immortal words: 'Let us therefore brace ourselves to our duties, and so bear ourselves that, if the British Empire and its Commonwealth last for a thousand years, men will still say, "This was their finest hour"'.

On the very night of 18/19 June 1940, the Luftwaffe launched its most significant night attack on Britain so far. Approximately 60 He 111s from three KG27 Staffels headed towards targets in the Midlands. There was action all across East Anglia too, with aircraft shot down on both sides. Around 30 He 111s from three KG4 Staffels, now based at Merville in France, targeted the RAF bomber bases at Mildenhall

In the company of the superlative Spitfire, the Bristol Blenheim was used by both RAF Bomber and Fighter Commands and seen almost every day by Observer Corps Posts all over the country. Around 200 Mk. I bombers were modified into Mk.IF long-range fighters, the first delivered in September 1938. By 1939, at least seven squadrons were operating them as fighters. The aircraft proved slower and less manoeuvrable than expected, and by June 1940, daylight Blenheim losses caused concern for Fighter Command, and the aircraft was relegated to night-fighter duties. (Kevin Wright)

and Honington and the oil storage tanks at Thameshaven. Bombs would be dropped near Bury St Edmunds, Clacton and Southend. That night, the German squadron would lose six aircraft to the British defences. Three RAF Blenheims and two Spitfires were also lost.

'C' Crew at Bromley Centre had come on duty at 23.00hrs. They were soon experiencing a hectic evening, with their log recording: 'Numerous tracks of X-raids and other tracks bearing Centre letter and number appeared on the table between 23.09 18/6/40 and 01.30, 19/6/40. All records and reports left with Controller'.[20]

Over Norfolk, a 23 Squadron Blenheim was shot down by a He 111 gunner, killing the pilot. Another 23 Squadron Blenheim pilot saw the event and, just north-east of Kings Lynn, spotted a He 111 caught in searchlight beams. During five attacks, Flt Lt Duke-Wooley and his gunner hit the aircraft, knocking out one engine, but were also hit several times themselves. The Heinkel force landed in shallow water off Blakeney Point in Norfolk.

Below the battle was P2 Post at Cley-Next-the-Sea. It was sat in a very exposed, open coastal position with good visibility. Some days earlier, it lost all its windows when they were blown out by a string of German bombs that had landed just 150 yards from the Post. But in the early hours on 19 June, they witnessed:

> A Heinkel coming in from the sea was intercepted by one of our fighters; a running fight took place between Wells and Cley, and the Heinkel was hit and burst into flames. It circled, and the pilot baled out over the sea, while the aircraft crashed on Cley beach. The pilot's cries for help were heard by the Observers on duty, and they 'phoned the Coastguards, who got out a boat and rescued the men.[21]

The aircraft was a He 111-H4 (fuselage code 5J + DM) of II/KG4. The captured men included KG4's new *Gruppenkommander*, Major Dietrich Freiherr von Massenbach, *Oberleutnant* Ulrich Jordan, *Oberfeldwebel* Max Leimer and *Feldwebel* Karl Amberger.

Meanwhile, in south Essex that night, German bombs were dropping across a considerable part of the county, causing disruption and damage, most seriously on Canvey Island. In the Bromley Group Log, the Canvey Post reported a loss of communications due to enemy action. The damage was extensive, including bombs hitting the local gas and electrical supplies: 'Observer from O2 rang up from Benfleet and reported that a bomb had dropped in the road at Northwich Corner, Canvey Island, with the result that all telephone lines from Canvey Island were out, including those from O2'.[22]

Near Chelmsford, another KG4 He 111 was part of the Luftwaffe bomber force destined to strike at RAF Mildenhall and Honington. Shortly after midnight, caught in the beams of multiple searchlights, the Heinkel was shot down by an RAF fighter, causing it to crash in the grounds of the Bishop of Chelmsford's residence. Its demise was witnessed by the Observers on duty at the Hatfield Peverel Post (G3):

> It was a clear night, with everything illuminated brightly by a moon almost at full, when about 30 enemy bombers came in up the Thames estuary. One of these was engaged at about 16,000 feet. The Heinkel burst into flames, and the parachute of a German airman became entangled in the tail of the aircraft as it fell. Coming down in a steep spiral, the aircraft crashed near Chelmsford.[23]

Bromley Groups P3 Post at Vange, near Basildon, also appears to have witnessed the demise of the Heinkel, reporting it to the Bromley Centre:

> 00.30 P3 report plane crashed approximately M1713, apparently as a result of engagement by Spitfire (up from Rochford). Reported to Crash Officer.[24]

The Spitfire that shot down the bomber was being flown by the soon to become very distinguished fighter ace 'Sailor' Malan from, and later commander of, 74 Squadron. He described the bomber's final moments: 'The enemy aircraft went down in a spiral dive, searchlights and I followed him right down until he crashed in flames near Chelmsford'. During that same sortie, Malan shot down another KG4 HE 111, this time near the Cork Lightship just off the Harwich/Felixstowe coast in view of the Felixstowe Post.[25] After the Ministry of Shipping gave its permission, the Post had only just moved to the top of the Martello Tower there, also used by the Coastguard. It had previously been sited in a position about a half-mile in from the coast and with no visibility of the sea.[26]

Another KG4 Heinkel was brought down at Fleam Dyke, near the Cherry Hinton Post in Cambridgeshire, after a running battle with a 19 Squadron Spitfire and a 23 Squadron Blenheim. Another crashed on the French side of the English Channel as it headed back to base.

The wreck of the 'Blakeney Heinkel', that crashed close to the P2 Post (Cley in Norfolk) on 18/19 June 1940. The wreckage would remain there until 1969, when it was finally removed. (NARA)

4
THE BATTLE OF BRITAIN

As the summer of 1940 unfolded and Luftwaffe attacks intensified, the Observer Corps across Britain was still expanding, on duty night and day. Radio Direction Finding was on constant watch, and RAF fighter squadrons, at maximum readiness, were stretched to the limit attempting to intercept and destroy an enemy that held the initiative in deciding when and where he would strike. As it was the RAF's 'finest hour', it was also the 'forged in battle' moment for the Observer Corps.

For historical purposes, the Battle of Britain has long been depicted as comprising distinct elements. Whilst useful for analysts today, in many respects it fails to adequately capture the fluidity of operations in a constantly evolving situation, rather than the German campaign being clearly defined and backed by a well-defined strategy. Action caused reaction and counter-reaction. Ignoring this fails to recognise the dynamic and uncertain course of events at the time.

During the summer of 1940, several shifts in German high-level policy redirected Luftwaffe operations. Initially harassing Channel and North Sea shipping and British coastal ports the Luftwaffe moved on to *Adlertag* (Eagle Day) and the switch to a large-scale assault on RAF airfields from 13 August 1940. In September, mass attacks on London followed.

Whilst the 1940 German air offensive against Britain was far from a clear, closely planned, well-defined strategy, the objective was to achieve air superiority. To wipe the RAF from the skies and clear the way for a planned invasion across the English Channel.

For the Observers in fields and on rooftops, the frequency of German air attacks brought ebbs and flows to their activity levels. While the action up to early summer 1940 was concentrated in coastal areas, in July and August 1940, inland Posts became much busier, as enemy air attacks struck further inland. As the Observer Corps covered almost the whole country (except for the north-west of Scotland and Northern Ireland), they not only continued to track aircraft, but also rendered quick reports of associated activities, including bombs dropped, crashed aircraft, and bailed out aircrews. Coastal Posts were frequently in a position to not only report attacks on shipping, but alerted the sea rescue services that saved many aircrews lives.[1] Indeed, the coastal Posts were considered so busy, with their additional responsibilities, that instead of the usual two Observers on duty, ACM Dowding requested permission from the Air Ministry to allow Posts in Maidstone, Horsham, Winchester, Colchester, Bury St Edmunds and Yeovil to be allowed a third person on duty at all times.[2]

From *Adlertag* onwards, the German plan developed a more systematic pattern. By day, Observer Corps Southern Area Groups were busy as intensive attacks were directed against No 11 (Fighter) Group's airfields. At night, the Northern and Midland Areas were busiest with attacks on industrial areas in Merseyside and the Midlands. In the two weeks up to the end of August, German air force sorties totalled around 8,000. By night, there were often around 200 enemy aircraft in action over Britain.[3]

As German fighter pilot ace and squadron commander during the Battle of Britain, Adolf Galland later described:

> Up to this time, the Battle of Britain was nothing more than a succession of small engagements. Plans for future large-scale operations were closely related to projects involving ground forces. Using tactics that were altered continually, the Germans initiated a course of action designed to undermine and eventually bring about the collapse of British defences.[4]
>
> The High Command of the Luftwaffe and the combat units were very surprised to discover that the British already had an excellent and complete radar network which enabled them to detect the approach of German aircraft. This showed that the far-sighted and methodical British had done their utmost to make the latest technical developments available to their air defences.[5]

At the same time, other, more widely spaced targets were struck by the Luftwaffe. 'By now Observer Corps Groups, particularly in the manufacturing areas and around the great ports, had had a considerable amount of experience in tracking and distinguishing friend from foe'.[6]

All of these factors were reflected in the levels of activity at Centres and Posts. The workload could be quiet, only to spike as a raid approached, calm somewhat after the attack, then to increase again as another wave of German bombers headed into the battle. In bad weather, when the Luftwaffe stayed on the ground, shifts could feel long and monotonous, leading to boredom, or provided welcome relief.

Posts came in all shapes and sizes. In urban area they were often on the roof of public buildings or industrial sites. (Picryl)

Posts in rural areas could be in the corner of a convenient field, near a telephone pole and surrounded with makeshift protection. (Picryl)

THE ROC SPITFIRES

In May 1940, the newly appointed Minister of Aircraft Production, Lord Beaverbrook, launched the Spitfire Fund. The cost of an aircraft was set at a nominal £5,000, and the public was invited to donate towards their purchase. All sorts of towns, groups and clubs raised money by all possible means, not just in Britain, but from all parts of the Commonwealth. Astonishingly, around 1,500 Spitfires would eventually be 'bought' with public subscriptions, most bearing the names of the donating cities and organisations.

The Observer Corps was not to be outdone and set in motion its own Spitfire Fund. A large sum of money was raised amazingly quickly, and by November 1940, some £9,350 had been raised. The first £5,000 was sent by Commandant Warrington-Morris to Lord Beaverbrook in the same month. A second Spitfire would follow.

The first Observer Corps Spitfire IIa, P7666, was delivered to 41 Squadron at RAF Hornchurch in November 1940, complete with the Observer Corps crest and name. (Via Picryl)

The first ROC funded aircraft was a Spitfire IIa serialled P7666. It was delivered to 41 Squadron at RAF Hornchurch in November 1940, bearing the Observer Corps crest and name. It was very soon in action. On 23 November 1940, a message from HQ 11 Group Fighter Command to the Southern Area Commandant confirmed an engagement between Sqn Ldr D Finlay, the CO of 41 Squadron and pilot of P7666, when he shot down a Me 109 although his aircraft was itself damaged by enemy fire.[7] Rapidly repaired, just two days later, on 27 November, Finlay scored a second victory in the Observer Corps Spitfire, shooting down another Me 109, this time off Dover.

The RAF sent a message to the Corps: 'Your Spitfire, presented to the nation and flown by the Officer Commanding 41 Squadron, destroyed its second Me109 today. That is two Huns in consecutive engagements. Got any more like this one?'[8]

The Royal prefix was later painted on the aircraft. Later transferred to 54 Squadron, the aircraft flown by Plt Off J Stokoe was shot down over the North Sea near Harwich on 20 April 1941. The air-sea rescue service safely recovered him.

The second Spitfire IIa purchased was P7837. It served with 616 Squadron and was later passed to 310 (Czech) Squadron at RAF Dyce. Unfortunately, the pilot, Plt Off Vladimir Zoral and the aircraft were lost in a flying accident close to RAF Dyce on 19 November 1941, when practising a glider attack.[9]

In 1985, the RAF painted one of its Battle of Britain Flight Spitfires in 41 Squadron and ROC markings to celebrate the 60th Anniversary of the Corps. Pictured here at the 1987 RAF Fairford International Air Tattoo. (Kevin Wright)

Assembling the Air Picture

Observer Corps Groups around the south and east coasts of Britain entered a period of intense activity during the Battle of Britain. That was especially true for the Groups surrounding London from mid-August 1940. Under the pressure of heavy air attack, the Centres' plotters and tellers struggled to cope with the incessant stream of information from the Posts and to relay relevant details to the RAF.[10]

The flow of reports into and out of the Centre could continue unabated for hours at a stretch, and did so almost every day, when the weather suited Luftwaffe attacks. Observer Corps Centre crews often finished their shifts exhausted. The job of plotting and tracking the raiders had to be done calmly, carefully, but with great speed. It called for careful concentration amid the noise, bustle, and excitement of battle.

The impressions from the diary of an unnamed Centre Observer, newly recruited in the summer of 1940, describing his first entry into the 'Ops' Room at Watford, are hard to better:

The plotting table and dais for the Group Controller at an unspecified Centre before the issue of uniforms. (Picryl)

> Advancing gingerly a few steps into the room, I saw what appeared to me to be a roomful of lunatics playing a game of devil's Ludo. About a dozen men were around an irregularly shaped table, some seated, some standing, others leaning across the Table to push coloured counters from one point to another. All were talking, some into their telephones, some to the men next to them and some, it seemed, with one side of their mouths into their phones whilst with the other side maintaining an argument with their neighbours. All the time they were busy with their game, pushing coloured counters hither and thither on the squared board, putting new ones on, moving little lettered blocks, keeping the pattern forever changing.
>
> On three sides of the Table, a few feet away, was a raised platform on which sat other men variously occupied, either talking into telephones, or scribbling busily into books or on little pads of paper. One thing they had in common with the men at the Table was that they were all talking, and from time to time, one of the scribblers (or both) would tear a sheet from his little pad and wave it aloft, shouting hoarsely.
>
> This madhouse appalled me. The lack of ventilation, the terrible intensity of the occupants, and the fact that not one person had taken the slightest notice of me, drove me nervous and shaken to retreat to the saner atmosphere of the ante-room, where I strove desperately for a few minutes to summon enough courage to go back to that weird pandemonium.

He continued his description:

> The peculiar conditions described resulted from the fact that about 25 men were working at high pressure in a comparatively small room, and though, to the layman, there existed neither method nor sequence, the trained eye could observe much resemblance to a shunting or marshalling yard, only instead of sorting trucks and wagons for despatch along the correct routes, these men were dealing with reports of invading aircraft. Doubtless, the varying states of undress and the queer assortment of clothes added to the strange picture, but the work was conducted in accordance with the arranged schedule. The fat man in grey flannels and open shirt is seated at the Table immediately under the Recorder's dais, and is repeating the report he has just received from George Two Post.
>
> '7911 West, nine at 15, Me 109s, and He III, 7507 West, five at 12'. The fat man pushes two counters on the squares 7911 and 7507 on the grid in front of him, and calls to the plotter seated on his left. 'Bill, the 'Dons' will have these in a minute; better take over'.
>
> Simultaneously, the 'Dons' start plotting, all three Posts in the cluster giving readings, while the line of counters creeps over the Table indicating the passage of the raiders. The fellow, in a summer golf jacket, across the Table, puts down a counter indicating the arrival of six Hurricanes over the 'Johnny' Posts and so the stage is set for the interception. The Tellers in the gallery above the Table watch the counters being laid, and through the open line to the RAF Sector 'tell' the plots of the raiders and fighters. Thus, the picture is built up both at the Centre and at the RAF Ops room. If the enemy hoped in any way to surprise the defences he was doomed to disappointment. Whilst his aircraft were still over the Continent (indeed, in many cases, as soon as they were airborne), our RDF was picking them up, and this undoubtedly was one of the crucial factors of the situation, as by its aid ample warning was received on the passage of aircraft flying across the English Channel.[11]

FLARING TROUBLE

Far away on the estuary of the River Orwell, in Suffolk, is the small village of Woolverstone, where an Observer Corps Post was established in 1929. From there, it would have been possible to detect aircraft flying up the river towards Ipswich, the nearby RAF station over the river at Martlesham Heath, and to provide visual coverage of both Harwich and Felixstowe naval ports and the seaplane base. Less than four miles away, at Shotley, was HMS *Ganges*, a large naval training base.

Jack Barrington Snell had joined the Corps in 1928, becoming the Woolverstone Post's Head Observer. The now 37-year-old Jack was on duty in the summer of 1940 as the Battle of Britain intensified. He had gone on late duty at the Post on 14 July. Recorded in the 18 Group Log later on 15 July 1940, is the following message:

> 15.15 Message from OGO [Observer Group Officer] No 18 Group phoned to N Weald. "Head Observer, J1, Woolverstone Post, Mr JB Snell was on duty at his Post at 12.30 AM this morning when a Chief Petty Officer and nine other Petty Officers and ratings returning in taxis from Ipswich to Shotley Barracks, seeing a flare lit at Woolverstone Post, surrounded the Post. The Chief Petty Officer, thinking presumably that the Head Observer, who was lighting the second flare, was a fifth columnist, shot him with a revolver, wounding him in the thigh and finger. Mr Snell has been removed to the Hospital."
> (Signed) V Sandiford, Major [12]

After being shot, Jack was taken to the nearby HMS *Ganges* hospital for treatment.

In spring 1943, the Post was moved to a much 'safer' location, less than half a mile away, to the roof of nearby Woolverstone Hall, which the Admiralty had requisitioned. From the roof, the Post had an unhindered view over the River Orwell. Head Observer Snell was awarded the British Empire Medal in the January 1946 New Year's Honours List 'For maintaining an extremely high standard of efficiency and excellent qualities of leadership'.[13]

Sometime after Head Observer JB Snell was shot, the Woolverstone Post was moved to the roof of the nearby Woolverstone Hall, which gave it an unrivalled vantage point. After the war, the London County Council used it as a boys' boarding school, with the Post still on the roof of the Hall. (LCC)

Unfortunately, trouble with the military was not limited to Suffolk, and other incidents were reported from several locations across the country. In June 1940, the 17 Group, C2 Post at Elstree, in Hertfordshire, reported frequent troubles with the Army and LDV members. On one night, soldiers from the Kensington Rifles, who had been lectured that day on the possibility of parachute landings guided by flares, were told to take aggressive action if they saw such activities. They challenged the Post Observers on no fewer than six occasions, with rifles and fixed bayonets. At another time, a party of Gordon Highlanders thought the Observers, dressed in their civilian clothes, were a Gypsy encampment and proved difficult to convince otherwise.

However, the real fear, expressed by the Head Observer, was that, blinded by their flares, the Observers might be 'shot up' by soldiers who would stalk the Post by creeping along an adjoining ditch, causing the Post members to return fire. The Head Observer sought a military guard to be stationed at the Post to prevent further incidents.[14]

The Pattern of Air Attacks

We can gain a broader understanding of the daytime pattern of German air attacks during the Battle of Britain by examining a snapshot of the records for a single day, in this case, 18 August 1940, sometimes referred to as the 'Hardest Day' of the battle. The recorded tracks numbered around 2,600 enemy sorties, but, allowing for some double-counting, a more reasonable total was probably around 2,000. German records appear to indicate much lower numbers, about 970 sorties.

The German targets for that day included RAF airfields at Biggin Hill, Kenley, North Weald, Ford, Thorney Island, Hornchurch and Gosport, Liverpool Docks with severe damage to the Poling radar station. The bombers were Ju 88s, He 111s, and Do 17s with Bf 110s and Bf 109s providing fighter cover. The losses, for both sides, were the heaviest for a single day during the Battle of Britain.[15]

Table 2 indicates the Observer Corps Groups involved in reporting on a single day's raids. It omits small-scale and reconnaissance missions by German aircraft.

He 111s in large numbers often spearheaded the daily air raids on Britain; their distinctive shape made them easily recognisable. (Via Picryl)

Table 2: Pattern of German Daytime Air Raids on Britain, 18 August 1940.[16]

Time	Location	Observer Corps Groups
11.00 hrs	Dover and East Kent	Maidstone (1), Horsham (2), Bromley (19)
11.00 – 13.00 hrs	Activity off Lands' End	Truro (20)
13.00 hrs	Newcastle and Sunderland	North Riding Yorkshire (9), Durham (30)
13.30 hrs	Scarborough and Hull	North Riding Yorkshire (9), East Riding Yorks & North Lincs (10)
15.00 hrs	Essex	Colchester (18), Bromley (19)
15.30 hrs	Dover	Maidstone (1)
17.00 hrs	Isle of Wight and inland	Horsham (2), Winchester (3)
18.00 hrs	Dover and inland	Across to Croydon and Farnborough Maidstone (1), Horsham (2), Winchester (3), Bromley (17)

Around 250 German aircraft were involved in the 17.00 hrs attack on the Isle of Wight. Later that day, under the cover of darkness, there were further raids in the areas around Sheffield, Leeds, Hull, Sealand, Colchester, Canvey Island and Manningtree. A RAF training airfield at Windrush, Gloucestershire, was also struck.

Precise figures for the actual aircraft losses that day are still difficult to establish definitively, but amounted to around 70 aircraft on the German side and 30 RAF machines. Given the German determination to catch the RAF on the ground that day, only eight were said to have been destroyed on the airfields attacked. Both RDF and the Observer Corps were credited with providing sufficient warning to the airfields to allow them to get their aircraft airborne in time. Although significant damage was done to the British airfields, none was said to have been critical.

Target London

An account from Watford Centre continues:

> On Saturday, September 6, in daylight, a large enemy formation eluded RAF fighters. It made a heavy attack on the docks and warehouses in East London and along the Thames Estuary. The German bombers had a heavy fighter escort. In total, about 400 aircraft took part, causing considerable damage and massive fires in the Silvertown dock area. A night attack followed with another 250 bombers.

The Observer Corps communication system functioned efficiently, with details of the advancing bombers passed from Group to Group by the Inter-Centre Tellers. Guided by the river below, they bombed 'the wharves, docks and factories, and soon there was a continuous line of fires raging for over half a mile'. The bombers guided by the still burning fires from the afternoon's raids. The Observers on duty described it as 'a terrifying but marvellous spectacle. The fires were visible 30 miles away'.

The following night, the enemy repeated these tactics, with some of the fires still burning from the previous night, and had no difficulty in re-locating their target. From then on until late December, the Luftwaffe came to the London area almost every night. As it was described, 'The Battle of Britain was an attempt to smash the RAF, but the night bombing raids on London were designed to break the spirit of the people and to wreck and destroy their homes'.

> The night raids placed an enormous amount of work onto the Centre. Plotters, at times, found it quite impossible to handle the continuous mass of plots pouring in from Posts. Posts queued to pass their reports to Centre, the latter spent many hours in the sweltering heat and smoky atmosphere of a blacked-out Operations Room, everyone working hard, conducted with that fervour and zest given only in voluntary labour, recording every plot, keeping continuous tracks and holding the Post Observers' interest to ensure that they realised that their task was indeed worthwhile. The Centre plotter needed to be a mathematician, a diplomat, a stoic and a father all at once. Sometimes during these raids, they could hear, through the Post lines, the whistle of descending bombs close by.
>
> At the height of a blitz, public transport stopped, and any unfortunate Observers travelling to duty by this means were compelled to walk the remaining distance to their Posts, mostly in complete darkness and generally without meeting another soul.
>
> Nor was it pleasant to leave the family in the shelter at home, to go on duty for four or eight hours during an all-night raid, and then to go straight to work in the morning. Not too bad for one night, but certainly a bit tough when it occurred three or four nights a week.
>
> The Germans sometimes switched to night attacks on other towns, including the major attack on Coventry on November 14 and others, including Birmingham, Bristol, Sheffield and Manchester. On such occasions, the German bombers went straight across the Group in a continuous stream. So well-defined and constant was their passage that it became known to Watford Centre plotters as the 'bus route'. Some plotters, fond of their little joke, would place a line of counters in advance of the aircraft, maintaining that it 'saved a lot of trouble' but Duty Controllers took a poor view of this.[17]

Shot down on 18 August 1940, the wreckage of a Dornier Do 17Z-2 KG76 was at Leaves Green, near Biggin Hill. Ground defences and 111 Squadron Hurricanes brought the aircraft down during a low-level attack on RAF Kenley. (Crown Copyright)

ROOF SPOTTER I AND ROOF SPOTTER II

Two very active Observer Corps Posts throughout the war were in central London. During the spring and summer of 1940, Churchill had complained that the large number of air raid warnings affecting London, sometimes unnecessary ones, were severely disrupting government business and war work. He wanted a system that would provide a second warning once it was clear that attacks were headed towards central London. In response, the Observer Corps Southern Area established two 'special' Posts in the heart of the City that became key to the 'Government Subsidiary Air Raid Scheme'.

Initially using Class 'A' Observers, the roof watch began on 6 September 1940, near the height of the Battle of Britain, from a temporary position on top of the Air Ministry building (Adastral House in Aldwych). Two weeks later, two more permanent 'control towers', as they were described, had been readied in central London and designated 'Roof Spotter I' (RS I) and 'Roof Spotter II' (RS II). The Air Ministry Post was RS I. RS II was placed high on the roof of the 10-storey building at 55 Broadway, above St James Underground Station. The Observers at both locations performed very long duty hours, often 72 hours officially, plus many additional unofficial ones. In addition to the Class A Observers, later several Class B men were recruited to serve at both locations. Most of the men for these crews were drawn from the Horsham Group. Others came from the Watford, Winchester, and Colchester Groups, with the crewing reportedly remaining very stable through to the end of the war.[18]

However, the purpose of 'Roof Spotters' was very different from that of standard Observer Corps Posts. Once properly established, the two Posts each possessed plotting maps covering over 15,000 square miles of the country and could show movements as far afield as the Isle of Wight to Dover, Mildenhall in the north, and Northampton and Basingstoke in the north and west, respectively. The information was passed to them from Group Centres via two control points (described only as 'Guns') that provided raid bearing and distance information, so they knew which direction to look for the approaching enemy aircraft. Once they were sure that the enemy was heading for central London, they issued their warning, which rang alarm bells in vital buildings across the City. These were in over 400 locations, including Downing Street, Buckingham Palace, Parliament, Adastral House, Ariel House and many key points, mainly in the Whitehall and Kingsway parts of the City, an area of some 12 square miles. Once sure the danger had passed, they could cancel the alarm.

RS I and RS II saw a lot of action, especially during the Blitz, which included 57 successive nights of bombing in 1941 and numerous other heavy attacks. With a grandstand view of events, they witnessed attacks that damaged the House of Commons and other important buildings later in April and May 1941. During one of these raids, the side of Adastral House was struck, but the resulting fire was quickly put out. At Broadway, there were incendiary bomb incidents. From June 1944, attacks were mainly by V-1s, of which approximately 2,340 would hit London.[19]

In June 1944, when V-1 'Diver' attacks began, the two Posts became extremely active again. Six V-1s were said to have exploded within 200 yards of RS II. Another missed the Air Ministry Roof Spotter Post by yards to explode in the road between Adastral House and the BBC's Bush House at Aldwych on 30 June 1944. 'Due to the height of the building and the absence of the windows, the Post escaped serious damage, though the duty men received a severe shaking'.[20]

In addition to the two Roof Spotter Posts, there were other 'standard' Posts in Central London, including high on top of the University College London Senate House, temporarily requisitioned by the Ministry of Information, also at Highgate and Stratford and others further out from central London.

The scene seconds after the V-1 explosion at Aldwych on 30 June 1944, close to the Air Ministry Roof Spotter Post and Bush House, home to the BBC's European House. Official figures counted 46 dead and approximately 200 injured casualties. (Via Greg Funnell)

Carefully managed official pictures from the area surrounding the explosion show property damage. Still, none show any damage to the Air Ministry or other sensitive buildings in the area. However, this photographer's image appears to have captured perhaps the only known view of the RS Post on the Air Ministry roof, with even what seems to be an Observer looking down on the scene below. (UPI)

Left and above: Images from central London, from RS II, the Charles Holden designed building at 55 Broadway and home to London Transport. (Crown Copyright)

Taken from the Roof of the Air Ministry Building in September 1940, the temporary Roof Spotter I Post was used for a few weeks whilst a more permanent 'control tower' was being constructed. (Crown Copyright)

Written by an Observer at RS I who witnessed the inferno in central London: 'One of the unforgettable memories of the Blitz was the great fire raid on the City of December 29, 1940. That night, the wind came from the west, giving us an unrestricted view of the vast area of flame. How St Paul's escaped in that blazing inferno we could never understand'. (Crown Copyright)

On 15 September 1940, an RAF Hurricane flown by Sgt Ray Holmes of 504 Squadron attacked a Do 17 which had already been damaged by fighters from another squadron, causing an engine to fail. Finally, over the City, the pilot, Obst Lt Robert Zehbe, bailed out. Two unarmed 50kg bombs fell from the stricken bomber into the grounds of Buckingham Palace. Attacking the Dornier again, Holmes's wing struck an object, probably part of the Dornier, causing him to spin out of control and forcing him to bail out at low level. Later, hero-seeking journalists retold the story, saying Holmes had deliberately rammed the German bomber to save the Royal Family and the Palace. Observers from the Temporary Post witnessed the whole event, the bombs falling, and the bomber, minus its tail, dropping close to the entrance of nearby Victoria station. (Crown Copyright)

Italian Air Force Raids

Italy had declared war on Britain and France on 10 June 1940. Five days later, RAF Fighter Command began sending messages to Observer Corps Centres describing the markings of Italian Air Force aircraft in case they attacked Britain.[21] However, it was not until September 1940, towards the end of the main phases of the Battle of Britain, that the Italians deployed a combined force of around 200 fighters, bombers, and support aircraft to bases in Belgium. Over the next few weeks, the unit, known as the *Corpo Aereo Italiano* (CAI, Italian Air Corps), was readied to take part in operations against Britain. Their first major operation was an unsuccessful night raid on Harwich on 25 October 1940. Small operations continued over the next few weeks, their initial fighter sweeps, sometimes going unopposed until anti-aircraft gunners finally identified them as 'hostiles'.

Initially, identifying the Italian aircraft was a challenge for Post Observers, unfamiliar with the appearance and sound of the 'new' aircraft and without proper guidance to aid recognition. 'They knew they were something strange, but could not give any opinion as to what they were'. On hearing one approaching aircraft, it was described to Norwich Centre by a Post as 'He's a rum'un Centre, sounds like a blinkin humming top'.[22]

The most significant attack by the CAI took place on 11 November 1940. It was also the best-documented account of an Italian attack by the Observer Corps. An extract from the Colchester Group Centre Log for that day illustrates the uncertainty caused by the CAI's early attacks with its CR42 fighters and Fiat BR 20 bombers:

> 14.02 Informed Uxbridge – Raid 42R in M7969 appears to be down – column of smoke and Hurricane circling – apparently a Dornier.
>
> 14.09 Informed Uxbridge that post H2 [Grundisburgh in Suffolk] thinks the first plane down in M96 was an Italian biplane; the second was a Junkers 88. Later reported that the supposed Italian plane fell on land. Uxbridge asked us to see that the wreckage of this plane was guarded. Suffolk police say they have six crashes reported to them – all hostile – and are investigating.
>
> 14.28 To Uxbridge – plane brought down in M9167 proved to be Italian. Pilot still alive, also the other plane brought down (a bomber) was Italian. Two men baled out, their parachutes failed to open.
>
> 14.50 Uxbridge asked us to ascertain whether the pilot of the Italian plane crashed M9167 was Italian or German.
>
> 14.52 Informed Uxbridge, pilot was definitely Italian.
>
> 15.37 Passed following additional report from H2 Post to Uxbridge – The Italian fighter was a Fiat 42 – the pilot says there were 22 Fiat fighters escorting German bombers, but would not state the number of bombers. Uxbridge observed that our post should not have been able to get this.[23]

Amid the turmoil of the Battle of Britain, some humorous incidents were captured as well. One Post reported an aircraft altitude of 10 feet. When that was queried by the Centre, the 10 feet was repeated, and the Centre asked if the aircraft was 'hedge hopping'. The Post reply was 'No, it is on the back of a lorry going down the Great North Road'.

In another incident, an Observer gave a lift to an RAF Flying Officer and was subjected to 'a flow of language against the Corps'. It turned out that living some distance from his home, and away on a course, he 'contrived to fly his Hurricane home for the weekend'. On his return, the Station Commander sent for him, asked what he had been doing and detailed the exact route he had flown home and the time of landing. 'It was you damned Observer blokes I hadn't reckoned with'. That explained his annoyance with the Corps.[24]

Secretary of State for Air, Sir Archibald Sinclair, gave a much more public and generous recognition of the Corps' work in a radio address transmitted by the BBC on 1 September 1940. He said:

> The work of the Observer Corps always exacting becomes more arduous as the air fighting becomes more intense. In all weathers night and day you keep unceasing watch and by your vigilance and faithful devotion to your duty you are making an indispensable contribution to the achievements of our fighter pilots. Their victories are your victories too, so I send you this message of thanks and congratulations on your successful performance of the important task which has been entrusted to you.[25]

On 11 November 1940, 22 Italian CR42s took off from Belgium at 1200 hours. One aircraft, MM5701, flown by 23-year-old *Sergente Pilota* Pietro Salvadori, suffered a broken oil pipe and fell behind the rest of his formation as his engine began to overheat. He just managed to reach the coast in Suffolk at Orfordness, and must have touched down very carefully on the shingle beach close to the lighthouse. Remarkably, the aircraft suffered only minor damage; it was later repaired, becoming 'BT474', moved to Farnborough, and later served with the RAF's 1426 (Enemy Aircraft) Flight from RAF Duxford for evaluation and recognition training purposes. It was later displayed in the Battle of Britain Hall at the RAF Hendon Museum. (Crown Copyright)

Pilots from 32 Squadron 'B' Flight rest at RAF Hawkinge in July 1940. From British Pathe, *Time to Remember – Standing Alone*, 1940, summarises a typical day in the Battle of Britain. It covers the main elements of the British air defence system, including the Observer Corps and the Italian raid in November 1940. (Crown Copyright)

Observers march past the Cenotaph in London. The designation of 15 September as Battle of Britain Day in 1943 involved a contingent of Observers, as part of the major parade outside Buckingham Palace. (Crown Copyright)

5
KEEPING TRACK OF THE ENEMY

The RAF's history of the ROC during the Second World War effectively encapsulates the key role the Corps played in the Battle of Britain, particularly given the limitations of RDF at the time:

> For steady, accurate plotting and estimation of the heights and strength of enemy formations. Quick and accurate recognition of whether the aircraft was hostile or friendly was of paramount importance, as was the ability to identify the varying types. It may be truly said though, that in cases where successful interceptions were made and where aircraft were shot down by our fighters overland, a very high proportion of the credit was due to the Observer Corps, linked up as it was with the whole system of defence, and providing at that time the only means of tracking down and intercepting aircraft by day, and the principal means by night. It must be remembered, too, that once enemy aircraft had passed inland from the RDF area, the plots and tracks provided by the Observer Corps furnished the information on which decisions were made as to the issue of Air Raid Warnings, which were, at that time, issued centrally, from Headquarters, Fighter Command.[1]

Assembling the Picture

The integrated air defence system developed under Fighter Command, begun in the mid-1930s, had become far more complex with the outbreak of war. It had developed multiple input points and many 'customers'. In addition to collecting the data, it had to be accurately reported, coordinated, and quickly distributed. Whilst that description is straightforward, the reality of making it work was highly complex. Vast amounts of information flowed up, down and across the system. With so many input points, there were many opportunities for confusion and mistakes. That the whole system functioned so effectively is to the enormous credit of its designers and all those who made it work on a day-to-day basis throughout the war, not least the GPO engineers who installed lines and repaired damage.

It is too complex to describe the operation and procedures of the entire system in detail here. Still, we can get a reasonable understanding from a simple description of the main Observer Corps elements and their interconnections, and of the procedures that also evolved, by following the progress of an imaginary German raid approaching the east coast from France. At the Posts, their first positive indication of a raid could be the sound of engines or a visual sighting. If the system were working well, RDF would already have provided the Group Centre with a warning of an approaching raid, which would have been forwarded to the coastal Posts.

When the enemy aircraft were seen, their track matched, and the number of aircraft reported, information on their passage would be passed to adjacent Observer Corps Groups, Fighter Command, Groups and Sectors and other 'customers' such as the air raid warning organisation, guns and searchlight units and other RAF Commands. All this had to be done using just voice and teleprinter links. A large raid might split into different elements, heading for separate targets that would all have to be tracked, reported, and handed over to other Groups as they approached their targets. In addition to enemy movements, there were those of friendly aircraft. These might be returning from sorties over the sea or continent, on training flights, or heading home being lost or damaged and in need of assistance.

A diagram from 17 Group illustrates the flows of information in and out of their Centre during the war. Plots from ROC Posts alone were said to reach 1.5 million in a 24-hours. (*Observers' Tale*, p.7).

The Filter Room

The RAF Filter Room was key in the transmission of data within the air defence system. They were vital in assembling the vast array of information into actionable form. Rapidly passed to Commanders in HQ Fighter Command, and their subordinate Fighter Groups, it meant they could monitor the whole air battle, using the information provided. Speed and accuracy were the key. In the Filter Room, information was plotted from RDF stations, the Observer Corps, and advanced flight information received from RAF Bomber, Fighter, and other Commands regarding their planned aircraft movements and patrols.

This information was sorted and consolidated into track form and passed forward to Fighter Command Operations Rooms, US Defence Wing HQ, RAF Commands, Groups and Sectors, Intruder Alert and the Observer Corps. The Corps could compare data provided from the Filter Room with that reported locally by Posts. This was especially important as contacts passed inland over the coast and Posts. Information on contacts not detected by RDF

An excellent Air Ministry Training film on 'The Scope and Purpose of the Filter Room', produced late in the war, describes how the system worked and briefly outlines its interaction with the ROC. (Crown Copyright)

could be fed up the reporting chain. The Filter Room was incredibly busy plotting tracks, and it could become overloaded with data; in such cases.

Liaison Officer

At each Fighter Command Group Headquarters, there was an Observer Corps Liaison Officer (OCLO, later ROCLO). His job was to watch the Fighter Group's plotting table and deal with any questions or issues arising within the Group and the coastal Observer Corps Centres to which his Group was connected.

Their priority task was to use their dedicated line through to the Centres to report the early RDF detection of approaching Luftwaffe raids while they were still out at sea. As these 'X' tracks passed overland and into neighbouring Groups, the OCLO ensured tracking continuity. He also checked that tracks were not 'lost' or misidentified. Other tasks included passing messages or instructions from the Commandant ROC or Fighter Command through to Centres. During the course of the war, the Liaison Officers tasks grew to include passing to the Fighter Group 'Any information of interest received from Centres, including reports of bombs dropped, aircraft crashes, the dropping of parachutes, and events at sea seen by Posts, even sightings of enemy submarines, the dropping of mines by aircraft, casualties to vessels or aircraft'.[2]

The Post Instrument

To calculate the position of an aircraft Posts used their 'Post Instrument' of which there were different iterations over the years. The most widely used was designed by R B Pullin & Co in 1934, which replaced an earlier, less sophisticated, 'pantograph' type instrument.

When not in use, the Post Instrument was kept boxed and had to be unpacked with the chart table and mounted onto a tripod. Each chart table was unique to the location for which it was designed. It was divided into grid squares and had to be correctly aligned with key local geographical features, such as church spires or buildings. Minimal additional key features would also be marked on the table, such as other Posts or coastal outlines, as well as a circle marking a five-mile distance around the Post, the 'sound line'.

To be plotted accurately, the aircraft had to be effectively triangulated by knowing either its height or its distance from a known ground feature. It was a practical application of trigonometry learned at school. When an aircraft was sighted, the No. 2 Observer would estimate its height. This technique required practice and experience to do accurately. He would set the estimated height on the instrument's height column, adjusting it with a small wheel. The optical sight was pointed at the aircraft. The bar was mechanically connected to a vertical pointer that indicated the aircraft's position on the instrument table map grid. The Post Observer would then report the grid square, along with the height and number of aircraft for each sighting, to their Centre. The initial height estimates could be refined during ongoing plotting through communication between the Centre and other Posts in the cluster on the same telephone circuit until the aircraft disappeared.

The main modification to the Post Instrument during the war was the addition of a 'Micklethwait' height corrector from 1940 (named after Observer Micklethwait, who invented it). It significantly improved aircraft height estimation, essential for accurately determining an aircraft's position. This device worked based on knowing if the aircraft being tracked was flying directly over a known visible feature – often another Post. When a Post reported an aircraft overhead, the Micklethwait slider from the adjacent Post could be adjusted to give a much more precise altitude estimate. The instrument could also be used for sound reporting, but required a different calculation technique. In post-war years, as aircraft flew faster, new tables and instruments were used.

Sound Reporting

If visually sighting and identifying aircraft could be challenging, the nature of British weather made the problem even more complex. Cloudy or wet weather always placed constrained opportunities for visual observation, and the chances for good, clear night observation were even more limited. In these circumstances, the only alternative

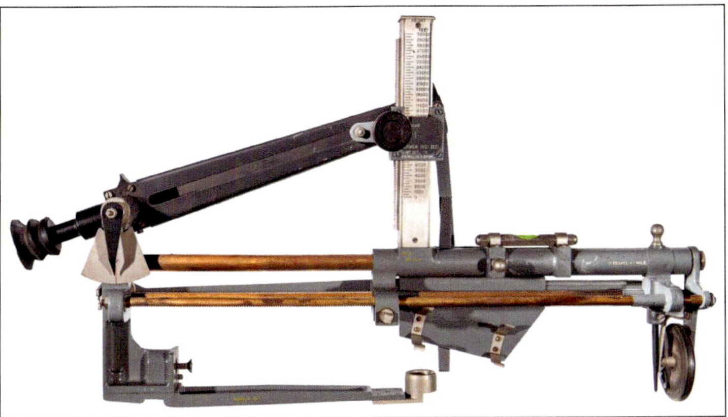

Side on view of a Post Instrument (RAFM)

A clear view of a Post Instrument in use, showing the map table, optical sight and height adjuster. (Open source)

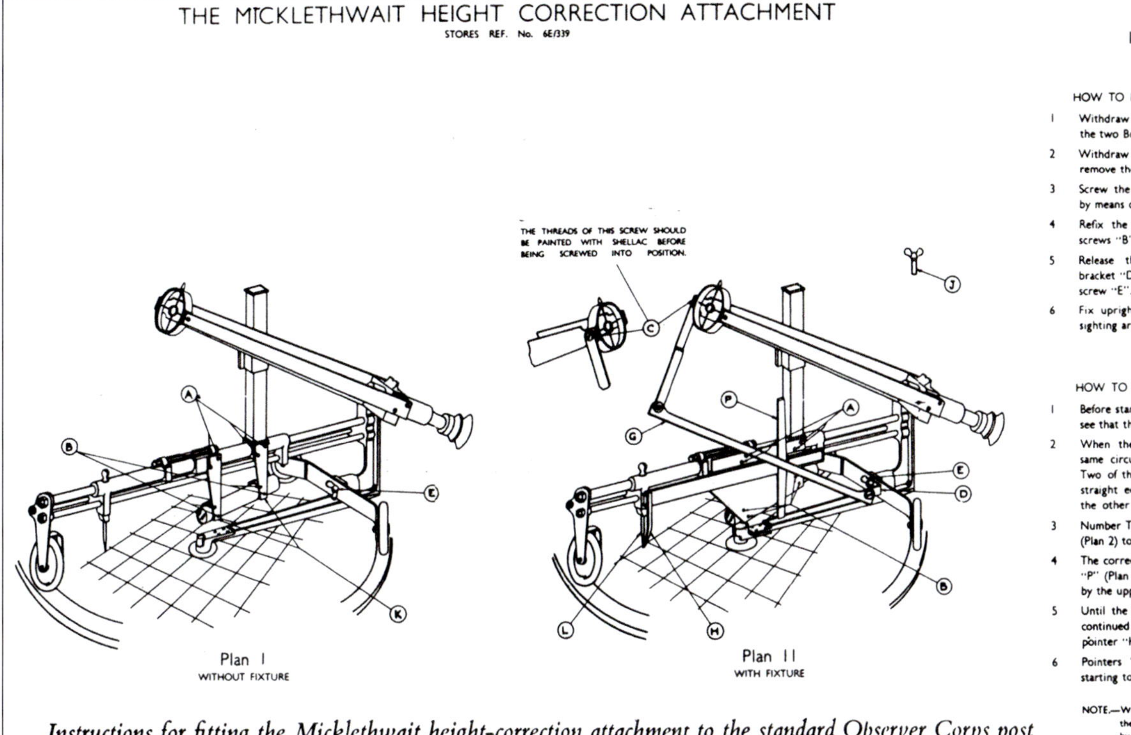

THE MICKLETHWAIT HEIGHT CORRECTION ATTACHMENT

STORES REF. No. 6E/339

THE THREADS OF THIS SCREW SHOULD BE PAINTED WITH SHELLAC BEFORE BEING SCREWED INTO POSITION.

Plan I
WITHOUT FIXTURE

Plan II
WITH FIXTURE

INSTRUCTIONS.

Part I.

HOW TO FIT TO OBSERVER INSTRUMENT

1 Withdraw four screws "A" (Plan I) and remove the two Brackets "K".

2 Withdraw the four screws "B" (Plan I) and remove the two clips for torch.

3 Screw the height corrector on to the Instrument by means of the four screws "A" (Plan 2).

4 Refix the two torch clips by means of the four screws "B" (Plan 2).

5 Release thumb-screw "E" (Plan 2); slip the bracket "D" behind it; then tighten up thumb-screw "E".

6 Fix upright arm or height corrector to top of sighting arm by means of screw "C" (Plan 2).

Part II.

HOW TO USE THE HEIGHT CORRECTOR.

1 Before starting to plot an aircraft it is necessary to see that the pointers "H" and "L" are aligned.

2 When the Post overhears another Post on the same circuit plotting the same aircraft, Number Two of the Post Crew joins up, by means of a straight edge, the positions on the Post Chart of the other Post and the plot given by that Post.

3 Number Two of the Post Crew moves Pointer "H" (Plan 2) to the straight edge.

4 The corrected height is then shown on the scale "P" (Plan 2) at the point at which it is intersected by the upper edge of the moving arm "G" (Plan 2).

5 Until the aircraft is out of sight, plotting can be continued without further adjustment by utilising pointer "H" instead of pointer "L".

6 Pointers "H" and "L" must be aligned before starting to plot another aircraft.

NOTE.—When the instrument is dismantled and placed in the transit case, thumb-screw "E" must be replaced by thumb-screw "J" in order to keep bracket "D" in position.

R.B.P. & Co. Ltd. 2438K

Instructions for fitting the Micklethwait height-correction attachment to the standard Observer Corps post instrument. The diagram was issued in August 1940 by the manufacturer, R. B. Pullin and Co. The attachment was designed by a member of the Corps after whom it was named

Details of the Micklethwait Correction Attachment (Wood, p.76)

was sound plotting. Trying to identify an aircraft's position accurately by its engine noise alone was always much more challenging than visual identification.

Sound plotting had always been a part of Corps activity, but there was very little that could be done to train Observers in this skill. The accuracy and value of these sound plots came to be judged primarily a matter of experience. Some Groups were more skilled than others, and individual Post members possessed very variable skill levels.

The advent of war brought a generally increased proficiency in sound reporting. Civilian aircraft operations all but disappeared. In the early stages of the war, Posts sited close to RAF airfields often became familiar with the particular engine noises of the aircraft types based there, even if just at the level of being able to distinguish locally based aircraft from 'others'.

As the German air offensive developed, Posts beneath the regular routes of German bombers heading for London or targets in the Midlands soon came to recognise their distinctive tones. The value of the sound plots generated often facilitated tying up RDF detected raids once they had passed over the coast, enabling continuous tracking. However, many Posts, if they were located close to built-up areas with road noise, ports, industrial areas or close to railway lines, found sound plotting close to impossible.[3]

Nevertheless, Fighter Command was still keen to have the sound plots that the Observer Corps could provide, even accepting the limitations involved, as T E Winslow recorded:

> Tracking by night was, naturally, largely by sound, and Observers became increasingly proficient at this branch of their work. At that time, it was the practice, when plotting by sound, only to give the track of the aircraft and to omit estimates of height, strength and direction of the enemy raiders. As these last three items of information were naturally of great value to the Royal Air Force, Sectors continually asked that estimates should be given, while the Observer Corps were reluctant to attempt to supply this information owing to the possibility of considerable error.

> However, the Operational Research Section of Fighter Command had a higher opinion of the Observer's capabilities than they had themselves. During the second and third weeks of August, 1940, the scale of attacks markedly increased both by day and night, and most of the Observer Groups received considerable practice in tracking. This was particularly true of the Groups round the great ports and the principal manufacturing areas of Great Britain including: Leeds, Bristol, Portland, Birmingham, Portsmouth and many other places.[4]

The anonymous 16 Group historian recorded some details of the night activity over Norfolk in 1940:

> With so much night activity, post Observers were getting good at identifying planes by sound. This is a thing which has got to be learnt by experience; it is most difficult to explain a certain sound in so many words, for the same identical sound will appear quite different to two different men. But our Norfolk fellows soon grasped the varying notes of the types which came our way, and they did not make many mistakes.[5]

As summer eased into autumn in 1940, the RAF's fighter pilots had deprived Hitler of the essential air superiority necessary to launch his invasion of south-east England. The Luftwaffe's operations reverted to coastal attacks and more night missions against cities and industrial centres as the Blitz continued in earnest.

As the shift in Luftwaffe activity gave a breathing space to the RAF's day fighter operations, it also reduced the intensity of Observer Corps activity. Now the greater effort was directed to tracking enemy night bombing, which provided some opportunity to reflect on the reporting procedures and practices that had evolved since the start of the war.

Aircraft Recognition and Identification

Whilst the work of the Observer Corps had proved of great importance, the basis of aircraft reporting had changed little since it was first formed. Towards the end of 1940, the Battle of Britain had brought into the open the potential importance of high-quality aircraft recognition for passive and active air defence operations, which had been so much neglected before the war.

However, as previously mentioned, aircraft reporting from Posts was based on a simple assumption: that all Posts could be asked to do was to report aircraft movements. Their status as 'hostiles' or friendlies would ultimately be determined by Fighter Command, who had information from Sector Controls, RDF and the Observer Corps Centres. There were four simple categories: 'Friendly Fighters', 'Bombers', 'Hostiles', and 'Unidentified'. This was incredibly simplistic. For reporting purposes, all bombers were to be regarded as hostiles. Up until the Nazi occupation of France, Belgium and the Netherlands, any single-engined aircraft was to be classed as a friendly fighter based on the premise that German fighters did not then have the range to reach Britain.[6]

Not expecting Observer Corps Posts to at least attempt aircraft identification by type was a gross underestimation of many Post members' skills. It was a situation in which official neglect and low priority attached to aircraft recognition from the 1920s were far outpaced by the practical, if unofficial, skills and experience accumulated by thousands of Observers (and many others) across the entire country who eagerly watched the skies. These difficulties experienced by the Observer Corps were also faced by the Army's anti-aircraft gunners, searchlight operators and naval gunners.

When aircraft recognition was more properly taught, models became widely used as training aids. (Key Publishing)

It was the existing, personally and unofficially acquired aircraft recognition skills of many Observers, and their desire to improve them even further, that eventually pushed officialdom to act. They then began to recognise aircraft identification as a valuable, sometimes vital skill, an important asset, the importance of which extended far beyond the Corps.

Even from the 1939 Colchester Group Centre Logs, there are instances where aircraft are identified, and sometimes misidentified, by type, especially the many Bristol Blenheims engaged in daily training and operational missions. Many aviation enthusiasts among the Observer Corps were already keen readers of aviation magazines such as *The Aeroplane* and *Flight*, as well as the non-official recognition pamphlets and books that had begun to appear.

In December 1939, members of the Winchester Group took the initiative by organising a meeting attended by 40 Observers at the Corona Café in Guildford High Street. There, Peter Masefield, the technical editor of *The Aeroplane*, and a key protagonist in the art of aircraft recognition, gave a lecture on the topic. They also held their first recognition test using 34 six-inch-square images of aircraft. The idea was an instant success, and the group was formalised as 'The Hearkers Club', meeting monthly. Peter Masefield soon gave the

Peter Masefield had a long career as a pilot, journalist, civil servant, and government adviser. When he was the editor of *The Aeroplane*, he was pivotal in advancing the techniques and skills of aircraft recognition, which stimulated many Corps members to develop their skills. (Picryl)

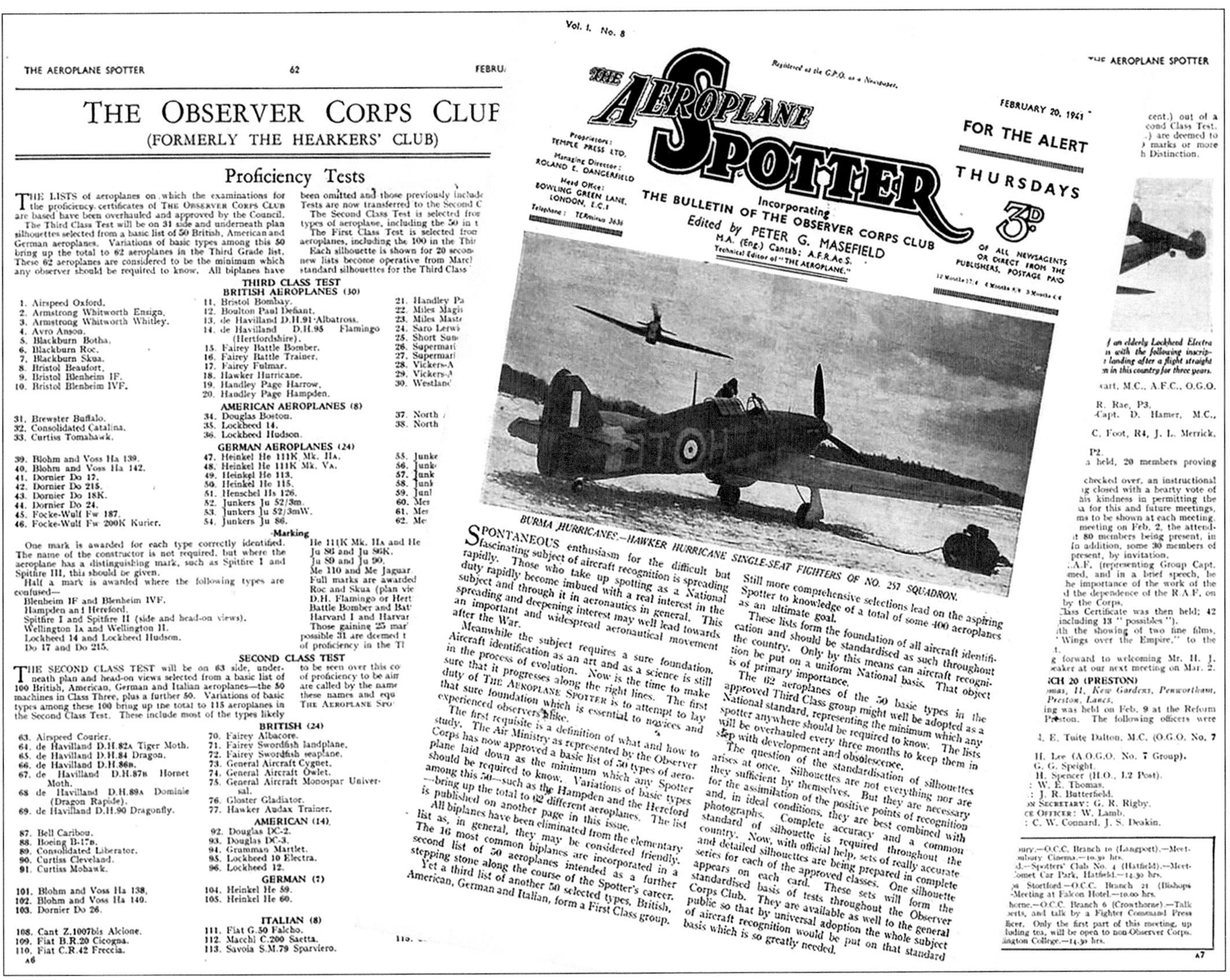

THE AEROPLANE SPOTTER 62 FEBRU

THE OBSERVER CORPS CLUF
(FORMERLY THE HEARKERS' CLUB)

Proficiency Tests

THE LISTS of aeroplanes on which the examinations for the proficiency certificates of THE OBSERVER CORPS CLUB are based have been overhauled and approved by the Council.

The Third Class Test will be on 31 side and underneath plan silhouettes selected from a basic list of 50 British, American and German aeroplanes. Variations of basic types among this 50 bring up the total to 62 aeroplanes in the Third Grade list. These 62 aeroplanes are considered to be the minimum which any observer should be required to know. All biplanes have been omitted and those previously include Tests are now transferred to the Second C

The Second Class Test is selected fro types of aeroplane, including the 50 in t

The First Class Test is selected fro aeroplanes, including the 100 in the Thi

Each silhouette is shown for 20 secon new lists become operative from Marc standard silhouettes for the Third Class

THIRD CLASS TEST
BRITISH AEROPLANES (30)

1. Airspeed Oxford.
2. Armstrong Whitworth Ensign.
3. Armstrong Whitworth Whitley.
4. Avro Anson.
5. Blackburn Botha.
6. Blackburn Roc.
7. Blackburn Skua.
8. Bristol Beaufort.
9. Bristol Blenheim IF.
10. Bristol Blenheim IVF.
11. Bristol Bombay.
12. Boulton Paul Defiant.
13. de Havilland D.H.91 Albatross.
14. de Havilland D.H.95 Flamingo (Hertfordshire).
15. Fairey Battle Bomber.
16. Fairey Battle Trainer.
17. Fairey Fulmar.
18. Hawker Hurricane.
19. Handley Page Harrow.
20. Handley Page Hampden.
21. Handley Pa
22. Miles Magi
23. Miles Mast
24. Saro Lerwi
25. Short Sun
26. Supermar
27. Supermar
28. Vickers-A
29. Vickers-A
30. Westland

AMERICAN AEROPLANES (8)

31. Brewster Buffalo.
32. Consolidated Catalina.
33. Curtiss Tomahawk.
34. Douglas Boston.
35. Lockheed 14.
36. Lockheed Hudson.
37. North
38. North

GERMAN AEROPLANES (24)

39. Blohm and Voss Ha 139.
40. Blohm and Voss Ha 142.
41. Dornier Do 17.
42. Dornier Do 215.
43. Dornier Do 18K.
44. Dornier Do 24.
45. Focke-Wulf Fw 187.
46. Focke-Wulf Fw 200K Kurier.
47. Heinkel He 111K Mk. IIA.
48. Heinkel He 111K Mk. VA.
49. Heinkel He 113.
50. Heinkel He 115.
51. Henschel Hs 126.
52. Junkers Ju 52/3m.
53. Junkers Ju 52/3mW.
54. Junkers Ju 86.
55. Junke
56. Junk
57. Junk
58. Junk
59. Junl
60. Me
61. Me
62. Me

Marking

One mark is awarded for each type correctly identified. The name of the constructor is not required, but where the aeroplane has a distinguishing mark, such as Spitfire I and Spitfire III, this should be given.

Half a mark is awarded where the following types are confused—

Blenheim IF and Blenheim IVF.
Hampden and Hereford.
Spitfire I and Spitfire II (side and head-on views).
Wellington IA and Wellington II.
Lockheed 14 and Lockheed Hudson.
Do 17 and Do 215.
He 111K Mk. IIA and He
Ju 86 and Ju 86K.
Ju 89 and Ju 90.
Me 110 and Me Jaguar.

Full marks are awarded
Roc and Skua (plan vie
D.H. Flamingo or Hert
Battle Bomber and Bat
Harvard I and Harvar

Those gaining 25 mar possible 31 are deemed t of proficiency in the T

SECOND CLASS TEST

THE SECOND CLASS TEST will be on 63 side, underneath plan and head-on views selected from a basic list of 100 British, American, German and Italian aeroplanes—the 50 machines in Class Three, plus a further 50. Variations of basic types among these 100 bring up the total to 115 aeroplanes in the Second Class Test. These include most of the types likely to be seen over this co of proficiency to be air are called by the name these names and equ THE AEROPLANE SPO

BRITISH (24)

63. Airspeed Courier.
64. de Havilland D.H.82A Tiger Moth.
65. de Havilland D.H.84 Dragon.
66. de Havilland D.H.86B.
67. de Havilland D.H.87B Hornet Moth.
68. de Havilland D.H.89A Dominie (Dragon Rapide).
69. de Havilland D.H.90 Dragonfly.
70. Fairey Albacore.
71. Fairey Swordfish landplane.
72. Fairey Swordfish seaplane.
73. General Aircraft Cygnet.
74. General Aircraft Owlet.
75. General Aircraft Monospar Universal.
76. Gloster Gladiator.
77. Hawker Audax Trainer.

AMERICAN (14)

87. Bell Caribou.
88. Boeing B-17B.
89. Consolidated Liberator.
90. Curtiss Cleveland.
91. Curtiss Mohawk.
92. Douglas DC-2.
93. Douglas DC-3.
94. Grumman Martlet.
95. Lockheed 10 Electra.
96. Lockheed 12.

GERMAN (7)

101. Blohm and Voss Ha 138.
102. Blohm and Voss Ha 140.
103. Dornier Do 26.
104. Heinkel He 59.
105. Heinkel He 60.

ITALIAN (8)

108. Cant Z.1007bis Alcione.
109. Fiat B.R.20 Cicogna.
110. Fiat C.R.42 Freccia.
111. Fiat G.50 Falcho.
112. Macchi C.200 Saetta.
113. Savoia S.M.79 Sparviero.
115.

A6

Vol. 1. No. 8

Registered at the G.P.O. as a Newspaper.

THE AEROPLANE SPOTTER

Incorporating
THE BULLETIN OF THE OBSERVER CORPS CLUB
Edited by PETER G. MASEFIELD
M.A. (Eng.) Cantab: A.F.R.Ae.S.
Technical Editor of "THE AEROPLANE."

Proprietors: TEMPLE PRESS LTD.
Managing Director: ROLAND E. DANGERFIELD
Head Office: BOWLING GREEN LANE, LONDON, E.C.1
Telephone: TERminus 3636

FEBRUARY 20, 1941
FOR THE ALERT
THURSDAYS
3D
OF ALL NEWSAGENTS OR DIRECT FROM THE PUBLISHERS, POSTAGE PAID

BURMA HURRICANES.—HAWKER HURRICANE SINGLE-SEAT FIGHTERS OF NO. 257 SQUADRON.

SPONTANEOUS enthusiasm for the difficult but fascinating subject of aircraft recognition is spreading rapidly. Those who take up spotting as a National duty rapidly become imbued with a real interest in the subject and through it in aeronautics in general. This spreading and deepening interest may well lead towards an important and widespread aeronautical movement after the War.

Meanwhile the subject requires a sure foundation. Aircraft identification as an art and as a science is still in the process of evolution. Now is the time to make sure that it progresses along the right lines. The first duty of THE AEROPLANE SPOTTER is to attempt to lay that sure foundation which is essential to novices and experienced observers alike.

The first requisite is a definition of what and how to study. The Air Ministry as represented by the Observer Corps has now approved a basic list of 50 types of aeroplane laid down as the minimum which any Spotter should be required to know. Variations of basic types among this 50—such as the Hampden and the Hereford—bring up the total to 62 different aeroplanes. The list is published on another page in this issue.

All biplanes have been eliminated from the elementary list as, in general, they may be considered friendly. The 16 most common biplanes are incorporated in a second list of 50 aeroplanes intended as a further stepping stone along the course of the Spotter's career. Yet a third list of another 50 selected types, British, American, German and Italian, form a First Class group.

Still more comprehensive selections lead on the aspiring Spotter to knowledge of a total of some 400 aeroplanes as an ultimate goal.

These lists form the foundation of all aircraft identification and should be standardised as such throughout the country. Only by this means can aircraft recognition be put on a uniform National basis. That object is of primary importance.

The 62 aeroplanes of the 50 basic types in the approved Third Class group might well be adopted as a National standard, representing the minimum which any spotter anywhere should be required to know. The lists will be overhauled every three months to keep them in step with development and obsolescence.

The question of the standardisation of silhouettes arises at once. Silhouettes are not everything nor are they sufficient by themselves. But they are necessary for the assimilation of the positive points of recognition and, in ideal conditions, they are best combined with photographs. Complete accuracy and a common standard of silhouette is required throughout the country. Now, with official help, sets of really accurate and detailed silhouettes are being prepared in complete series for each of the approved classes. One silhouette appears on each card. These sets will form the standardised basis of tests throughout the Observer Corps Club. They are available as well to the general public so that by universal adoption the whole subject of aircraft recognition would be put on that standard basis which is so greatly needed.

Front cover of a February 1941 edition of *The Aeroplane Spotter*, an aircraft recognition journal incorporating the ROC Club Bulletin. (Kevin Wright)

concept a much wider readership when he published a full-page article on the new Club in an edition of *The Aeroplane*. It immediately sparked interest around the country and abroad. Masefield also began a public campaign on 'The vital importance of positive identification of British and foreign aircraft by Britain's defence forces and therefore the need for more information on aircraft recognition'.

The magazine soon began to describe aircraft recognition techniques and to publish aircraft silhouettes and quiz-type pictures of German and Allied aircraft, with answers provided the following week. Where images of real aircraft were lacking, scale models were substituted.[7] Soon, recognition tests were devised for different skill levels and became highly competitive. Individuals progressed from 'elementary' to 'intermediate' and eventually 'advanced' stages. Developments came quickly. Monthly meetings became weekly, so many people attended that they had to move to bigger accommodation at Guildford Technical College. New branches of the club immediately sprang up at Shirley (Surrey), Hendon, Liverpool, Evesham, Crowthorne, Southend and Angus. Exclusive to members of the Observer Corps, by spring 1940, it was even producing its own magazine, *The Hearkers Club Bulletin*.[8]

The Observer Corps leadership saw the immediate success of the Hearkers and, short of resources, the Club persuaded them to take on the initiative, renaming it the 'Observer Corps Club'. Management was passed to the Corps, and some funds were made available to purchase slides and materials. Also significant was a petrol grant that allowed Observers to attend one branch meeting per month.

The success of aircraft recognition publications, in particular *The Aeroplane*, drove further developments. In its first edition, on 2 January 1941, Peter Masefield announced a new magazine focused solely on aircraft recognition. To be called *The Aircraft Spotter*, the first edition was an eight-page issue that immediately sold out and received sackfuls of congratulations. Within the first month, it was adopted by the War Office and Air Ministry, who ordered subscriptions for Anti-Aircraft Command and RAF stations, and it became the official journal of the Observer Corps Club.[9] In addition to the recognition materials, the magazine also carried news from Observer Club branch meetings. The magazine continued in print until 1948. The soon-to-be Royal Observer Corps Club (ROCC) grew rapidly and at its peak in late 1942 had 191 branches. In September 1941, the ROCC launched its own magazine, the *Journal of the Royal Observer Corps Club*. It was also available to outside organisations and was in high demand.

These semi-official publications encouraged the production of commercial ones, in particular the *Observer's Book of Aircraft* that later became much more widely known. It first appeared in 1942 as the *Observer's Book of Airplanes*, published by Frederick Warne, with subsequent editions in 1943 and 1945. In later years, when the books were published annually, copies continued to be made available to ROC Posts.

Front cover of the Christmas 1942, and final edition of *The Journal of the ROC Club*. (Kevin Wright)

Members of the police and Home Guard by the wreckage of Part of the Me 110 successfully tracked across Scotland by Rudolf Hess when he defected in May 1941. (Crown Copyright)

Rudolf Hess

One of the most documented incidents involving the Observer Corps' aircraft tracking was the defection of Rudolf Hess and his flight across Northern England and Scotland on 10 May 1941. Reported in detail by Derek Wood, he records how the aircraft was first tracked off Northumberland at 22.10, flying at 12,000 feet, and designated as 'Raid 42'. The ROC Post at Embleton (A2), part of 30 Group, provided a sound plot of the aircraft at 22.23 hrs. Descending as it gradually headed westwards, the aircraft passed A3 Post at Chatton where it was visually identified as a Me 110 by the Post's Head Observer.

Passing into the airspace watched by 31 Group at Galashiels, the Posts at Jedburgh and Ashkirk plotted it. After being lost for a while, the track reappeared in the 34 Group's (Glasgow) area. There was some confusion because the RAF controller refused to accept that the aircraft was a Me 110, instead believing it to be a Do 17. ROC plotters at Glasgow calculated the aircraft's speed at 300mph, much too fast to be a Do 17, which was actively derided by the RAF, and the Corps was told to keep the Do 17 designation. The RAF launched a Defiant night-fighter from Prestwick to intercept the 'Dornier', which it failed to do.

Other ROC Posts identified the aircraft as a Me 110, including West Kilbride (G3) Post that saw it at an extremely low level. Soon after passing out over the coast, the aircraft turned back inland on an irregular course before someone baled out, and it crashed in a field at Eaglesham, in sight of H2 Post, at 23.09. The Home Guard and local police were called.

Assistant Observer Group Officer Major Graham Donald, responsible for H2, set out from central Glasgow, the short distance to Eaglesham, saying to his Group Controller that the RAF could be told, 'If they cannot catch a Me110 with a Defiant, I am now going to pick up the bits with a Vauxhall'. The aircraft's single occupant soon gave himself up and was handed over to the Home Guard. Before long, Major Donald recognised the German prisoner, who had given his name as Alfred Horn, to be Rudolf Hess. Not believed by the police or Army

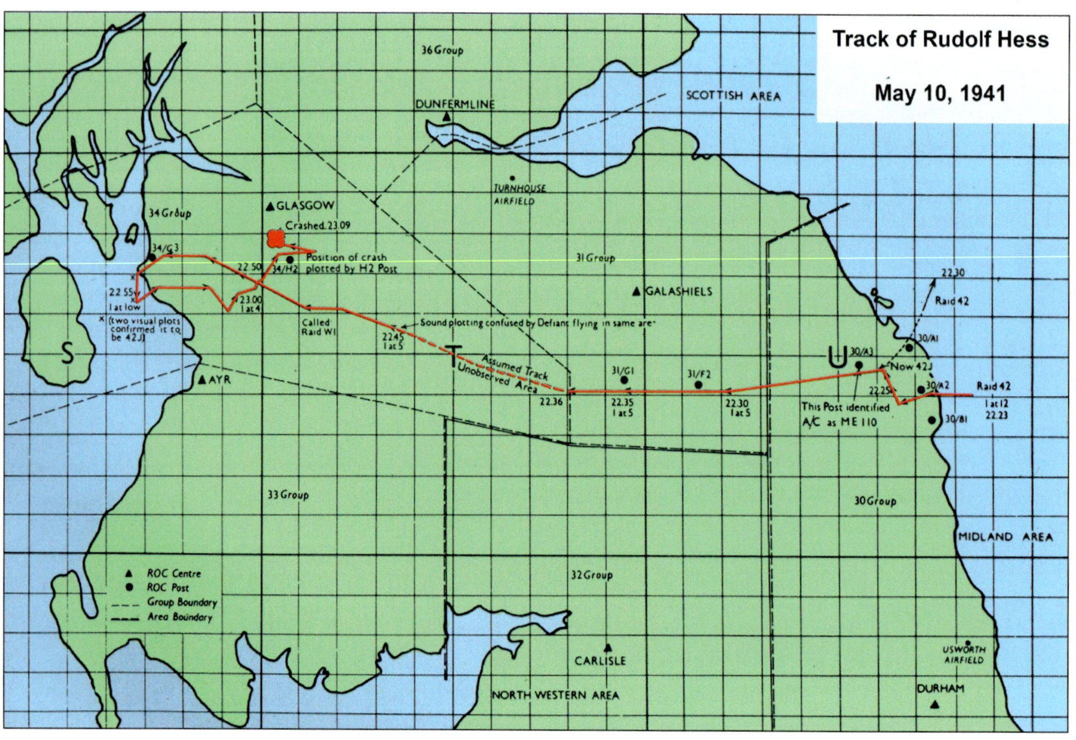

The route of Hess's Me 110 was accurately identified and tracked by the ROC. (Wood, p.3)

Intelligence, Donald's identification was not confirmed until nearly two days later.[10]

In a confidential letter to Air Cde Warrington, sent a few days later on 14 May 1941, Major Donald gave a more personal account of events. He clearly felt the Corps' role in events was far more creditable than that of the police, RAF and Army saying:

The one efficient unit of Britain's air defence at least was aware that a Messerschmitt 110 was over Scotland (all other reports said a Dornier 215), reported to the police and the Home Guard, where it crashed, and also reported that the pilot was Rudolf Hess. The one efficient unit, I am proud to say, is 34 Observer Group of the Royal Observer Corps.[11]

AN RAF LIAISON OFFICER'S VIEW

With such sudden, and to a significant extent public, attention drawn to aircraft recognition skills, it finally began to attract official interest. In December 1940, Sqn Ldr McNeil, the Group Intelligence Officer at HQ 11 Group Fighter Command, received a detailed account of his duties from an RAF Flight Lieutenant recently appointed as the RAF Liaison Officer to the Observers Corps Southern Area.

He outlined one of his primary responsibilities to provide 'Instruction to the Observer Corps in the recognition of aircraft'. He identified some of the difficulties Posts faced in achieving a better distribution and greater uniformity in training. In his description of the Hearker's Club meeting that he attended (probably the November 1940 end-of-year meeting), he wrote, 'There were probably 150 people present, but not all were Observers, a number of troops being included'. Though appealing to the enthusiastic, it could not 'touch the majority of men in out-of-the-way posts'. He further explained that while Posts had official copies of AP1480 and AP1764, most also subscribed to *The Aeroplane*. He also noted the uneven quality and distribution of aircraft recognition materials among and between Posts. Some Observers did only night or weekend duty, making training difficult. Similarly, this made scheduling time for Post-lectures on the topic difficult, as did the many remote Post locations. These remote locations posed additional concerns: they were often where aircraft recognition was poorest, yet their very remoteness made recruiting more accomplished 'spotters' more difficult. In such situations, lifting the standard of aircraft recognition was most challenging. More powerful field glasses were suggested to aid in identifying high-flying aircraft.

There was also the observation that the most accomplished individuals in aircraft recognition were those with the most practical experience and exposure to the greatest variety of aircraft types. Where some Posts were used to seeing just one type of aircraft, be it fighters, trainers or bombers, on sighting a different aircraft type, they would often experience some hesitancy in identification. The official AP1480 and AP1764 publications could not be removed from the Posts. As a result many individuals resorted to the private purchase of some of the publicly available aircraft recognition books.

His final summary is telling of the high spirit among Corps members: 'Wherever I have been, I have found the Observer Corps incredibly keen. All they ask is to be made use of for the purpose of destroying the enemy'.[12]

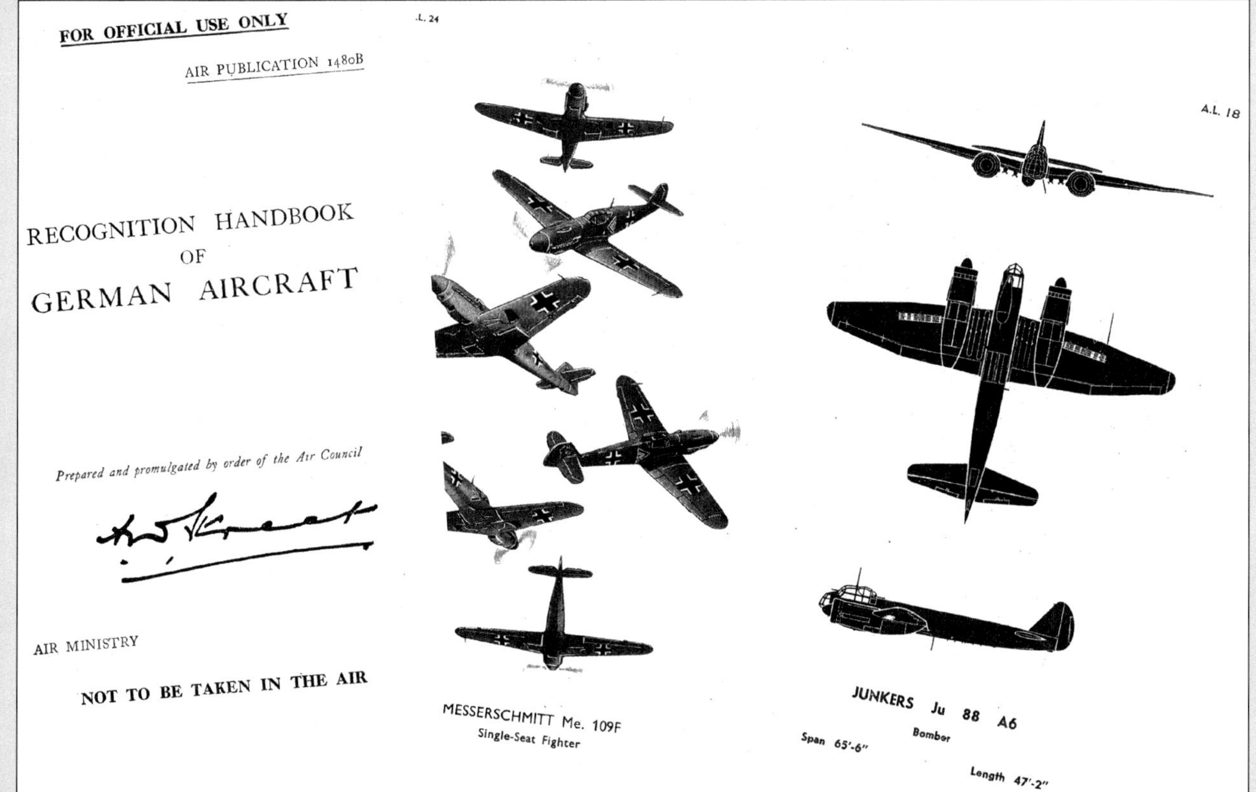
FOR OFFICIAL USE ONLY

AIR PUBLICATION 1480B

RECOGNITION HANDBOOK OF GERMAN AIRCRAFT

Prepared and promulgated by order of the Air Council

AIR MINISTRY

NOT TO BE TAKEN IN THE AIR

AP1480 was one of the official aircraft recognition publications issued to the services and the Observer Corps. It contained sections on aircraft from different countries and generalised material about aircraft recognition techniques. The quality of AP1480 significantly improved as the aircraft recognition received greater official attention. (AP1480, Crown Copyright)

6
ROYAL CONNECTIONS

From the start of the war, the monarchy took on a heightened importance as the symbolic face of the nation. Their official duties and private activities sometimes brought them into contact with the Observer Corps. It would even result in the construction of a Post on the roof of Windsor Castle. Official recognition of the Corps' important work came with the granting of the 'Royal' prefix in 1941, acknowledging their work during the Battle of Britain. Official duties sometimes brought photographers to record events, but most occasions were much more informal and largely private.

Inspection Tour

Between 29 and 31 October 1940, the King visited the Eastern Command in East Anglia for an official inspection tour. The central part of his visit was to inspect the large number of troops in the region, including a sizeable contingent of Australian soldiers and their Headquarters in Lexden Road, Colchester.[1] Visits were also scheduled to the 18 Group Observer Corps HQ in Colchester on 31 October. The previous day, the King had visited a local Post, most likely E3 at Braintree. The visit produced some images that were widely published in the press.

The Sandringham Estate

The royal estate at Sandringham in Norfolk was the location for 16 Group's O3 Post. On its nominal role were five members who also worked on the estate. Recorded in the Group history:

> On December 30, 1939, the King, together with the Queen, Princess Elizabeth and Princess Margaret, inspected the Post and spent some considerable time enquiring into the operations and conditions of the post; the two members on duty, Obs WG Brooks and Obs FJ Bone, had the great honour to receive their majesties on the post stand, were impressed by The King's knowledge of modern types of aircraft.
>
> The Queen expressed thanks that the Observer Corps was in existence and ready at the commencement of hostilities, and thanked us for our pre-war voluntary training.
>
> On leaving, HM the King was asked to sign on and off in the duty register. Their majesties were each presented with Observer Corps lapel badges.[2]

The 16 Group's history recorded another occasion when the men at O3 received another royal visit:

> **A Command Parade**
> In January 1941, on a cold, frosty morning, with snow on the ground, the parade being inspected by HM The King and HM The Queen, who shook hands and spoke to each member. HM The Queen showed great concern whether our uniform and great-coats were thick and good enough to withstand the weather to which our duty exposed us; but Her Majesty was satisfied on being informed that a thick battle-dress was in the course of being issued. Unknown to members at the time, a photograph to record the occasion was taken of the parade. The Inspection was a great honour for the Post and the Observer Corps generally.[3]

A difficult to reproduce image of the King inspecting the O3 Sandringham Post in January 1941. (Winslow)

The Windsor Post

However, soon the Royal Family would host a Post at Windsor Castle. Apart from prestige reasons, the rationale for wanting to use

In late October 1940 some effort was put into preparing the Observers to meet His Majesty, with both men given matching overcoats, berets and armbands to provide some unusual uniformity at the time. Air Cde Warrington-Morris accompanied the King. (Crown Copyright)

the castle as a vantage point was a clear one. It dominates the local area, as one of the Post Observers said:

> Considering that the tower stands 400 feet above river level, and is tall enough for one to pick out landmarks in a dozen counties, it was a cosy nest. Watch-keeping from such a vantage point was a rare experience, pleasant when there was work to do, and fascinating in the idle moments. At all seasons and at all times there was beauty and enchantment – wondrous cloud effects, glorious sunrises and equally magnificent sunsets. The toil of two hundred stairs could never dim the eye to the appreciation of such a prospect.[4]

The earliest written record we have of the plans for the Observer Corps to open a Post there comes from a letter dated 30 April 1943, from Lord Wigram (Deputy Constable of Windsor Castle from 1936 to 1945) to Captain Harrison at ROC Southern Area HQ.[5] The precise choice for the Post location was either the top of the castle's 'Round Tower' or the 'Brunswick Tower', the two highest points in the castle. There was some prevarication over which would prove best, since the Round Tower was in use by the Castle Guard and already had a local link to the nearby anti-aircraft battery. Eventually, the ROC expressed a preference for the Brunswick Tower. Against ROC policy elsewhere, dispensation was given by HQ ROC for the Post to provide the Windsor Castle Switchboard with incendiary and 'early warning of hostile activity' when required. The Post construction costs were to be borne by the Castle authorities. By late August 1943, the Post was almost ready for use, with operations to begin on 1 September 1943.[6]

Given the importance of the location, the Post Head Observer would have to be an exceptional individual. Fortunately, Observer Lieutenant (Obs Lt) KF Sworder (Capt Kenneth F Sworder, DSO, RN) was the Observer Group Officer responsible for the area. As a Group Officer, he had played a significant role within the 17 Group before the war in situating Posts in London. In discussion

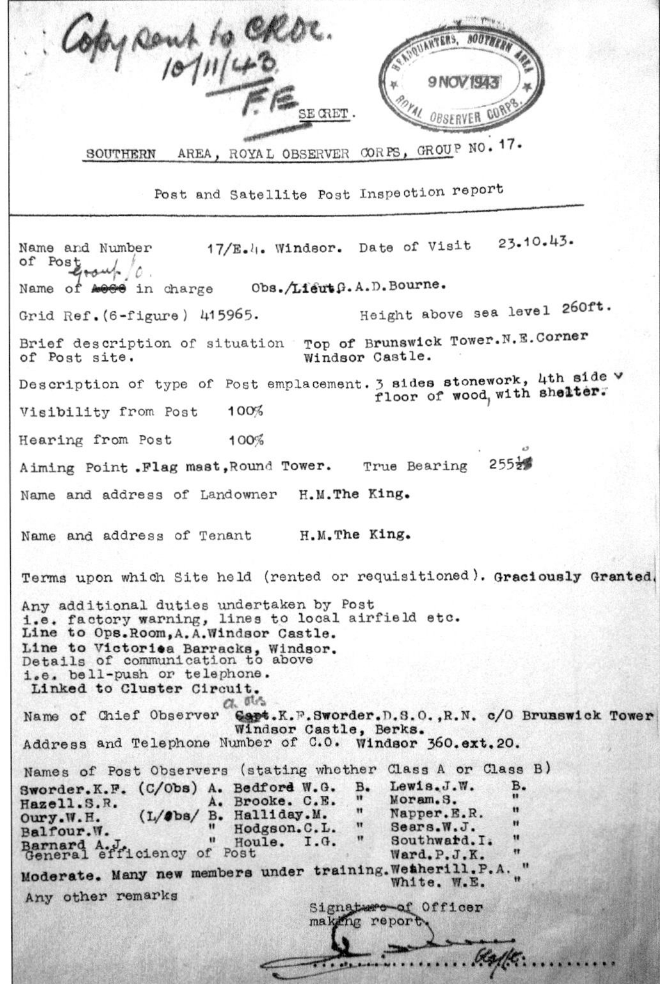

Copy sent to CROC. 10/11/43. F.E.

HEADQUARTERS, SOUTHERN AREA 9 NOV 1943 ROYAL OBSERVER CORPS

SECRET.

SOUTHERN AREA, ROYAL OBSERVER CORPS, GROUP NO. 17.

Post and Satellite Post Inspection report

Name and Number of Post 17/E.4. Windsor. Date of Visit 23.10.43.

Name of ~~AOCC~~ Group /O. in charge Obs./Lieut.G.A.D.Bourne.

Grid Ref.(6-figure) 415965. Height above sea level 260ft.

Brief description of situation of Post site. Top of Brunswick Tower.N.E.Corner Windsor Castle.

Description of type of Post emplacement. 3 sides stonework, 4th side & floor of wood, with shelter.

Visibility from Post 100%

Hearing from Post 100%

Aiming Point .Flag mast,Round Tower. True Bearing 255½°

Name and address of Landowner H.M.The King.

Name and address of Tenant H.M.The King.

Terms upon which Site held (rented or requisitioned). Graciously Granted.

Any additional duties undertaken by Post i.e. factory warning, lines to local airfield etc.
Line to Ops.Room,A.A.Windsor Castle.
Line to Victoria Barracks, Windsor.
Details of communication to above i.e. bell-push or telephone.
Linked to Cluster Circuit.

Name of Chief Observer ~~Capt~~ Ch. Obs. K.F.Sworder.D.S.O.,R.N. c/O Brunswick Tower Windsor Castle, Berks.
Address and Telephone Number of C.O. Windsor 360.ext.20.

Names of Post Observers (stating whether Class A or Class B)

Sworder.K.F. (C/Obs)	A.	Bedford W.G.	B.	Lewis.J.W.	B.
Hazell.S.R.	A.	Brooke. C.E.	"	Moram.S.	"
Oury.W.H. (L/Obs/	B.	Halliday.M.	"	Napper.E.R.	"
Balfour.W.	"	Hodgson.C.L.	"	Sears.W.J.	"
Barnard A.J.	"	Houle. I.G.	"	Southward.I.	"
				Ward.P.J.K.	"
				Wetherill.P.A.	"
				White. W.E.	"

General efficiency of Post
Moderate. Many new members under training.

Any other remarks

Signature of Officer making report.

When the ROC adopted a new Post, the Group Officer was required to complete an Inspection Report to ensure everything was in order. The unique nature of the Windsor Post produced a unique report. Obs Lt GAD Bourne would later take part in 'Seaborne' and the D-Day landings. (TNA, AIR 2/19920)

The ROC Post, erected on the top of the Brunswick Tower at Windsor Castle, gave an unparalleled view over the surrounding countryside. (*Observers' Tale*)

with ROC Southern Area HQ, he dropped his rank and became the full-time Head Observer for the new Post. His deputy was Leading Observer WH Oury, a local chartered accountant. The men for the Post were to be specially selected from existing members of the Slough Post, which was being closed down and regarded as being poorly sited. New entrants were drawn from nearby Windsor and Eaton, and their suitability vetted before they were accepted as Post members.

Recorded in the *Post Stories* of 17 Group, there are further details of engagement with the Royal Family written by Obs FR Hazell:

> On all sides, the hand of friendship was extended, and the memory of this kindness will be cherished by all. The King and Queen took a keen and active interest in the work of the Post and the comfort of its members. Their visits, with the Princess Elizabeth, during the flying bomb attacks, were proud moments in the life of E4; moments which may be justly regarded as an honour and a tribute to the whole Corps.
>
> First personal contact with the Royal Family came on Christmas Day, 1943. In the late afternoon, as dusk was falling, the writer was trudging manfully up the hill through Lower Ward when he had the unexpected privilege of meeting the Queen and the two Princesses. Most people will agree that a smile and a greeting from the Queen of England were more than just recompense for the ill-luck of a Christmas night duty, but the conversation which followed was especially interesting, in as much as it showed that the Royal Family were better acquainted with the work of the ROC than some who should have known all about it, and were much concerned for the comfort of its members.
>
> This royal interest was demonstrated on various occasions by invitations to the Princesses' pantomime and to the Royal Household Ball; by pieces of cake that appeared on Royal Birthdays, and by eager inquiries about any new or unidentified aircraft that happened to be passing. And then, as the war in Europe drew towards its close and the Head Observer, Captain Sworder, DSO, RN, retired after twelve years' service with the Corps, he was received by His Majesty, who thanked him for 'the magnificent work which you and your crew have done during the past nineteen months'.
>
> Operationally, E4 was a Post of more than passing importance. To the south, it was separated from the Winchester Group by a thin neck of the Bromley table, and westwards it abutted on to Oxford. This junction of territories, and the commanding view afforded by the Post, required the utmost vigilance to avert overlapping. It was not unusual to see mass raids in four different groups, and there were occasions when upwards of eight hundred aircraft could be seen spread out across the sky. Conversely, there was the bogey of the single machine which could leave the Winchester table, flash across the Bromley area and enter the Watford Group before Bromley had time to do much about it. In addition to the usual run of aircraft and the commonplace incidents that made up the day's work, E4 had its quota of 'friendlies' which shattered the peace by suddenly dropping bombs, and 'hostiles' which surprised observers by proving incapable of offensive action. The returning bombers, which sounded 'rather rough', were legion, but there were the obvious 'lame ducks', and, sad to relate, one of these – a badly damaged Mosquito – crashed, with the loss of its crew, on the King's golf course only a few hundred yards from the Post.[7] In spite of valiant efforts by both Post and Centre this was failure, grim and tragic. It was also a reminder that many crippled aircraft had been spared a similar fate through the devotion and the efficiency of the Corps – and therein was some comfort and inspiration.

A Summer Night

Whilst under attack by the enemy's flying bombs in June 1944, members of E4 Post on Windsor Castle's Brunswick Tower went into action in the presence of the King, Queen and Princess Elizabeth. The King was impressed by the prompt and accurate tracking of the flying bombs. The Corps, by arrangement between Centre and E4, was asked to warn the castle defences of the approach of Divers until the military authorities had organised their own system.

The post-war 17 Group history recounts two occasions when the Royal Family visited the Windsor Post. Obs FR Hazel was again on duty on Sunday evening, 18 June 1944. He was an 'A' Class Observer, and on duty with him was Obs Reverend Donald Southeard. As Obs Hazell recounted:

> This was a perfect summer's evening. V-Is had been coming over the London Area for the past hour, and more than a dozen had crashed within sight of the Post. The door below the surround suddenly slammed, and investigation disclosed one of the 'Pages of the Presence'. His message was short but startling: 'Their Majesties are coming to visit the Post. You may expect them in one minute'. There was just time to push the 'News of the World' out of sight behind the wireless. Mercifully, the plotting instrument was immaculate. Number Two Observer hurriedly, but circumspectly, put Centre wise; said something about VVVIPs, and hoped for the best. A moment later, footsteps were heard approaching. After opening the wicket-gate to the surround and letting in the visitors, the Observers came smartly to the salute. His Majesty was accompanied by the Queen and the Princess Elizabeth, and the Queen's nephew, the Hon Andrew Elphinstone. With them was Obs Duncan Balfour, who was in the restroom below when the royal party arrived.
>
> The Observers on duty were very soon put at their ease by the note of complete informality which their Majesties introduced. The actual ROC job on the Post was first explained at the King's request. Both he and his party showed great interest in the plotting that was done.
>
> Whilst inspecting the cubbyhole, complete with its car seats as armchairs, his Majesty found a pack of ROC test photographs, which he examined with much interest, pointing out certain types of aircraft then regarded as obsolete. Both he and the Princess were able to identify correctly almost every photograph on sight. Suddenly, there was a query by the King which called for quick thinking.
>
> He asked, "What is that plane that always looks as though it is flying upside down?" During another conversation, the Princess looked up and said, "Are you going to plot that Wellington?" Number One did some quick work with the binoculars and was able to give Number Two, "Wellington. Over post north-east-one at nine".
>
> Towards dusk, another flock of V-1s were plotted coming in, and the Duty Controller arranged a running commentary of plots from the time of crossing the coast onwards. This, with the aid of the Post map, made it possible to follow the course of each flying bomb. More than one was seen to be

On 31 December 1943, B-17 Flying Fortress 42-31178, from the 324th Bombardment Squadron, 91st Bombardment Group at RAF Bassingbourn in Cambridgeshire, was one of 572 aircraft sent to bomb French targets in the Bordeaux and Cognac areas. Fifteen aircraft never returned, and a further 75 were damaged, including 42-31178.

Bad weather and low cloud gave poor visibility, made worse by high winds. The pilot, 2nd Lt Wayne D Hedglin, had to land the aircraft without the aid of radio communication. Lost, approaching darkness, and running low on fuel, the aircraft had to land somewhere. At 17.30hrs, the plane was seen following the Thames. An eyewitness at the time said that 'it had only three working engines and just missed chimneys of houses by inches'.

The aircraft eventually made a wheels-up landing on Long Mead, adjacent to the Windsor Road, roughly three miles from the Windsor Post. Despite extensive damage, the remaining fuel on board did not ignite, and all 10 crew escaped unscathed. The crew were relieved to be in England rather than occupied France, as they had feared. The airmen were taken to the Bells of Ouseley public house in Old Windsor, from where they could telephone their home base. With little else they could do until morning, the crew spent New Year's Eve celebrating with the locals.

The crew inspect the wreckage of their aircraft. (William D Pulliam)

B-17 42-31178 from the 91st Bombardment Wing crashed near Windsor Castle on 31 December 1943. (William D Pulliam)

heading for the Post, but even so the royal visitors put on steel helmets with great reluctance. Divers crashed within the sound circle but there was no immediate danger. 'It was all but dark at 23.15 hours when both Post torches were brought out to illuminate the Post log-book while the visitors signed their names, and left the Observers to their vigil'. The following evening at much the same hour, but giving the Post rather longer notice, the ROC was again honoured by a visit from their Majesties and the Princess Elizabeth. The Chief Observer (Captain Sworder) was on duty with Obs Hazell. During this visit, there was very little flying, either friendly or hostile, nor was the weather so good. Nevertheless, the visitors stayed for more than half-an-hour chatting informally on many subjects".[8]

After the end of the war, the Castle authorities unilaterally decided that the ROC Post was no longer needed. By September 1945, it had been demolished, much to the surprise of Post members and without consultation with the ROC or Air Ministry.[9] If only for prestige reasons, the ROC was keen to maintain a presence at the castle. Soon, rapid, adroit lobbying secured the hoped-for response, when on 23 December 1945, a note was received from the castle stating, 'His Majesty has approved of the re-establishment of the Royal Observer Corps Post on the Brunswick Tower'.[10] When the Corps adopted the nuclear role in the mid-1950s, a non-standard underground Post was created within Windsor Castle.

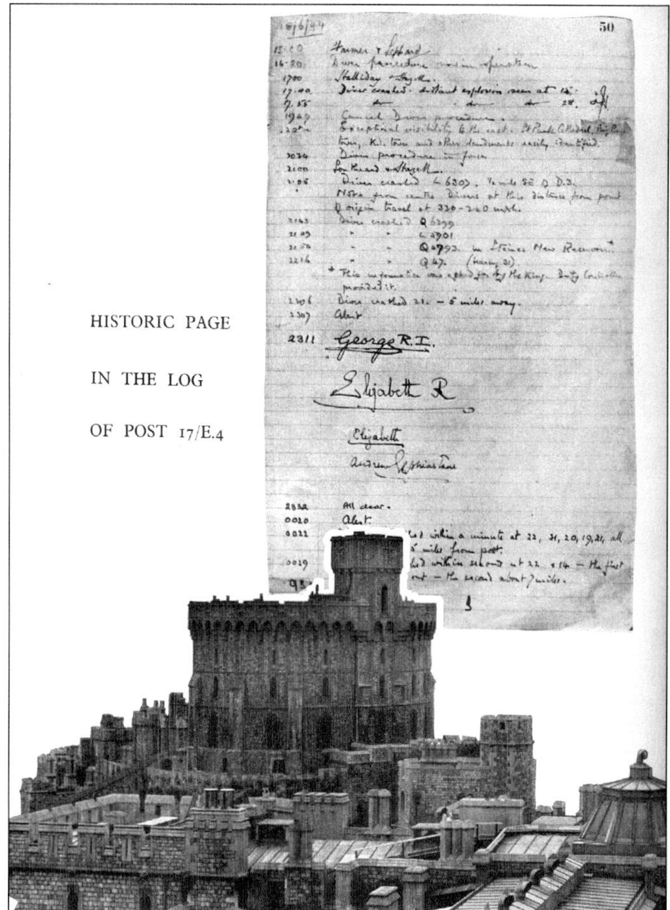

The signatures of the King, Queen and two Princesses in the 17/E4 Windsor Post Log from 18 June 1944. (*Observers' Tale*)

Displayed for the public outside Windsor Castle in October 1940, this captured Messerschmitt Bf 109E-1 was placed there and admittance charged to raise funds for the local Spitfire Fund. (Picryl)

BECOMING 'ROYAL'

In the House of Commons on 9 April 1941, 'soft' questions to the Secretary of State for Air, Sir Archibald Sinclair, allowed him to make a formal announcement that the Observer Corps was to be granted 'Royal' status:

> I am happy to inform the House that, in recognition of the valuable services rendered by the Observer Corps over a number of years, His Majesty the King has been graciously pleased to approve that the corps shall henceforward be known by the style and description of 'The Royal Observer Corps'. I have recently had under review various questions relating to the status and conditions of service of the Corps, and I have arranged to place in the Library, for the convenience of Members, a summary of conclusions on the main points of principle and detail, and of the action that has been taken or is in progress.

When the Observer Corps was granted its 'Royal' status, a small segment was carried by a British Pathe newsreel, mainly using previously published footage. (Pathe News)

Members of the Corps widely welcomed the granting of Royal status and gave them a public standing that had been sadly lacking for so long. It was an honour that came to be much valued and 'will always stand as evidence that those in authority recognised…the work which Observers all over the country were so wholeheartedly performing'.[11] However, recognising the volunteers' work was just the first step in a range of extensive changes that would come to the Corps over the next couple of years.[12]

7
WOMEN TO THE RESCUE

Before the war, discussions of allowing women to join the Observer Corps had been halted by Sir Hugh Dowding, after many senior Corps officers raised objections because of the disruption they believed it would cause. However, women were now undertaking all sorts of war work, and WAAFs (Women's Auxiliary Air Force) were being employed in RAF Operations Rooms with great success. It belatedly led to the recognition that women had much to offer the Corps.

Following the July 1941 decision to allow women to be enrolled in the Corps, small numbers began to join. The Centres were immediately more attractive to young women living in towns and cities, as the distances to travel were generally shorter. Still, it was not unusual for those living in outlying areas to sometimes cycle considerable distances into town to do their shifts at Group Centres.

Domestic conditions were poor at many of the original Centres located in small, cramped GPO premises and other small adapted buildings. Later, when some of the new purpose-designed Centres became operational, the situation improved significantly. On Posts, where conditions were generally far more basic, the number of women Observers was proportionally much smaller.

There was also some caution and even resentment towards the presence of women among some male Corps members. Soon, these male bastions were eroded, especially in the Centres, many of which would never have functioned at all without the significant numbers of women that eventually joined the ROC. Male behaviour and language had to be improved, accompanied by a preparedness to work alongside the women and to soon have female officers.

One notable early woman recruit was Chief Woman Observer Flora Macdonald. Formed in 1941, she became the Controller of the smallest ROC Group, No 40, at Portree on the Island of Skye. It had just five Posts, some Coastguard watcher posts and a Wireless Observer Unit.[1]

Even as women began to be recruited for the ROC, the Army tried to force the Air Ministry to instead accept 'men of low medical category' from the Army rather than release them, in an effort to divert women away from the Corps to serve elsewhere. Fortunately, the Chief of the Air Staff rejected the idea because, as he said, 'No one with an intimate knowledge of the duties which the personnel in the ROC's Centres have to discharge could suppose that the use of these men could do other than reduce the present operational efficiency of the Centres'.[2]

Recruiting More Women

In 1941, the Ministry of Labour became heavily involved in directing potential female recruits towards the ROC. They sought to provide the Corps with 1,400 women to replace 840 mainly part-time men. The remaining 560 were considered necessary to bring the organisation up to its full operational establishment. By May 1943, after six months' work, the equivalent of some 700 full-time women had been recruited, but the inflow was slowing. Needs were said to be greatest in the areas covered by 11 Group Fighter Command and to a slightly lesser extent 10 Group. The need was becoming even more urgent because the Corps was soon to take on the new task of operating the Decentralised Air Raid Warning Scheme from August 1943. To overcome the shortage, proposals were made to attach some WAAF personnel to the ROC, in a scheme to enable young women to defer their conscription for some time before entering the WAAF 'proper'.

The ROC began recruiting women from several sources simultaneously. The direct recruitment of 'immobile women' under 35 aimed to attract those who were married or had some caring responsibilities. As well as the Deferred WAAF Scheme, there was another devised under the Association of Girls' Training Corps, plus a direct publicity campaign aimed at recruiting girls under 18 and a half. Up to 460 WAAFs would be employed in ROC Centres on a 'temporary basis' for the rest of the war, as recruiting sufficient members via other means continued to be a recurring challenge at several locations.[3] The deferment option was particularly attractive to some young women, as it allowed them to meet their conscription obligation by joining the WAAF, while remaining at home by serving in the Observer Corps at a local Centre.

From RAF experience during the Battle of Britain, it was recognised that women were far more effective as plotters than most men, and soon many Observer Corps Centre crews became predominately female. (Crown Copyright)

Training

Training Centre plotters and tellers in earlier years had been largely unsystematic, dependent on the Controllers and Assistant Controllers, and the skills of other plotters. Stemming from the Ambler reorganisation, Memorandum No. 5 spelt out the new requirements:

2. The work of plotters on ROC Centre Tables exactly corresponds with that performed by RAF and WAAF plotters on Filter-room tables; the high standard of qualifications required and the great care taken in selecting and training Filter Room personnel is well known, and the requisite qualifications, selection and training for the equivalent ROC duties should be no less exacting.
3. It is not intended to press for all recruits to be sent for training to the Leighton Buzzard Training School as it is felt that a satisfactory compromise can be effected by appointing one Woman at each ROC Centre who, before her appointment, will attend and qualify at the School and will thereby be able to give instruction herself on RAF lines: this technique and method is increasingly necessary for the ROC to adopt.[4]

Duties of Centre Instructor (Woman)

i) To attend and pass the WAAF Filterers' course at Leighton Buzzard.
ii) To attend any other course away from their Centre as required from time to time by her Group Commandant.
iii) To select and give preliminary instruction to recruits, (to make them competent in one duty only).
iv) To give special instruction on the subjects taught at the WAAF course to any members sent to her for that purpose by the Centre Controller.
v) To exercise a general supervision of the welfare of the Women Observers of the Centre and to advise the Group Commandant and Centre Controller on such matters when required.[5]

Female Officers

The first female officer was appointed to serve at HQ ROC in 1943, but it was immediately evident that a single one was inadequate. After some disagreements, by October 1943, the number of women, particularly in the Centres, and the need to quickly train them, saw the Air Ministry accept the need for more 'women supervisors', although they were to be of NCO rank.[6]

That was also soon recognised as being inadequate 'Due to the fact that of the numbers employed in Centres, 60% of the whole-time personnel are women, a further 1,084 are employed part-time, and a further influx in considerable numbers is expected as a result of the recruiting campaign about to be launched'.

To aid recruitment and retention, because of high turnover expected among the younger women, the Ministry of Labour and National Service recommended that serious efforts 'Be made for the proper reception, interviewing and selection of the women candidates and it was agreed between all concerned that only a woman could do this properly'. Instructions were issued to all Group Commandants to select a Woman Observer from the Centre personnel and detail her, as a temporary measure, to undertake those duties after a short course of instruction. It was initially expected that this would meet immediate needs, 'But since the wastage rate amongst the class of women now employed is high, and may be expected to continue so, there is a permanent need for such a woman'.

The tasks for the proposed 'Group Officers (Women)' was to include, the interview and selection of women Observers, their initial training, welfare work (including travelling, duty patterns, working conditions and so on). Externally they would liaise with the Ministry of Labour, Women's Voluntary Services and work in an advisory capacity to Group Officers employing women on their Posts.[7]

The case had to be made several more times, against the Air Ministry which insisted that the new positions be found within existing officer allocations. Initially known as Women Personnel Officers, it took until February 1944 for the Air Ministry to finally approve the 39 new Observer Lieutenant (second class) positions, excluding the very small 40 Group.[8]

Watford's Reaction

The doubts expressed about the arrival of women at Watford Centre were probably similar to those felt across much of the Corps, with an initial hesitancy soon followed by acceptance of the new reality:

> The decision to employ women as Observers was the obvious solution but, it was not greeted with any marked enthusiasm, and some die-hards who failed to appreciate the seriousness of the manpower shortage deplored the fact that the sacred precincts of the Ops Room were to be invaded by females.
>
> As might have been expected, the girls turned up, did a good job, and in no time, everyone was perfectly happy.

In just five months by Christmas 1941, five of the six Centre crews were said to be 'strongly feminised', with two having more female members than men.[9]

Norwich Group

In the autumn of 1943, 16 Group (Norwich) was representative of those across the country experiencing personnel shortages in their Centres and the efforts made to resolve them. There was a national advertising campaign explicitly aimed at attracting women to the Corps. In Norwich, it resulted in a rush of applicants, but as it turned out, 'many were called, but few were chosen' as recorded in the Group history:

> **Campaign for Girls**
>
> Girls had been joining in a steady flow, but not in the numbers required, so in November a nationwide press advertising campaign was launched in the press, encouraging girls to enrol in the ROC.
>
> The result in Norwich was staggering – the steady flow was transferred overnight into a torrent. Girls of all ages, shapes, shades, trades, professions, married girls, single girls, country girls, city girls, rich girls, poor girls, converged on Headquarters in such numbers that three officers were engaged, severally and unceasingly, interviewing the would-be Observers. The total number of applicants was over 600. Of these, for one reason or another – perhaps we set our standard rather high – only 35 passed through the probationary period, and became full-blown Observers. Of course, it is hardly necessary to state that those 35 were really good.[10]

However good the 35 were, the Group was still short of Centre personnel. In early 1944, Norwich managed to attract some of the sought-after WAAFs, too:

> The almost complete metamorphosis of the Centre was increased with the arrival of 16 WAAF, who were to take duty in the Ops Room, and, as fast as the work went, be just like any other ROC member. Corporal D Brown was in charge of the party somewhat later, Sgt E Scullion arrived on the scene. They

> had a brightening effect, particularly on the male members of the crews, and five of them, Cpl Brown and LACWs M Banks, G Pay, F Pells, and J Wales, remained faithful to No 16 Group till the end.[11]

There was particular praise for the WAAF's at Watford Centre, where the work had become more exacting than it was in the pe-war period, and so it was 'essential to provide detailed instruction'. Of the young women themselves, it was said:

> They proved to be excellent at all these tasks. At the Long Range Board, they were superb, as their work during the Flying Bomb attacks abundantly proved. At 'Telling' they were excellent, for they possessed nice, clear young voices and were more easily audible than the men…The members of the WAAF were especially welcomed at Watford, and by their genuine desire for comradeship and sincere determination to cooperate, they endeared themselves to all Observers.[12]

The recruitment of 'local' WAAFs was initially intended to be a temporary measure, but for many of the girls involved, it ended up as a long-term arrangement, continued until the end of the war.

It had taken several years before women were allowed to join the Observer Corps, but it was the manpower shortage that finally made it happen. However, there can be no doubt that, without these women, the Centres at least, could never have functioned as successfully as they did for the rest of the war.

It was hoped that posters like these would attract women to join the ROC as part of a major recruitment campaign. (Picryl)

In this publicity image three women Observers are at an ROC Post. The reality was that few women became Post Observers, with less civilised working conditions and no doubt a little resentment shown by some men who regarded their Post as a male preserve. (Crown Copyright)

8
REORGANISATION AND RENEWAL

1942 was a landmark year for the Observer Corps. Not only was there a change in the tempo of operations, but there was also the implementation of a major organisational restructuring process, begun in 1941, which gathered pace during 1942 and 1943. It took place at the same time the Corps continued to play a crucial part in the air defence of Great Britain.

Some changes were forced by circumstances, mainly a shortage of available people, and others were necessary to improve efficiency. Combined, they transformed an organisation, designed in peacetime, that had now been tested in battle. It now needed to incorporate the lessons learned from the intense months of the Battle of Britain and the Blitz and readied for a new phase in the war. In today's terms, it was a process of modernisation and professionalisation. Many of the organisational changes ushered in would stay with the Corps for the rest of its existence into the 1990s.

The Start of Change

Aviation magazines like *The Aeroplane* and *Flight* featured advanced aircraft recognition and catered to the air-minded. Many Observer Corps members read both, which also carried readers' letters. In early 1941, several letters were published by Corps members bemoaning its many administrative deficiencies.

A file at the National Archive simply titled 'Observer Corps Committee' opened in 1941 and contains transcripts of some of these letters that made their way to the attention of the Under-Secretary of State for Air, Mr Balfour. They were taken sufficiently seriously, or at least provided a pretext, for the Secretary of State for Air, Sir Archibald Sinclair, to establish a committee to 'Review the present status and conditions of service of personnel of the Observer Corps in the light of present conditions and to make recommendations'.[1]

The committee was a high-level one, comprising Balfour; the Air Member for Personnel; Permanent Under-Secretary (Sir Arthur Street); the Air Officer Commanding (AOC) Fighter Command; Air Cde Cunningham from Fighter Command; Corps Commandant Warrington-Morris; and Mr IVH Campbell from the Air Ministry, Department S5.

The committee was empowered to examine the central question of the Corps' status, including the grievances raised publicly. At their first meeting on 29 January 1941, the main topics to be addressed by the committee were comprehensively outlined by the AOC Fighter Command, Air Marshal Sir Sholto Douglas. These mainly revolved around many long standing issues, such as the status of the Corps, protective clothing, payments if injured on duty, training, its title and the list of grievances presented by Mr Balfour from issues raised in letters to MP's and published in newspapers and magazines. Some of these were acknowledged by Home Security Minister Mr Mabane, who was also attending, and believed them to be caused by the way the Home Guard had been established, which had advanced it over the other civil defence services and indeed the Observer Corps. Committee members were much in favour of keeping the Corps a civilian organisation but that its status be elevated, for which the consideration of granting it a 'Royal prefix' would play a significant part, especially given that it had already 'won its spurs' during the Battle of Britain.

The second committee meeting on 5 February 1941, took a very positive approach to addressing the issues under discussion. In five weeks, by 26 February 1941, it held its fifth meeting and had submitted its recommendations to Archibald Sinclair for his action.[2] A separately prepared, very detailed report by the RAF Inspector General had also been written following his visits to Centres and Posts. The vast majority of the Inspector General's report covered issues raised in the committee.[3] Many of the topics in it informed future developments, but it still took until June 1942 for widespread change to gain traction.

Organisational Change

Before the organisational review process had gained serious momentum, there was an early indication of two main goals for future change in a Minute from Fighter Command to the Air Ministry. First, a reorganisation of the Corps was necessary to

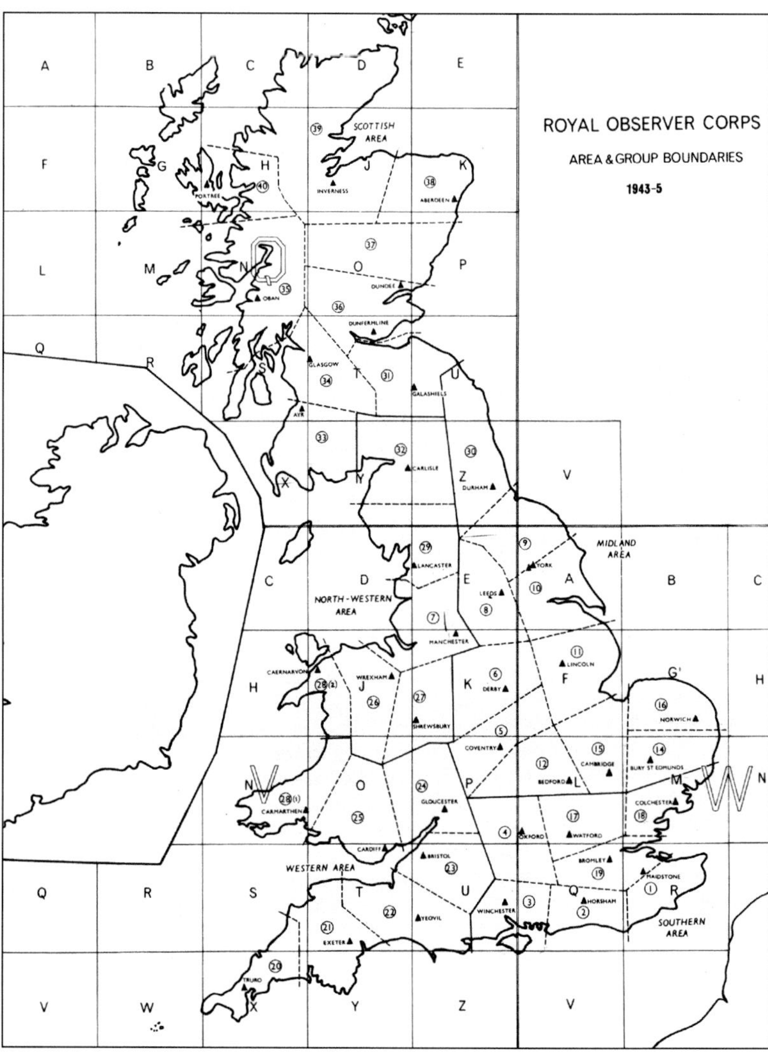

Realigned ROC Group and Area boundaries created by the Ambler reforms in 1943. (Wood, p.177)

UNIFORMS (AGAIN)

The vexed issue of uniform had been rumbling on since before the war, and the universally hated 'boiler' suits issued in 1940 had caused near mutiny in places. The question of the Observer Corps uniform even reached Parliament on several occasions. On 21 August 1940, there was an exchange between the MP for Lincoln, Walter Liddall, and Sir Archibald Sinclair, Secretary of State for Air:

> **Mr Liddall**
> Asked the Secretary of State for Air whether he has considered the resolution passed unanimously at a meeting of Head Observers held in Lincolnshire, on 21st July, 1940, protesting against the boiler suit uniforms which have been issued; whether he is aware that everyone declines to wear them; and will he, in order to strengthen the *esprit de corps* of all Posts, provide Observers with an Air Force blue uniform in two pieces?
>
> **Secretary of State for Air**
> I am aware of the resolution referred to. I cannot agree that the present type of uniform, which is intended for working purposes only, is as unpopular as the Honourable Member suggests. Certain improvements, moreover, are under consideration, which should remove any reasonable grounds for criticism. The introduction of a completely new type of uniform would involve heavy expenditure, which I do not think could be justified in the present circumstances.
>
> **Mr Liddall**
> Is the Minister not aware that the dye from these overalls has ruined many observers' suits, and why should not a two-piece uniform of Royal Air Force blue be distributed to the men?
>
> **Secretary of State for Air**
> It certainly seems that the question of the dye should be considered when deciding on any improvement to the uniform. I shall be glad to consider any suggestions that the Honourable Member may make.

Liddall suggested that the Observers wanted an RAF-style battledress uniform. The exchange was rounded off with some flippancy by MP Robert Gibson:

> Would not the appearance of the uniform in question be relieved by the wearing of a Carnation?[6]

On 9 April 1941, Sir Archibald Sinclair placed in the House of Commons Library a summary of his decisions relating to the review of the status and conditions of service in the Observer Corps.[7] A few days later, this formed the main content of an instruction from Commandant Warrington-Morris sent to Area Commandants. It was intended to settle the many, sometimes very vocal, grumbles around the Corps. Included within it, the issue of uniform was again raised. It largely defended the use of overalls on cost grounds and suggested their practicality for slipping over civilian work clothes rather than a battledress uniform. However, it also proposed a 'new pattern one-piece uniform, which is an improvement upon the present pattern and can be termed somewhere midway between overall and battle dress' to be described as a 'uniform' rather than 'overall'.

That solution proved only a temporary one. Eight months later, on 8 December 1941, Harold Balfour announced in the Commons that 'A blue uniform of the battledress type has now been approved for wear by members of the Royal Observer Corps. It is expected that the issue of this uniform will begin about the end of February'.[8]

The issue of uniforms caused vast expenditure of time and effort from its formation in 1925 until the decision to authorise the issue of a full RAF-style uniform in December 1941. Although often worn in very individual ways, uniforms brought a long-sought-after standardisation. (Picryl)

improve efficiency, the process to be kickstarted with a conference involving Fighter Command, the Home Guard, ROC and S.5 at the Air Ministry. A second internal goal was to 'cut out the dead wood' from the existing organisation, to be led by the Air Ministry.[4]

'Professionalisation' of the Corps

One early proposal to reform manpower requirements would have completely changed the balance and character of the Observer Corps. The proposed goal was to free extra personnel from the Observer Corps, who would then be available to join the Home Guard or other civil defence organisations. The suggestions would have made the vast majority of Observers full-time, with only a small part-time reserve.[5]

At the time, there were around 34,000 male and 500 female members of the ROC. Of those, only around 4,000 were 'A' (full-time) Observers; the rest were 'B' (part-time). They were spread between 40 Centres and 1,375 Posts. This translated to around 20 or so personnel on each Post and six crews of 25 to 30 men and women at each Centre.

The new proposal foresaw a requirement for just 11,000 personnel, of whom 3,600 would work in Centres, plus a part-time reserve of approximately 3,000 to cover the sickness and leave of full-time personnel. Superficially, it appeared to offer substantial manpower savings of around 17,000 people. The proposal further suggested that women be employed to the 'maximum extent possible' in the Centres and that Posts be manned by physically fit individuals, all of whom were to be trained for static defence duties in case of invasion. However, to avoid losing experienced, trained personnel, this would have meant persuading (or conscripting) approximately 10,500 part-time Observers to become full-time Class A members. Even leaving aside that many of these individuals already worked in reserved civilian occupations and many others lived in remote locations where extra billeting arrangements might be necessary for any full-time personnel drafted in to serve there, the disruption would have been enormous.

It is difficult to determine from the official papers whether this was a serious suggestion or a 'straw man' argument, one intended to highlight the potential for massive disruption and to dissuade the authorities from drawing on the Observer Corps to provide extra manpower for other home and civil defence tasks.

Whatever else was going on, strong tea was ROC fuel, and a kettle and teapot always had to be withing reach. Importantly, he is still connected to his Centre with his headphones. (Picryl)

A New Type of Commandant

There was also to be a change at the top, with an initiative to find a new Corps Commandant, to be selected by the CinC of Fighter Command, Air Marshal Sholto Douglas. He had replaced Sir Hugh Dowding in November 1940. In a diplomatically phrased letter to the new Chief of the Air Staff, Sir Charles Portal, Douglas outlined the case for the replacement of Air Cde Warrington-Morris as ROC Commandant:

> As I told you in the course of conversation a few days ago, I think that the time has come to make a change in the post of Commandant of the Royal Observer Corps. Air Commodore Warrington-Morris has now held this post for six years. He has done excellent work, and has been responsible for the expansion of the Royal Observer Corps from a small organisation covering a limited area to an organisation which comprises the whole of the British Isles. This has been a considerable administrative undertaking. He has also done good work in the development of the operational procedure for the tracking and reporting of aircraft.
>
> On the other hand, I feel – and this opinion is, I believe, shared by certain members of your staff and by Lord Sherwood [Under-Secretary of State for Air] that it would be of benefit to the Corps to have a new Commandant. Six years is a long time to remain head of an organisation such as the Royal Observer Corps, and there is a natural tendency on the part of the individual who has held such a post so long to adopt a conservative outlook and to resist changes in administration or operational procedure which may, in fact, be advisable owing to a change of circumstances. I think that it is now advisable for a fresh brain to be brought to bear on the many intricate problems which the progress of the war has brought to the Royal Observer Corps.[9]

Within Fighter Command, there were growing high-level views that a major reorganisation of the ROC was due. In searching for a suitable replacement for Warrington-Morris, Sholto Douglas concluded that 'None of the senior officers of the ROC is entirely suitable to fill the post. They are all somewhat elderly, retired officers of the RAF and Army who have been associated with the ROC for many years. I feel that a younger man with a fresh outlook is required'.[10]

As the ROC was now an integral part of Fighter Command activities, it needed to be closely aligned with their needs. Following a Prime Ministerial edict, there were efforts to reduce the manpower and resources devoted to the air defence of Great Britain. Fighter Command itself was being stripped of Operations Room staff, so more efficient working methods had to be devised. There were even suggestions to disband the Corps and hand over its responsibilities to the Army, particularly its searchlight units. However, the conclusion on this suggestion was that 'The Royal Observer Corps is an essential concomitant of the air defence of this country, and cannot be dispensed with'.[11]

Sholto Douglas had already identified a prospective new Corps Commandant, then Group Captain Geoffrey Hill Ambler. It was an inspired choice. Ambler had previously served with the Royal Auxiliary Air Force and so 'he knows therefore something of handling a semi-military organisation'. Aged 37, at the time he was the CO

The issue of RAF-style battledress in 1941 finally settled the long-running argument about uniforms for the ROC that had been much prevaricated over since the late 1920s and had only grown more serious after the outbreak of war in September 1939. (Artwork by Renato Dalmaso)

Most female ROC members during the Second World War served in Group Centres where conditions could be hot and stuffy. The work they did was directly comparable to that done by members of the Women's Auxiliary Air Force at RAF Sector and Group HQs. Many Centre crews would become predominantly composed of women by the end of the war. (Artwork by Renato Dalmaso)

For some formal occasions and visits to their rural Posts, Observer Corps officers found greatcoats and protective boots were a necessity for crossing muddy fields during the cold, wet winters. Following the fall of France in 1940, when invasion was a real possibility, some officers were issued with revolvers. (Artwork by Renato Dalmaso)

From their North German coast base at Jever, on 16 October 1939, 12 Ju 88s from the recently formed *1 Staffel* of *Kampfgeschwader 30* attacked ships in the Firth of Forth and the Royal Navy Base at Rosyth. Observer Corps Posts from the Dunfermline and Galashiels Groups monitored the air battle as Spitfires from 603 (City of Edinburgh) Squadron shot down this aircraft four miles North of Port Seton. (Artwork by Jean-Marie Guillou)

On 18/19 June 1940, a German night raid was intercepted near King's Lynn in Norfolk. A 23 Squadron Blenheim shot down the Heinkel 111 from KG4, which crashed in shallow water close to P2 Post at Cley-Next-the-Sea. Post members notified the local Coastguard, and they rescued the German airmen, including KG4's new *Gruppenkommandeur*, Major Dietrich Freiherr von Massenbach. (Artwork by Jean-Marie Guillou)

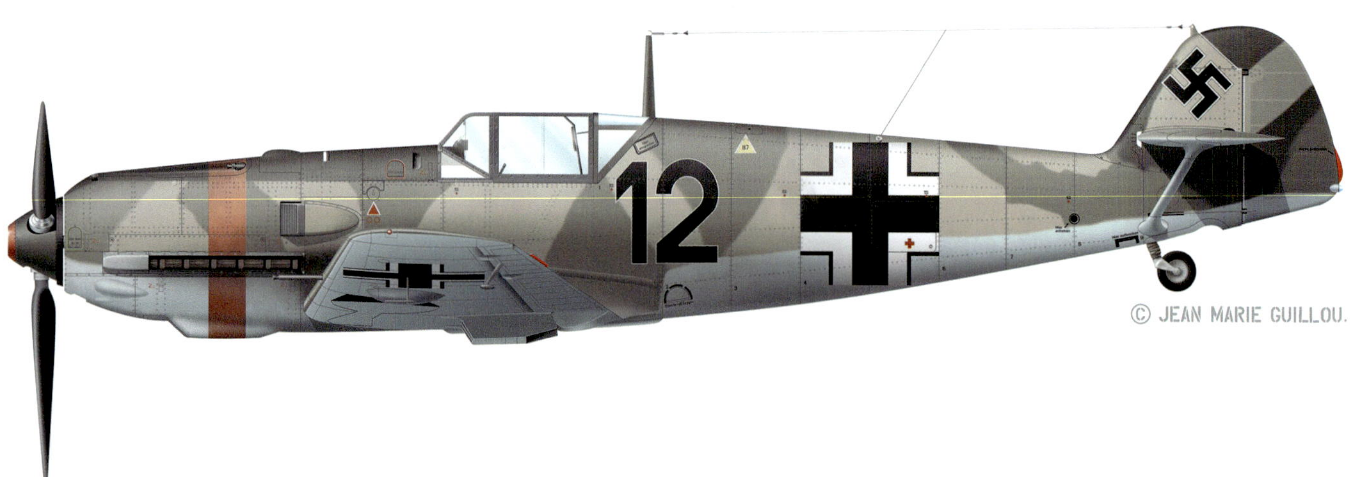

On 23 November 1940, the Royal Observer Corps funded Spitfire P7666, flown by 41 Squadron CO Sqn Ldr D Finlay, shot down a Bf 109 over the Channel. Although not definite, crash records indicate that this was most likely a Bf 109 E4 from II/JG53, which had taken off from its base at Berck-sur-Mer, in the Pas-de-Calais region. The aircraft was being flown by Fw Josef Wurmheller. Damaged by the RAF aircraft, it ditched into the Channel, with the pilot rescued by the Luftwaffe's *Seenotdienst* (Sea rescue service). (Artwork by Jean-Marie Guillou)

On 10 May 1941, the ROC tracked the progress of the defecting Rudolf Hess's Bf 110 more successfully than the disbelieving RAF. Assistant Observer Group Officer Major Graham Donald quickly travelled to the crash site from the Glasgow Group HQ. He talked with the Bf 110's single crew member, who claimed to be Hauptmann Alfred Horn. Donald identified him as Hess, but neither the police nor Army Intelligence believed him, and it took them nearly two more days to confirm he was right. (Artwork by Jean-Marie Guillou)

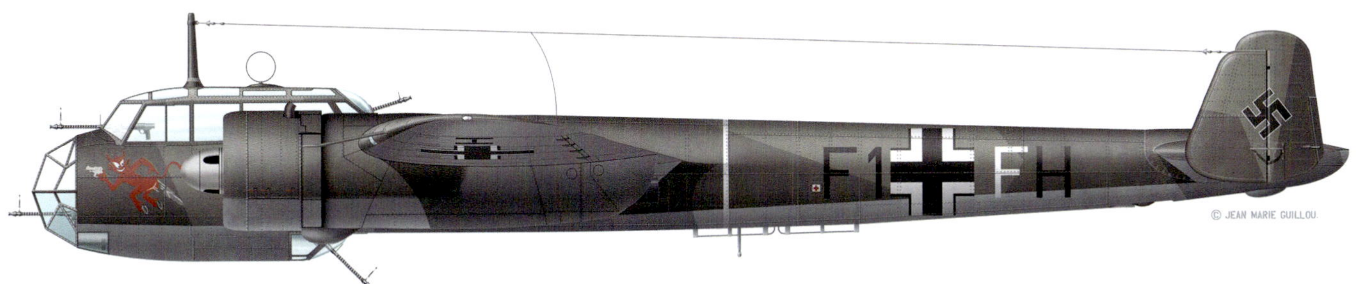

At the height of the Battle of Britain on 15 September 1940, RAF Hurricane pilot Sgt Ray Holmes collided with an already damaged Do 17 that had dropped bombs on Buckingham Palace. The collision caused the bomber to crash near the Victoria Railway Station, close to the RS II Observer Post, high on 55 Broadway above St James's Underground Station. (Artwork by Jean-Marie Guillou)

In the autumn of 1940, the Italian Air Force entered the air war over Britain. On 11 November 1940, 22 CR42s took off from Belgium and were carefully tracked by RDF and then local Observer Corps Posts. CR42 MM5701, flown by *Sergente Pilota* Pietro Salvadori, suffered a broken oil pipe, causing his engine to overheat. Just managing to reach the Suffolk coast, he made a successful forced beach landing, causing only minor damage to the aircraft. Soon repaired, it was re-serialled 'BT474' by the RAF. It later served with the RAF's 1426 (Enemy Aircraft) Flight at RAF Duxford and went on to be displayed in the Battle of Britain Hall in the RAF Museum, Hendon. (Artwork by Jean-Marie Guillou)

In May 1940, Minister of Aircraft Production, Lord Beaverbrook, launched the 'Spitfire Fund'. The cost of an aircraft was set at a nominal £5,000, and the ROC raised enough money for two aircraft. The second was Mk IIa P7837 that went on to serve with 310 (Czech) Squadron. It was tragically lost in a flying accident on 19 November 1941, killing Pilot Officer Vladimir Zoral at RAF Dyce. (Artwork by Jean-Marie Guillou)

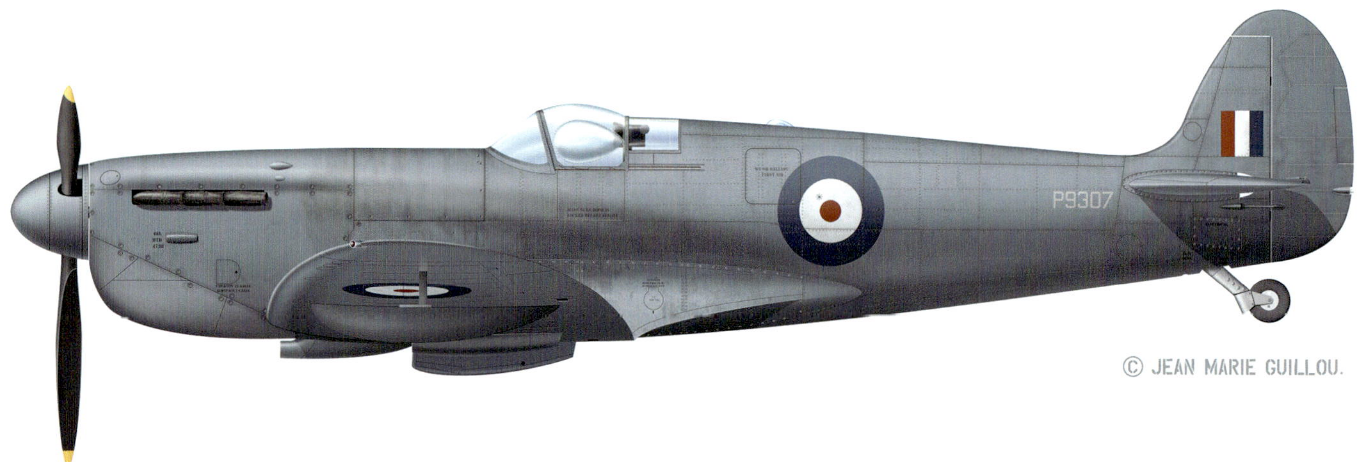

Early photo reconnaissance Spitfires became very active in the summer of 1940, collecting imagery over much of Western Europe newly occupied by Germany. These included Spitfire 1 (PR)C, P9307, from the RAF Photographic Development Unit (PDU) with its underwing-mounted cameras. The aircraft's movements were regularly pre-warned to coastal Observer Corps Groups to track their outbound and return progress and avoid misidentification as enemy intruders. Later in the year, the unit was renamed as the 'Photographic Reconnaissance Unit' and then 1 PRU. (Artwork by Jean-Marie Guillou)

On 6 September 1939, a flight of RAF Hurricanes from 56 Squadron based at North Weald were scrambled to intercept an incoming raid detected by an Army searchlight unit in Essex. With the intruders' progress mistakenly confirmed by RDF, more fighters were scrambled to intercept them. There were, in fact, no raiders, but the 56 Squadron Hurricanes were intercepted by Spitfires and two Hurricanes, flown by PO Rose and PO Hulton-Harrop, were shot down over Suffolk, killing the latter. The catastrophe resulted in a significant tightening of reporting and tracking procedures. (Artwork by Jean-Marie Guillou)

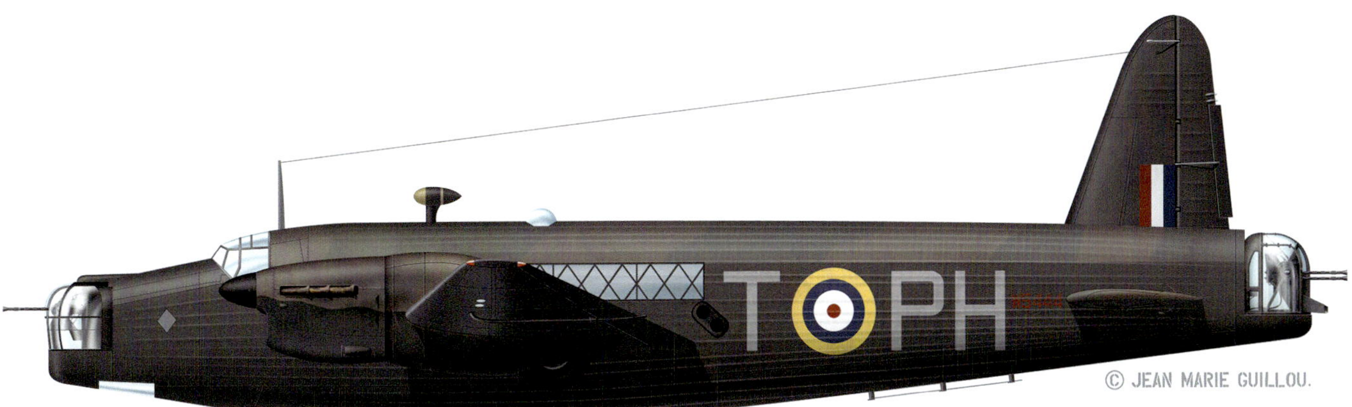

On 17 August 1941, Wellington MkII W5444, from 12 Squadron based at Binbrook, was seriously damaged in a bombing mission over Cologne. It crashed uncomfortably close to 16 Group, Q3 Post, at Melton Constable in Norfolk. The aircraft caught fire, but Post Observers managed to pull some of the surviving, but badly injured aircrew from the wreckage. Their bravery was later commended by Corps Commandant Warrington-Morris. (Artwork by Jean-Marie Guillou)

As the RAF and USAAF bomber offensive grew, many ROC Posts assisted returning damaged or lost bombers on their way home. Sometimes, it was just to report the crash site to police and military authorities. On 31 December 1943, 91st Bombardment Group B-17G Flying Fortress 42-31178, based at RAF Bassingbourn, was returning damaged from a large raid on targets in the Bordeaux and Cognac areas. Becoming lost, without a radio in the approaching darkness, and running low on fuel, it managed to force land on open ground within three miles of the ROC Post sited on top of Windsor Castle. (Artwork by Jean-Marie Guillou)

USAAF Ninth Air Force medium bombers, like this B-26 Marauder from the 397th Bomb Group at Rivenhall, were heavily engaged attacking targets in Northern France prior to D-Day. Some departing raids were so large that ROC posts had to employ 'mass reporting' procedures, rather than trying to count the huge numbers of aircraft heading out to attack German targets on the Continent. (Artwork by Jean-Marie Guillou)

'Operation Diver' became active in countering the German V-1 offensive that was launched soon after the D-Day invasion of France in June 1944. Observer Corps Posts in south-east England became key in detecting their approach to warn the defences. To speed the interception of the V-1s, the RAF quickly placed Forward Controllers at the ROC Maidstone and Horsham Centres, from where they used VHF radios to speak directly to RAF fighter aircraft intercepting the V-1s and alone accounted for the destruction of more than 200. (Artwork by Jean-Marie Guillou)

In early September 1944, the German V-1 offensive began to slow as Allied forces overran launch sites across France, Belgium and into the Netherlands. A new twist was to air-launch V-1s from specially modified He 111 bombers that carried a V-1 under their right wing. The bombers flew at low level over the North Sea, heading directly towards their designated target. To launch the missile, they would climb to around 1,500 to 2,000 feet, start the V-1's ramjet and release the weapon on its way. This method gave the defences very little warning of their approach, especially along the coasts of Norfolk, Suffolk and Essex. Over 1,200 V-1s would be launched this way between September 1944 and January 1945, mainly targeting London, Southampton, and Gloucester. (Artwork by Jean-Marie Guillou)

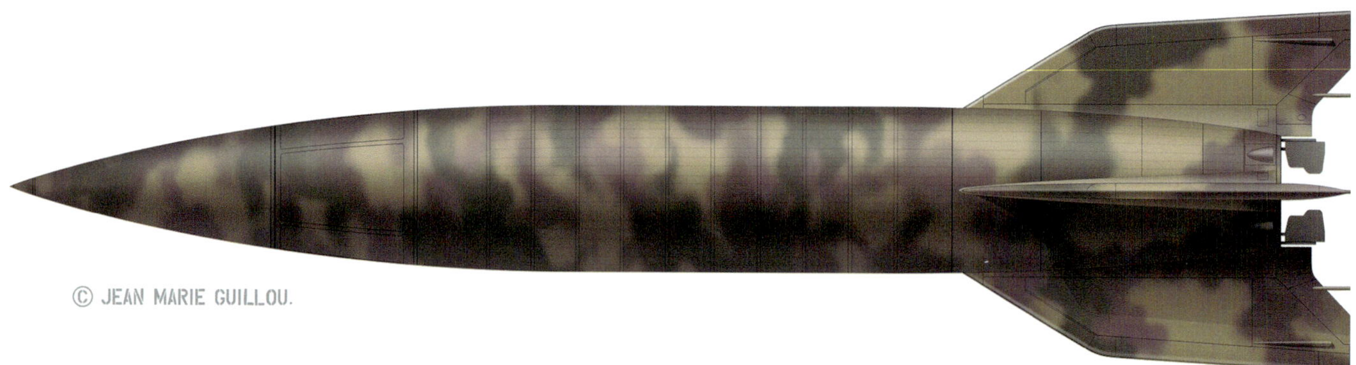

Even as the Allied ground advance pushed ahead, V-2 rockets continued to be launched in large numbers at British and Belgian cities, with 517 striking London. Defence against these powerful ballistic missiles was impossible. The best that could be done was for some ROC coastal Posts to sometimes warn of their launch when their rocket trails were visible as they soared high into the atmosphere when launched from bases in the Netherlands. After that, all that could be done was for Posts and Centres to record their impact. (Artwork by Jean-Marie Guillou)

of Fighter Command's Middle Wallop Sector. He was said to be a 'good administrator and is also an expert on Operations Rooms and Fighter Command operational procedure generally'. Rather than resign his RAF Commission to become the civilian Commandant of the ROC, Douglas proposed that Ambler be promoted to acting Air Commodore, given that he would be responsible for 34,000 full- and part-time Observers.[12] Ambler assumed his position as Commandant ROC on 25 June 1942. In doing so, the precedent was set that all future Commandants of the Royal Observer Corps would be serving RAF Air Commodores.

Air Cde Geoffrey Hill Ambler, as Commandant of the ROC during 1942–1943, ushered in major changes to the organisation and its operation. (Hamilton, p.111)

The Plan for Change

Air Cde Ambler produced his detailed recommendations for change in a memorandum to the Air Ministry Under-Secretary of State on 20 July 1942.[13] Drawn up after visits to some 17 ROC Groups, the proposals were ambitious and sweeping in their scope. It would see the Corps organisation much more closely aligned to that of the RAF. However, Ambler was pragmatic enough to accept that some proposals might need to be modified as events unfolded.

1. Reorganisation of HQ ROC

Ambler wanted HQ ROC staff divided into two halves, one for operations and the other for administration, as in the RAF, each to be headed by a Deputy Commandant. The Operations post was to be headed by an RAF Wing Commander who was fully conversant with all aspects of the Fighter Command system and responsible for the liaison work with the RAF Fighter Groups. He was to be supported by an Assistant, a full-time senior ROC officer.

2. Area HQs

He proposed that Area HQ's be reorganised on the same basis as HQ ROC, with one officer responsible for Operations and Training, the other for administration and organisation.

3. Group HQs

Amblers' proposals included a change to the existing organisation in which, within each Group, there were two parallel systems; the Centre Controller responsible for personnel within the Centre, and an Observer Group Officer responsible for all the Posts, with no one in overall charge. Ambler proposed a single Group Commandant in overall charge, accepting the initial difficulty of persuading one of the two current officeholders to step aside or take second place to the other.

4. HQ Locations

There was a recommendation to rationalise ROC Area boundaries to align closely with those of the RAF Fighter Groups and to co-locate Headquarters with the appropriate Fighter Group HQs. This was expected to achieve much closer RAF/ROC coordination. Similarly, at Group HQs where the Centre Controller and the Observer Group Officer were based, in separate geographical locations, they should be brought together.

5. Staffing

In addition to internal considerations, external manpower pressures played a significant role in proposals covering this area of the organisation. One of the most fundamental changes was 'the proposal for the future manning of Centres. Ambler described the work there as of exactly the same character as the work in any type of Fighter Command Operations room'. Based on his discussions with Centre Controllers and his RAF Sector Control experience, he suggested that the maximum age for men employed in Centres should be 40 to 45 years old, and for women, 30 to 35 years. Commandant Ambler and later Air Cde Crerar were very firm in asserting that women were far more adept at performing the tasks required in Centres than most men, citing the tremendous success of WAAFs employed in RAF Operations Rooms.

However, Ambler was not so keen on employing women with existing domestic responsibilities (often described as 'non-mobile women') as the place for 'such individuals would be in their homes during raids'. He also expressed the view that the number of available men in the 40 to 45-year age bracket would drop significantly as conscription laws widened the age range for individuals being called up for military service. While Class A Observers were exempt from call-up, those in Class B were not, and the end of deferment arrangements for some male conscription groups meant even more men were being pulled away from the Corps.

While these discussions were ongoing, the War Office was attempting to force the Corps to take on low-medical-standard (C3) personnel to serve in Centres. It was a suggestion rigorously resisted by Sir Sholto Douglas, saying, 'I am sure that members of the ROC would resent the drafting into their organisation of Army rejects, few of whom would be likely to be suitable for the work. (Unfortunately, C3 bodies usually go with C3 brains)'.

In September 1942, Douglas submitted to the Chief of the Air Staff, Sir Charles Portal, that, as most women over 20 were already being conscripted and that as all the services and industry were recruiting heavily from this pool, it was likely to be an unproductive avenue of recruitment for the Corps. For Douglas, another possible solution was to be permitted to recruit 17 to 20-year-old young women of 'the type recruited as WAAFs to serve in RAF Operations Rooms'. It would prove a contentious request. This would require the Air Ministry to modify the Corps' conditions of service and to be prepared to release the young women for conscripted service when they reached 20 years old. He asserted that it would be 'unwise for us to deny ourselves access to this constantly replenished supply of women, who can give us a couple of years of useful service' and that these experiences would make them more useful to the services afterwards. However, the Chief of the Air Staff and War Office both rejected his request on the basis that these Groups of women were already being fully recruited. Agreeing to drop these proposals and concentrate on the recruitment of 'non-mobile' women and perhaps some others was to be used as a bargaining chip to resist being required to accept the C3 category 'Army rejects'.[14]

6. Training

Another of the big changes was to make training compulsory, rather than voluntary as it then was, and to financially compensate members for it. Training was to be appropriately organised and conducted by Areas and Group HQs.

The training of Post Observers had been of variable quality across the Corps, dependent on the Head Observer and the capabilities of individual Post members. The review sought to improve and standardise the level of training among Post Observers. This goal was to 'institute and carry out a comprehensive system of training of ROC Post personnel', intended to 'establish a minimum standard of efficiency in Post Procedure and Aircraft Recognition'. Post Observers would be required to reach and maintain a minimum standard in both areas. Proficiency badges were also to be introduced for Observers who reached an appropriate standard.

7. Conditions of Service

The requirement for compulsory training also led to some more substantial changes in the conditions of service for ROC members. Ambler noted a significant difference in attitude, particularly regarding training, between the keenest members and those less so. There was a need for greater leadership, which he suggested came from the desire 'which is very much held in some quarters for the militarisation of the ROC on the lines of the Home Guard but related to the RAF in character'.

Another significant change was particularly aimed at reforming the officer structure, which Ambler (and others at Fighter Command and in the Air Ministry) regarded as a current weakness. He suggested that:

> Some of the higher officers of the ROC, I am afraid, depend on their retired rank of one of the Fighting Services, and seem to be ashamed to wear their ROC uniform. In my opinion this is a most undesirable condition both from the point of view of present and future policy. It is probable that in the measure of time it will be necessary to replace some Commandants, and Deputy Commandants, and I think that such replacements should be made from the resources of the ROC. The only qualifications being knowledge, experience and efficiency in ROC work.
>
> It, therefore, appears logical that ROC Officers should carry some kind of ROC rank, and that salaries should be applicable to rank, and appointment appropriate to rank. Such an arrangement would provide a normal ladder for promotion.

A requirement was also expressed to enable the organisation to more easily shed non-performing personnel, as the only usual recourse to secure their departure was to persuade them to resign. The terms and conditions for the organisation were formalised by the Air Ministry through a specific set of Regulations for the Royal Observer Corps (AP3306).

Amblers' recommendations were endorsed by Sholto Douglas when passed to Harold Balfour, the Under-Secretary of State (and First World War fighter ace) at the Air Ministry. The only notable addition was the suggestion to introduce NCO ranks to recognise the work of key Observers at Posts and in Centres.[15]

In August 1942, Sqn Ldr WHM Walker was appointed as ROC Deputy Commandant, and a strengthening of the disciplinary arrangements was approved under Defence Regulation 29B. On 21 October 1942, Amblers' reforms were given shape in a series of three memoranda issued by Sholto Douglas to the Air Ministry.[16] Each covered a specific subject:

Memorandum No. 1 Reorganisation of ROC Area Headquarters
Memorandum No. 2 Reorganisation of ROC Group Headquarters
Memorandum No. 3 Training of ROC Personnel

With some minor modifications, these were approved by the Air Council on 31 January 1943.[17]

Areas and Groups

After receiving Air Ministry sanction, the hard work really began implementing the changes Ambler wanted, dealing with the details and unforeseen issues that arose.

The reallocation of Groups to the new Area HQs was as shown in Table 3. No changes were to be made to the Western and Southern Areas, which already corresponded roughly with the Areas of 10 and 11 Fighter Groups, respectively.

Following on from this, the location of the ROC Area Headquarters was moved to co-locate with the appropriate RAF Fighter Command Group HQs as shown in Table 4.

Table 3: Reallocation of Groups to the new Area HQs

Scottish Area	to lose	No.36 Group, (Dunfermline)
		No.34 Group, (Glasgow)
		No.31 Group, (Galashiels)
Northern Area	to lose	No.32 Group, (Carlisle)
		No. 29 Group, (Lancaster)
		No. 8 Group, (Leeds)
		No.10 Group, (York)
	to gain	No.36 Group, (Dunfermline)
		No.34 Group, (Glasgow)
		No.31 Group, (Galashiels)
North Western Area	to gain	No.32 Group, (Carlisle)
		No.29 Group, (Lancaster)
Midland Area	to gain	No. 8 Group, (Leeds)
		No. 10 Group, (York)

Table 4: ROC Area Headquarters co-located with RAF Fighter Command Group HQs

HQ	From	To
Scottish Area Headquarters	Edinburgh	No. 14 (F) Group, RAF Inverness
Northern Area Headquarters*	Catterick	No. 13 (F) Group, RAF Newcastle
Midland Area Headquarters	Grantham	No. 12 (F) Group, RAF Watnall
Western Area Headquarters	Gloucester	No. 10 (F) Group RAF Rudloe
Southern Area HQ at RAF Uxbridge was already located alongside HQ 11(F) Group and Western Area with 9 (F) Group at Preston.		
*On 1 July 1943, the RAF's No. 13 Group was dissolved, and with it went Northern Area ROC, with its Groups reallocated to the Scottish and Midland Areas.		

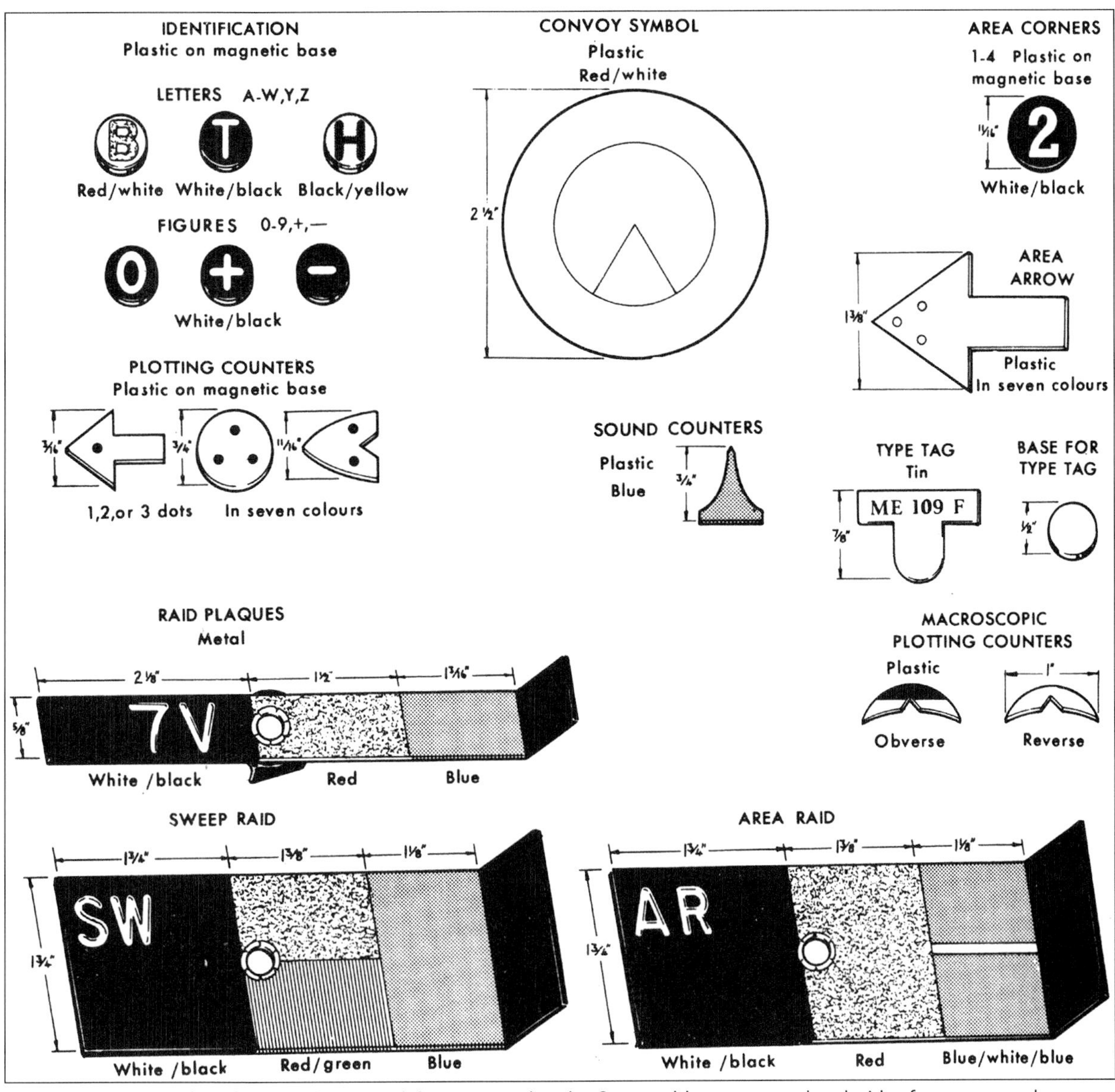

By 1942, the growing list of the ROC's responsibilities meant that the Centre tables were populated with a far more complex range of plotting counters than during the Battle of Britain. (Wood, p.154)

A Growing List of Responsibilities

In 1939, the role of Observer Corps Posts had been limited to reporting aircraft to Centres, and the Centres to 'tell' the information to RAF Fighter Groups and Sector Controls. By 1943, the responsibilities had grown enormously as Air Cde Ambler listed in a report to HQ Fighter Command. These included:

For Posts

i) Aircraft Recognition
ii) Liaison with Coastguards
iii) Satellite Posts
iv) Air Raid Alarm to factories
v) Air Raid Warnings (31 posts on the South Coast)
vi) Rockets for low-flying enemy aircraft (69 Posts)
vii) 'Darky' sets for communicating with aircraft lost or in distress, (29 posts scheduled, 16 fitted)
viii) Homing searchlights (107 Posts)
ix) Reports on aircraft in distress
x) GL (Gun Laying) sets (10 Posts)
xi) Passing of Army messages in anti-invasion operations
xii) Warnings to Home Guard
xiii) Warnings to Bomber Command, and others, by direct lines, to posts by local arrangements.

For Centres

i) Reports of bombs and flares
ii) Reports to Groups of air raid warnings originated by Posts
iii) Liaison between Alarm Controller at the Centre, and Posts
iv) GL interrogation
v) Air Raid warnings to Bomber Groups, etc
vi) Liaison with Gun Operations Rooms
vii) Liaison about aircraft in distress with Bomber Groups and Stations; and with Regional Commissioners, police, etc.

In addition to all this, Posts had, at fixed times, to give to Centres, and Centres to pass on to Fighter Groups fairly detailed meteorological reports.[18]

Forced Retirement

Overall, most of the changes introduced were received positively, as improvements in general efficiency, with some minor grumbles, but one issue caused considerable anger. The decision that male Centre members would be required to retire at 50 was resented by many.

Not limited by official constraints to stop public utterances, there were many letters to local MPs and newspaper editors. So much so that Sir Archibald Sinclair had to reply to questions in the House of Commons on the matter.[19]

The new age limit policy affected some 1,400 men, with 25 aged over 70 years old, 280 aged between 61 and 70 and nearly 1,100 aged between 51 and 60 years old. The expectation was that they would be replaced by 'immobile women' who would be more effective.[21] A better solution might have been to retain the over-50s on an annual basis, but the original line was held, and the older men were forced out, although some transferred to serve on Posts, which had a higher age limit.

At senior levels, the rearrangement of tasks and structures within Groups and Areas meant that some long-serving officers became redundant, whilst others were offered new positions or were redeployed.

One further issue that caused some initial consternation was the decision to make Post training an official responsibility. Ambler felt that this meant that the 'ROC Clubs' that trained and tested Post Observers in aircraft recognition should be disbanded. While the clubs persisted for some time, as the official aircraft recognition training and testing system ramped up, most of the recognition clubs declined quite quickly.

Testing

The advent of the Hearkers and ROC Clubs had introduced a system of aircraft recognition testing that members could take, with different levels of achievement. This arrangement was incorporated among the many other changes introduced by Air Cde Ambler. The new testing system required Post members to attain a proficiency in operational procedures and a high standard of aircraft recognition. At Posts, achieving high standards of aircraft recognition was the main emphasis.

First was the compulsory 'Basic Test', intended to ensure a minimum standard of competence, including a practical test using the Post Instrument. In addition to that, there was a written exam on Corps Standing Orders as they affected Post Observers and a written aircraft recognition test of approximately '50 operational friendly and hostile aircraft'. The pass level was set at 80 percent.

Beyond that, there was a voluntary 'intermediate' aircraft recognition test, with the 'pass' level set at 85 percent, based on a combination of around 100 silhouettes and photographs displayed via an epidiascope.[22]

Each year, there was also to be a voluntary annual 'Master Test', held throughout the Corps, the first taking place on 12 December 1943. This test was exceptionally tough. Out of 200 aircraft views, to pass the test at the highest level, Observers had to get 180 right. Whilst several hundred just missed the 180 mark, 71 did achieve it. The 71 were entitled to wear the coveted woven Spitfire badge on their uniform sleeve. Midland Area routine orders

ROYAL OBSERVER CORPS RANKS

ROC RANK	APPROPRIATE TO APPOINTMENT AS	INSIGNIA	AIR COMMODORE
OBSERVER COMMODORE	COMMANDANT ROYAL OBSERVER CORPS		AIR COMMODORE
OBSERVER CAPTAIN	DEPUTY COMMANDANT ROYAL OBSERVER CORPS AREA COMMANDANTS		GROUP CAPTAIN
OBSERVER COMMANDER	HQ OPERATIONS STAFF OFFICER DEPUTY AREA COMMANDANT GROUP COMMANDANT		WING COMMANDER
OBSERVER LIEUTENANT 1ST CLASS			
OBSERVER LIEUTENANT	ASSISTANT OPERATIONS STAFF OFFICER (HQ) GROUP CONTROLLER* *On Promotion		FLIGHT LIEUTENANT
OBSERVER OFFICER	MOBILE EQUIPMENT OFFICER GROUP OFFICER DUTY CONTROLLER ROC LIAISON OFFICER		FLYING OFFICER
CHIEF OBSERVER	HEAD OBSERVER (POST) ASSISTANT DUTY CONTROLLERS* POST CONTROLLERS* *Operations Room		SERGEANT
LEADING OBSERVER	DEPUTY HEAD OBSERVER (POST) FLOOR SUPERVISOR (OPERATIONS ROOM)		CORPORAL
OBSERVER	POST AND OPERATIONS ROOM OTHER THAN CHIEF AND LEADING OBSERVERS		AIRCRAFTSMAN

As the Commandant of the Corps is usually a serving Royal Air Force officer, he carries the rank of Air Commodore and not Observer Commodore

Table 5: Royal Observer Corps Ranks 1943[20]

FOREWARNED IS FOREARMED
ROYAL OBSERVER CORPS

ROYAL OBSERVER CORPS

This is to certify that

Observer. J. E. Jones.

of Post Y.2. Group 8.

has passed the Royal Observer Corps

Intermediate Test.

DATE. Dec. 17th 1944.

GROUP COMMANDANT.

The 1944 Intermediate Certificate for Obs J Jones from the Askern Post within 8 Group (Leeds). Passing at this level required a high degree of proficiency in aircraft recognition. (https://theddaystory.com)

soon after reflected 'In view of the exceptionally high standard of recognition ability required to pass, it can be said that successful candidates can be regarded as amongst the finest recognition experts in the world'.[23]

The New Commandant

Air Cde Ambler's term as Commandant ROC was due to end in mid-1943, and the Air Ministry considered extending his tour. Having instigated significant changes, they were keen to retain him to oversee their full implementation. However, the RAF insisted on Amblers' return to Fighter Command, so the Air Ministry had to search for a replacement.

Mr IVH Campbell, Private Secretary (S5) in correspondence to Parliamentary Under-Secretary Harold Balfour, was not shy in expressing his personal view that Ambler's replacement should not be a retired RAF officer:

> After what I have seen of the weak and faulty administration of some of the more senior retired RAF officers who have resigned, or been retired from the Corps during the last twelve months, I am convinced that it would be fatal to the new spirit of enthusiasm and initiative which has recently been created and is being fostered in the Corps if an individual were appointed from what I am afraid the rank and file of the Corps regard as a discredited field, viz, the retired officer class. I do not suggest that an altogether exceptional retired RAF officer might not fill the bill satisfactorily, but I think the psychological effect on the Corps of appointing a retired officer might be unfortunate, and we ought not to take the risk.
>
> There is no one in the Corps at present who is qualified to succeed Air Commodore Ambler.[24]

CinC Fighter Command endorsed that position; Sholto Douglas suggested that Gp Capt Finlay Crerar should become the new ROC Commandant. Now promoted to Air Commodore, Crerar would fill the position for the rest of the war from 24 June 1943 to 8 November 1945. He too had experience of working with 'semi-civilians' as the Commanding Officer of 612 (City of Aberdeen) Squadron of the Royal Auxiliary Air Force from 1937 to June 1940, before moving to serve briefly as a Station Commander and then at HQ RAF Maintenance Command.

Crerar's affirmation of the changes Ambler had started was very positive:

> It seems to me that the Corps is now on the threshold of bigger and better things. Its whole outlook has been radically changed and harmonised with that of Fighter Command, whose servant it is: its operational technique has been modernised, its equipment and accommodation re-designed and provided to set the stage for greater efficiency; and a machine for proper administration and operational control has been built, and manned by what is virtually a new corps of officers.
>
> Almost everything has been done to give it a new lease of life – almost everything: but one thing is apparent, the self-respect and confidence of the Corps is not what it was, and there is too a widespread feeling that authority is unnecessarily harsh and unsympathetic in its administration and its edicts. One hears repeatedly such remarks as "I wish there was someone up there who knows us and what we do". The remedy appears to me to be fairly simple. It is to administer the Corps through one of its own bodies, known and respected in the Corps.

The new Commandant appears well aware of the dissatisfaction caused by the policy of retiring the over-50s in the Centres, and some of the disgruntlement this had caused. He was also clearly cognisant of the need to have a deputy thoroughly versed in the life of the Corps to fill the gaps in his personal knowledge and experience.[25]

In a movie star pose, Air Commodore Finlay Crerar was Commandant of the Royal Observer Corps from 24 June 1943 to 8 November 1945. (Crown Copyright)

Before taking the proposal to the Air Ministry for the appointment of an ROC officer as Deputy Commandant, Crerar had already looked at a very well respected ROC officer, Col Angus Robertson. He had left the ROC in August 1943 to return to the family linen manufacturing businesses in Kirkcaldy. He had been the part-time Controller of Dunfermline Centre from September 1939 until August 1943, when he felt unable to take the Post on a full-time basis.

Having met Crerar, Robertson was clearly torn between his personal preference to return to managing the family business and his loyalty to the Corps, asking him to serve in such a key appointment. His self-effacement is obvious 'As you know, the appointment you outlined to me and which you asked me to consider came as a very great surprise…I can only wish I had as much confidence in my ability as you apparently have'.[26] However, Robertson accepted and served as Deputy Commandant until the end of the war in Europe.

While the organisational changes were being implemented, the skies still had to be watched while the organisation was still adjusting to the many recent changes.

9
THE WAR CONTINUES

Whilst internal change was planned and gradually put in place, the work of the Posts and Centres was continuous. However, after the Battle of Britain and the early stages of the Blitz, as the tactics of the air war shifted, so did the pattern and tempo of ROC operations.

19 Group Bromley Centre

The 19 Group Centre (Bromley) was established on the ground floor of Church House, in Church Road, Bromley, in 1938. It had functioned successfully until 16 April 1941, when, on one of the heaviest nights of the Blitz, some 450 bombers attacked London with high explosive and incendiary bombs.

Derek Wood reported in some detail the effects of the bombs that night on Bromley Centre:

> At 21.35 on April 16, a heavy bomb hit the parish church adjacent to the Centre, wrecking it completely. Simultaneously, a mass of incendiary bombs fell on Church House and nearby properties. 'F' Crew, under acting Duty Controller Mr DW Bowen, immediately put its fire squad into action and, with the help of the Home Guard, 16 incendiaries were extinguished or thrown out.
>
> Soon afterwards, the air conditioning plant began to blow smoke, and it was found that one incendiary had lodged in the gutter, and the fire was taking hold. The old building was highly combustible, and fire engines were unable to reach it because of debris.
>
> Within 20 minutes, the whole roof was ablaze, and it was clear that the structure would collapse. Bowen ordered his Crew to leave in small groups, each carrying as much equipment as possible. They ran through the gardens to the emergency centre 300 yards away in the old telephone exchange. There, they set up shop and prepared to take over.
>
> To avoid a break in reporting, the remaining members continued plotting at Church House, even though blinded by smoke and with lumps of the ceiling crashing down on the table. Finally, Bowen ordered a complete evacuation, and as he walked through the front door, the roof and the upper floors collapsed in a blazing ruin. Despite the chaos and the bombs still falling 'F' Crew got 19 Group back on the air.

Fortunately, though they must have been shocked, the crew managed to resume their work in the standby Centre. Eric Wilton, a Bromley Centre crew member, later wrote that:

> Thanks to the devotion of the Duty Crew and the courage of their Controller, the lapse of time during which the raid went un-plotted was only a matter of minutes. The back of the old telephone exchange, in which the Crew were now housed, was on fire. So was the Vicarage next door. A small party of volunteers tackled both these outbreaks, and shortly had them under control. By 22.45, when 'G' Crew took over, plotting and telling were proceeding smoothly on such lines as had not been destroyed by the fury of the flames and high explosive.[1]

On 7 October 1943, Bromley suffered during a second attack when a stick of four bombs fell around 60 yards from the Centre, which shook the building and broke windows.

Bromley was not the first Centre to be damaged. After a series of near misses from August 1940 onwards, the Coventry Centre (5 Group) was destroyed in the mass bombing of 14–15 November 1940. Situated on the ground floor of the Post Office, the area telephone exchange was on the floor above it. Although not directly hit, smoke and fumes were drawn into the ventilation system, and explosions shook the building. Many telephone circuits failed, as did the electricity, the crew having to work by candlelight. They stuck with their work through the night, and even a few relief men got through.[2]

The Groups That Never Were

As the Observer Corps had expanded during the mid-1930s, it was believed that Groups covering Wales and the west coast of England and Scotland were unnecessary, as they were unlikely to be attacked. Somewhat belatedly, it was realised that this was no longer the case and a further rapid expansion was initiated. However, Northern Ireland was still left behind in all these discussions. Believed to be largely out of reach of the Luftwaffe, its air defences were rudimentary and were only stepped up well into the war. In fact, no ROC presence would exist in the north until the nuclear age. However, files in the National Archive show the detailed planning that took place in readiness for the formation of two Groups during 1941.

As the province was relatively compact in size and shape, it was considered that control could be centralised with RDF, searchlight, fighter control, and other assets, all reporting to one location. The existing searchlight coverage, wireless observation units and the proposed extension of the RDF network were to be supplemented by additional resources. The whole topic was explored by a high-level meeting at the Air Ministry in London in May 1941.[3] The key areas for protection included Belfast and military assets such as RAF airfields and critical port facilities, including Belfast Lough, Larne, Lough Erne and Londonderry. The overall system was to be managed in the same way as in the rest of Britain, with Sector and Filter Rooms. The possibility of supplementing information from the Republic was also considered under reciprocal arrangements, but is not further described.[4]

RDF was seen as the key to the province's protection, in combination with Chain Home, Low, and Extra-Low stations on the eastern and northern coasts. Mobile units were set up at Crossmaglen and Newtonbutler to provide coverage to the south, over the Irish Republic, as it was thought that a southern approach route was a viable option for Luftwaffe bombers. There was also the possibility of providing inland RDF coverage. The main limitation was the availability of equipment capable of providing effective coverage below 3,000 feet (sometimes reported as 5,000 feet). However, another significant brake on all the planned measures was the poor state of the telecommunications infrastructure across Northern Ireland.

Preparation was well advanced by April 1941. ROC Area Commandants on the mainland were approached informally to see if they could suggest any possible names for appointment as Commandants.[5] The main consideration in choosing potential Post locations was having telephone exchanges and villages or towns to draw volunteers from. There were immediate concerns about recruiting sufficient Post personnel at locations close to the border.

Table 6: 1941 Proposed ROC Post Locations in Northern Ireland[6]

No 41 Group (Belfast)		
Bushmills	Bangor	Crossgar
Ballycastle	Coagh	Portaferry
Armoy	Crumlin	Armagh
Cushendall	Belfast	Banbridge
Cloughmills	Holywood	Dromara
Glenarm	Newtonards	Seaforde
Portglenone	Mill Isle	Markethill
Broughshane	Moire	Rathfriland
Larne	Lisburn	Ardglass
Magherafelt	Killinchy	Newton Hamilton
Toome	Kircubbin	Newry
Ballyclare	Moy	Newcastle
Antrim	Portadown	Warren Point
Carrickfergus	Saintfield	Kilkeel

No 42 Group (Londonderry)		
Magilligan	Draperstown	Dungannon
Coleraine	Castlederg	Derrygonnelly
Limavady	Newton Stewart	Ballygawley
Londonderry	Drumquin	Lisbellaw
Garvagh	Omagh	Fivemiletown
Claudy	Carrickmore	Caledon
Dungiven	Cookstown	Belcoe
Strabane	Kesh	Newton Butler
Cranagh	Fintona	

Some of the best images available of an ROC Centre Operations Room during wartime come from 19 Group Bromley. If accurately dated to 1943, then they must be of the Group's standby Centre after the destruction of the main one in April 1941. They show the cramped, improvised conditions in which the Observers were then working.

The 'balcony' at Bromley, from where the Controller and key staff can look down on the Group plotting table.

The tellers on the balcony were able to communicate with adjacent Groups and associated agencies.

The view of the plotting table from the Bromley balcony shows the improvised nature of the arrangements.

The upright mounting of the Long Range Board (LRB) in Centres saved a great deal of space. It gave Centre Controllers and crews a much wider appreciation of activity in adjacent areas. (Air Ministry Collection, via Picryl)

We get no direct indication of why the idea of setting up an ROC system across Ulster was ultimately abandoned, but perhaps a clue comes from a subsequent Air Ministry meeting in London on 30 June 1941. At the very beginning, the chairman's opening statement says:

> The Commandant ROC has visited Northern Ireland. The C-in-C Fighter Command had informed the Air Ministry that, in the light of the Commandant's report, he was not now in favour of establishing an Observer Corps organisation in Northern Ireland as had been proposed.[7]

Air Raid Warnings

The issuing of air raid warnings quickly became a controversial issue during 1940. A highly centralised system saw widespread warnings issued across the country. The public safety issue had to be balanced against the disruption that the frequent issuing of unnecessary widespread warnings caused to war production and the population in general. There were also occasions where the failure to issue sufficient warning resulted in extra loss of life. Although the responsibility of the Ministry of Home Security, the Observer Corps were often blamed for the failures in the warning system. The problem was so serious it reached Cabinet level on occasions during 1940 but was not satisfactorily resolved.[8]

One partial solution was to use the 'Alarm Controllers' to operate from Observer Corps Centres to provide 'a reliable secondary' warning when there was danger of attack on important industrial targets within the Groups area. If the system was to go ahead Fighter Command insisted that the it should be responsibility of Ministry of Home Security (MoHS) staff in Observer Corps premises, not the Corps itself.

The advent of the tip-and-run raids during 1942 posed another layer of difficulty, as they sometimes provided insufficient time to allow the issue of warnings to selected local industrial sites and then a wider distribution to the local public. A hybrid system was evolved where coastal Posts could issue a warning to the local town in the event of an attack. It also passed the warning on to its Centre, however, on occasions in Colchester it happened that this method meant that it failed to reach the wider public in sufficient time resulting in the absence of any public warning altogether. Local workers threatened strikes unless the public warnings were issued at the same time as the industry warning.[9]

The success of the Industrial alarm system, it heavily reduced the number of unnecessary alarms to factories, led to requests to widen it further. This was the devolution of the air raid warning system to Observer Corps Centres. Based in Group Centres, the Alarm Controllers (many being Corps members transferred to the MoHS for the Alarm work), would issue a local public warning of imminent air attack when they issued their industrial warning.[10] It was greatly aided by the ongoing reorganisation of the ROC, but especially with the advent of the Long Range Boards in Centres that gave Alarm Controllers a better indication, and longer warning, of approaching potential raids.

The 'new' system began operation in November 1943 at Truro,

The Alarm Controller at Bromley looks from the balcony at the Long Range Board by his switchboard to issue preliminary warnings. (Whitty)

rolled back along the south coast, up to Colchester, then westwards across the country to South Wales. From Bury to North Wales and then the northern part of the country ending at Inverness, completed on 14 April 1944. Groups would be aware of attack warnings from information told to them from adjoining Centres.[11] The work of the Controllers could involve difficult judgements, raids could fly feints as they approached a potential target and suddenly change course to strike a different target. Single German reconnaissance aircraft were generally ignored, but sometimes would turn out to be tip-and-run raiders and so mistakes were made. If warnings were made they needed to be done in a timely way. Too early and they would waste important production time. Too late would bring real disaster. However, the revised system was far more effective. These were especially important in the period of V-1 attacks, when the ROC displays made the Controllers job considerably easier than it could have been.[12]

Minister of Home Security Herbet Morrison visits Bromley Centre in 1943, in the company of Commandant ROC Finlay Crerar, and Obs Cdr Binyon, Group Commandant 19 Group. (Crown Copyright)

THE 'Y' SERVICE

Issued with special radio listening sets, the very secretive Radio Security Service, better known as the 'Y' Service, employed civilian listeners as 'Voluntary Interceptors' (VIs). They were typically radio 'hams' or those with specialist radio knowledge or experience who listened to German Morse and radio transmissions, recording and reporting what they heard. Sometimes this was done from home; for others, it required them working from a location where suitable equipment had been installed. At some RDF stations, Y Service listeners were employed to determine the geographic origins of German radio signals through triangulation. In some cases, the VIs were issued with ROC uniforms to appear to the uninitiated as Corps members and so allay local suspicion. That certainly happened at Aldeburgh in Suffolk, and no doubt other locations around Britain. The same thing also happened in Northern Ireland, which caused some questions and curiosity, simply because the Corps was not there and so immediately attracted unwanted attention, the complete opposite of what they sought to achieve![13]

Mr William 'Bill' Amos ran a radio shop in Haddington's Market Street in East Lothian. He used the shop as a cover, relying on an assistant to deal with customers while he worked upstairs as a secret Voluntary Interceptor. After the war, his service was recognised in the 1946 New Year's Honours list with the award of a British Empire Medal. At that time, and for many years afterwards, the work of the Radio Security Service remained secret, connected as it was with Bletchley Park. His British Empire Medal is listed in the *London Gazette* as 'William Alexander Amos, Observer, Royal Observer Corps', thus maintaining his fictional cover.[14]

Airways Corporation.
John ALTHAM, Foreman Plater, Grayson, Rollo & Clover Docks Ltd.
William Alexander AMOS, Observer, Royal Observer Corps.
Annie, Mrs. ANDERSON, Weaver and Weaving

The *London Gazette* entry for William Amos's BEM awarded in the 1946 New Year's Honours List. He had served as a member of the 'Y' Service, but to maintain their secrecy, he was described as a member of the ROC. (*London Gazette*)

The major changes to the Corps organisation and operations proposed by Air Cde Ambler took time to implement under Air Cde Crerar. During 1943 and 1944, they gathered pace and reached the 'frontline' at Centres and Posts.

New Centres

Ever since its inception, the Group Centres that were established were usually 'shoehorned' into repurposed existing premises, often small empty spaces in GPO telephone exchanges or sometimes other buildings that were deemed suitable before 1939. This was especially true of those created in the immediate runup to the outbreak of war. The experiences of the Battle of Britain and the Blitz, when some Centres received direct hits, and others were in high-risk locations, such as city centres and co-located with GPO telephone exchanges, posed significant vulnerabilities.

The arrangements for the provision of alternative emergency Centres in case the primary one was damaged or destroyed were even less satisfactory. These were widely neglected before 1941–42. In some cases, the preparations were extensive. However, in many cases, multiple difficulties had led to inadequate arrangements. Often, there were problems identifying available, potentially suitable alternate locations that were not themselves in vulnerable areas, or were not too close to the existing main Centre. In some cases, premises were earmarked as Alternate Centres but could not be accessed until an actual emergency occurred.

Amblers' report had recommended that new purpose-built Centres be constructed and that potential standby Centres be pre-identified. The growing number of tasks the Corps was accumulating, the introduction of female Observers, and other factors meant that the existing premises rarely remained adequate for the new circumstances.

The proposed solution was to provide a standard design and size for Centres to be used nationwide. It was a plan that was never fully achieved for several reasons. The basic idea of creating purpose-built premises, mainly in new locations, that incorporated proper plotting table space, a balcony, a GPO equipment room, appropriate domestic facilities, a canteen, and sleeping accommodation would have been a giant leap forward for the ROC.

However, implementing the plan proved far more difficult. It is very clear that at the beginning of 1942, the position on the provision of buildings and facilities for the ROC was highly unsatisfactory. Air Cde J Whitworth-Jones, the Director of Fighter Operations at HQ Fighter Command, attempted to take a grip of the situation. He defined the problem as stemming from the ROC's lack of a clear policy on what was actually needed, and from Fighter Command having to negotiate with several branches of the Air Ministry at once to get things done. When a concession was squeezed out of the Air Ministry, the RAF and ROC wanted them interpreted as a general policy to be applied everywhere. As Whitworth said, in a document he never intended for an official file 'We have decided to stop the rot'. Whatever his preferences for the documents' use, it captured the main problems very succinctly and provided a proposed solution. This was to agree a policy for moving forward via a conference of involved parties, agree a standard Centre design for the ROC, and to 'Give every Observer Corps Centre the once over and fix, once and for all, the building reconstruction and new amenities needed'.[15]

Over the following few months, there was a lot of official scurrying around to identify the main issues that needed attention. It was not that there was no work going on, but rather that it lacked clear direction or someone directly in charge of advancing it. Air Cde Whitworth-Jones Conference at the Air Ministry certainly pushed the issue forward. These included recognition that the efforts to provide some protective measures for existing premises had failed, which was significant because many of them were in particularly vulnerable areas liable to 'heavy blitz attack'. The proposed solutions were to build new Centres in locations where the existing premises were 'peculiarly vulnerable, accommodation inadequate; and alternatives, by way of requisitioning, are impracticable'. That the 'new buildings must provide the necessary degree of security' by virtue of their new location or by the provision of 'direct passive defence measures'. The meeting was also presented with a complete list, describing the present state of affairs for all the primary and alternative Centres. The list of Centres requiring significant attention was extremely long.[16]

A shot from the balcony of an unnamed new standard design ROC Centre in 1943. Even in the new Centres, the operations area was still quite small. (Picryl)

New 17 Group Centre

Plans for a new design of standard ROC Centres had been advanced before Whitworth-Jones's efforts to accelerate processes. The previous experiences of Corps Commandants Ambler and Crerar heavily influenced these designs. Among the first of these new Centre designs approved by Fighter Command in October 1941 were those for Watford and the two in York, all of which were completed during 1943.

The 'new' Centre for 17 Group at Watford was opened in August 1943. Originally in the GPO buildings in Market Street, Watford, it moved to new premises at Cassiobury Drive. In the remaining years of the war, Watford in particular, became a showcase, the location for many VIP visits, and, fortunately, the source of some of the best images available of the inside of one of the 'new' Centres.

The design plan for the new 17 Group Centre provides a clear picture of the external and liaison links now required of the ROC. Post reports were received at the Centre as before, and plotted on the table, and overseen by the Post Controller. Inter-Centre Tellers

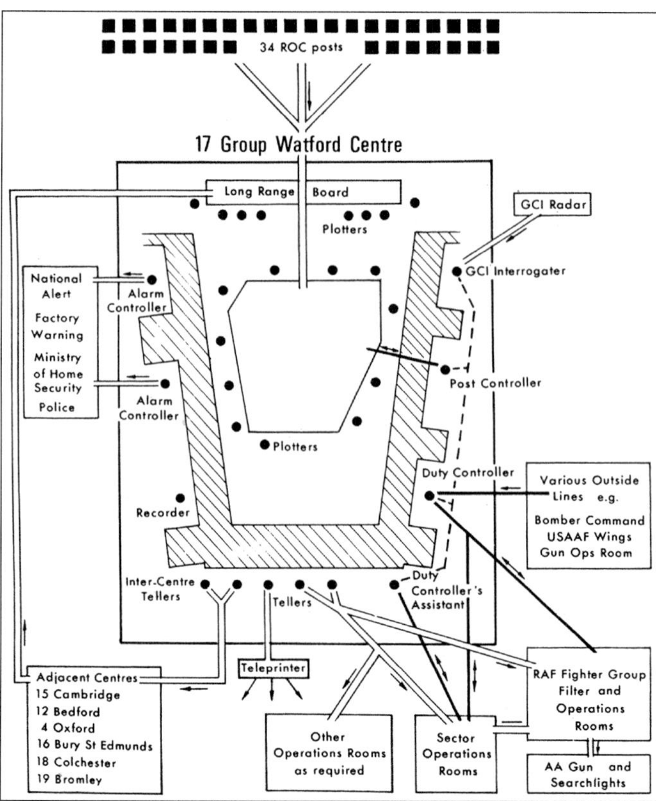

A schematic of a 'new' standard Centre Operations Room layout, in this case, Watford. It shows the Group's main positions and external communications links. (Wood, p.156)

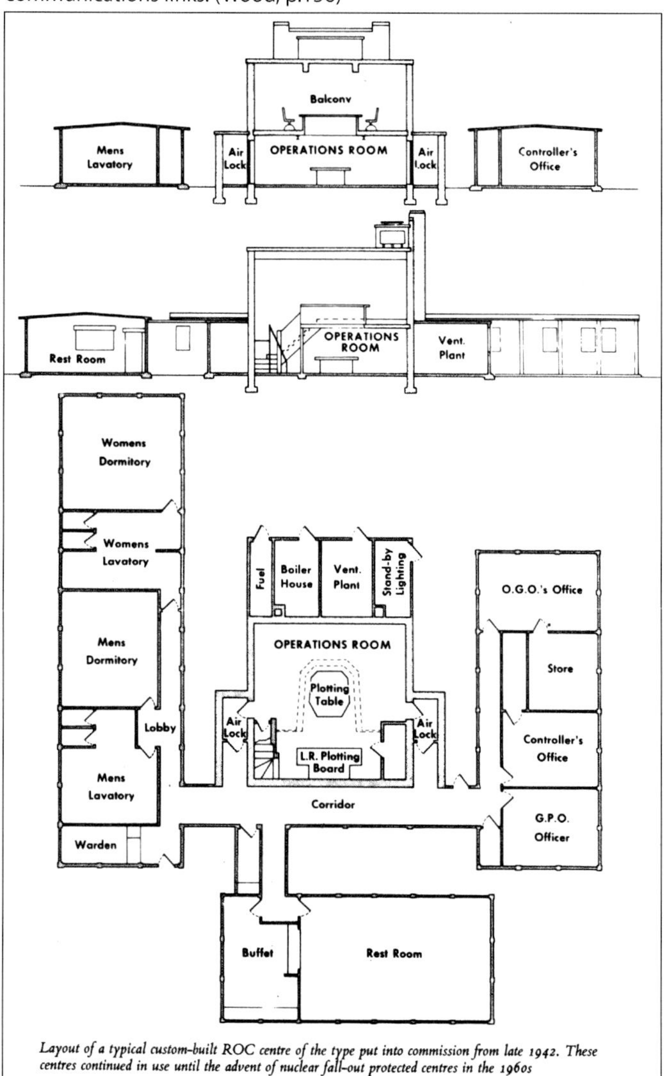

Layout of a typical custom-built ROC centre of the type put into commission from late 1942. These centres continued in use until the advent of nuclear fall-out protected centres in the 1960s

A plan of a standard design Centre showing the layout of the complete structure incorporating office and domestic accommodation. (Wood, p.188)

The new Watford Centre opened at Cassiobury Drive in August 1943. It was painted to resemble something other than an Observer Corps Centre. (*Observers' Tale*, p.21)

communicated movements with all the adjacent ROC Groups. The Long Range Board (LRB) had become increasingly important as the war progressed, providing early warning to the neighbouring Groups of approaching aircraft. Teleprinters disseminated 17 Group data to recipients through their connections. The two Alarm Controllers were now responsible for issuing air raid warnings from ROC Centres in conjunction with the Ministry of Home Security and Police.

There were also external links to RAF Fighter Group, Sector Operations, and Filter Rooms, along with the Army searchlights and anti-aircraft guns handled by the Duty Controller's assistant and tellers. In overall charge was the Duty Controller, who, in addition to having overall responsibility for the Group, could maintain direct external links with other organisations. These would include the RAF's Fighter Group Filter and Operations Rooms. Depending on the Group's location, they may also have links to local RAF and United States Army Air Force (USAAF) airfields, nearby naval units, and other high-priority agencies. The links to nearby USAAF and RAF airfields often proved valuable in helping to 'home' lost aircraft during training flights or those returning from operational missions.

Whilst Watford and some other Centre projects and relocations were completed, plans for many more never reached fruition for various reasons. Works at Cambridge, Exeter, Glasgow, Shrewsbury and elsewhere, all considered 'urgent', encountered severe delays. In Cambridge, it was simply finding a satisfactory new location to build a Centre. In Wales, the local authority described the Carmarthen Centre as a 'health hazard', but plans to modernise the building heavily were first delayed, then abandoned due to objections from the owner. In other locations, major works programmes were hit by escalating costs and bureaucratic issues, often leading to a rethink, scaling back, or their total abandonment. By the end of 1944 and in early 1945, several planned programmes were paused as their continued necessity was increasingly questioned, given that the potential threat to many areas of the country had significantly receded and the ultimate defeat of Germany imminent.[17]

The Long Range Board

One persistent issue for Observer Corps Centres was the handing over of tracks from one to another as they passed into or out of their area. All too frequently, it would end up in missed or duplicated tracks that caused confusion that took time to resolve.[18]

Warning of still-distant raids affecting adjoining Groups was valuable to everyone, not least the air raid warning system. It helped when raids crossed boundaries as handovers were less often missed and did not come as a surprise to the 'receiving' Centre, which was already aware of the possible approach. These weaknesses were well recognised and were addressed by HQROC Operating Instruction No. 46 introduced in January 1944 (and revised later that year) that would see the introduction of Long Range Boards across most of the Corps. However, the idea did not originate with Headquarters but was an initiative first tried at Watford Centre and led to an innovative method of mounting the display.

Existing ROC Centres were too small to accommodate significantly larger plotting tables, which would have been much more difficult for the plotters to work. Using smaller-scale charts on the existing tables would have made life more difficult for everyone. The solution was to create a near vertically mounted chart covering a much larger area and to position it so it was visible from the Controllers' balcony. It was to be manned by plotters fed by information from lines with adjacent Groups. An improvised prototype arrangement was set up at Watford during 1942 and successfully demonstrated to Air Ministry representatives and the Senior Air Staff Officer (SASO) at Fighter Command. The idea was quickly accepted and revised 'Long Range Boards' using a magnetic surface, and plaques appeared at all Centres.[19] At Watford, 'Tracks of the raiders were clearly displayed approaching the Group from the Colchester and Bromley areas, thus giving plotters ample time to warn the appropriate Posts of their impending arrival'.[20] It was also a system that helped facilitate the decentralisation of the Public Air Raid Warning system.

In addition to the internal organisational changes the ROC was making, changes in enemy tactics brought further alterations to the Corps' operations. The Nazi invasion of the Soviet Union in 1941 saw a diversion of Luftwaffe units and aircraft from the Western to the Eastern Front. No longer mounting mass raids of the scale seen during the Battle of Britain, it began to employ smaller-scale attacks.

Baedeker Blitz

In April and May 1942, the Luftwaffe launched a series of raids against British cities, including Norwich, York, Bath, Exeter and Canterbury, judged as of 'cultural and historic value', reputedly in retaliation for RAF Bomber Command's destruction of Lubeck.

On 23–24 April 1942, Exeter was the first city struck, followed by a second raid the following night. The bombers hit Bath and

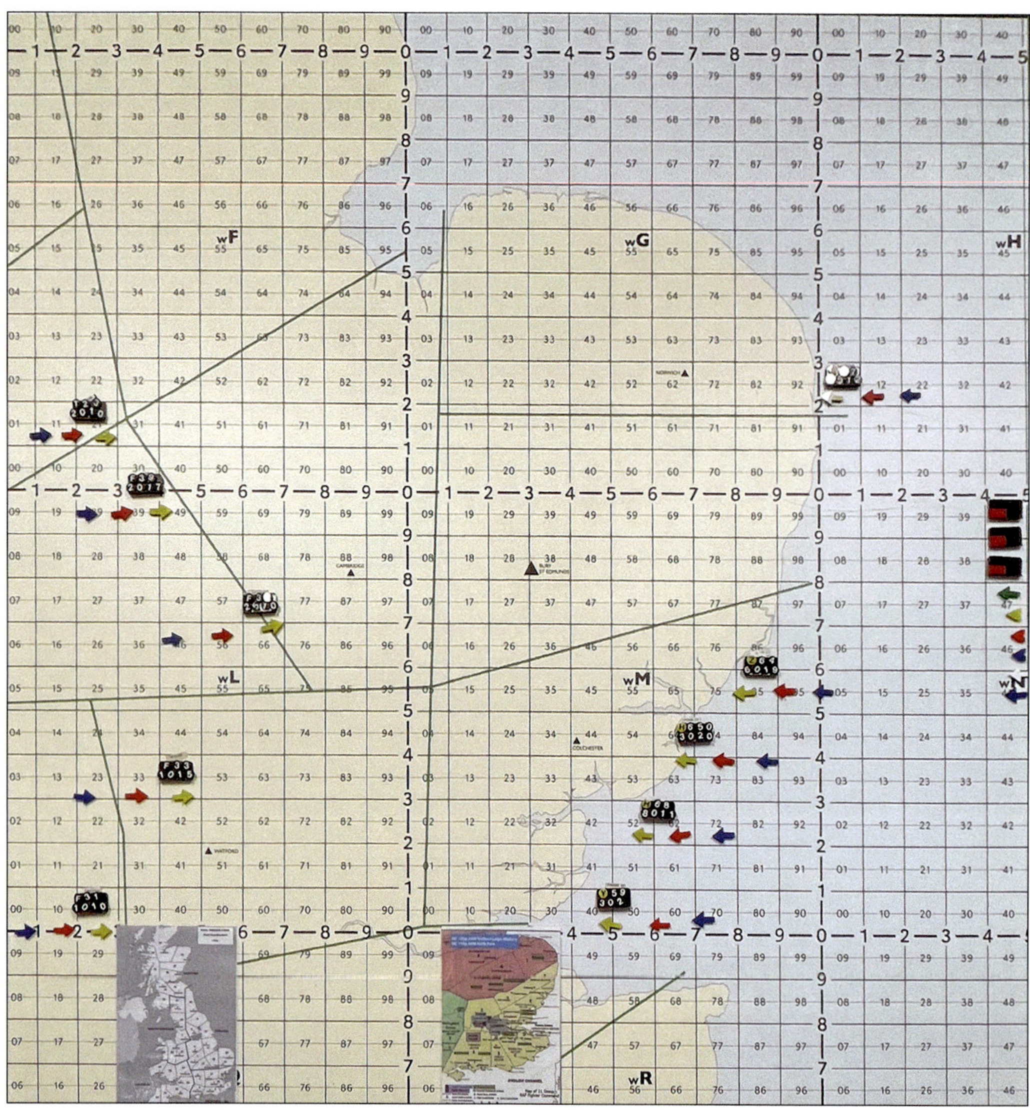

The introduction of Long Range Board enabled ROC Groups to have a much wider appreciation of the overall air picture as it affected adjacent Groups. This contemporary image comes from the recreated ROC Centre at the Bury St Edmunds Guildhall. (Richard E Flagg)

The introduction of the Long Range Board to Centres further reduced the available space, making conditions even more cramped. These were maintained by dedicated Observers who were fed with information by tellers in adjacent Groups. (Crown Copyright)

Bristol on 25–26 and 26–27 April, causing more than 400 casualties. Norwich was next, with the Luftwaffe aircraft arriving from over the sea on 27–28 April. In mostly small groups, and not clearly tracked, they came when the Group was in the midst of transferring from its old location to its new Centre at 'Fairfields'. The Luftwaffe struck from low level, saturating the aircraft plot over the city.

28–29 April saw York struck with major damage done to the city centre and 79 deaths. The air raid warning had not been passed until after the first bomb had been dropped. In some cases, the vulnerabilities of the ROC's existing premises were astonishing, the situation of 9 and 10 Groups in the city being a clear example:

> The two Observer Corps Centres in York are situated together in a hut on the bank of the Ouse in the very middle of the town, next door to the Guildhall and the GPO. The hut is of wood and contains both Centres, which sit in adjoining rooms. It is located in the very centre of the target on the most conspicuous landmark, namely, the river.

The Centres only narrowly escaped destruction when the bombs destroyed the Guildhall on 29 April. Indeed, one incendiary even landed on the roof of the wooden hut but failed to ignite. Through all this, both Centres continued operations.[21]

On 29–30 April, an attack on Norwich cut Centre communications when one bomb struck a main cable between the telephone exchange and the Centre. Controller Bill Scoggins that evening, noted that the Group had working links to only nine Posts; most of the Sector, liaison, and teleprinter lines were 'out'.

'F' Crew came on duty at midnight many members having to battle through the attack to get to their Centre 'Obs CH Caselton had been blasted off his bike', Scoggins noting that 'The very fact that they got to the Centre in the prevailing conditions, illustrates more clearly than anything we can say about how strong was the sense of duty in the Group'.

Despite working hard, the GPO engineers were unable to adequately repair all the damaged lines. So the crews returned to their old Centre, the 'Auto' telephone exchange, and worked from there. Some five miles apart, they said the distance felt more like 20. However, not everyone got the message. One Observer, now having failed to get the message of the move back, had to cycle back to the old Centre. He said:

> The air was filled with weird whistlings, and the next moment, a shower of incendiary bombs was falling around me. I rushed on, 'IBs' to the left of me, 'IBs' to the right of me, 'IBs' in front of me; I dare not look behind. Fires were springing up all around, and as I dodged one in the middle of the road, it scorched the leg of my trousers, and I thought I was on fire. I expected HEs at any moment.

Meanwhile, inside the Centre 'E' Crew had heard incendiaries hitting against the outside of the Ops Room.[22]

The Luftwaffe returned to Exeter on 3–4 May, causing heavy damage to the city centre and destroying the ROC's Alternate Centre there. The Commandant ROC visited the city on 4 May and, as a result, suggested building a new Centre outside the city and relegating the existing Centre to become the Alternate. Cowes on the Isle of Wight was hit on 4–5 May, and on 8–9 May, a return visit was made to Norwich, but most of the bombs were dropped on a decoy site to the east of the city.[23]

Later in the month, the target list widened to include attacks on Hull, Poole (twice), Grimsby, Canterbury (three times), and Ipswich. In June, the Luftwaffe incurred substantial losses as it went still further afield, but these attacks were neither as determined nor as successful as the initial ones. In each case, they caused significant casualties and some severe local damage, but did not achieve their overall objective of 'demoralising the enemy'.

On 28–29 April 1942, a Baedeker raid on York lasted an hour, killing 79 people and seriously injuring 90. Amid the widespread damage was the destruction of the city's Guildhall, close to which were the wooden Centre buildings of 9 and 10 Group, which miraculously survived. (Northern Echo)

The Baedeker raid on Norwich on 29–30 April 1942, caused significant damage in the city and disrupted the work of the ROC Centre. (Via English Heritage)

BULLSEYE EXERCISES

As part of ongoing training to better prepare their crews for operations Bomber Command instituted Exercise Bullseye. For the aircraft crews these were long-range and duration night navigation exercises. These could involve flying entirely overland within the UK, or out over the surrounding seas and then heading back in to 'bomb' the designated 'targets'. Those that flew over water towards the enemy coastline also served the purpose of being diversionary raids for the enemy air defence system to ponder as they approached.

To be successful, not only did the aircraft and crews have to perform satisfactorily, they had to be carefully coordinated with all the elements of the air defences. As well training the bomber crews, they also tested the searchlight units, to provide practice interception opportunities for night-fighters, and to 'provide practice for ROC Posts and Centres in night tracking, handing over tracks, plotting and telling'. There were different categories of Bullseye, that were intended to test specific components of the air defence system, organised either by HQ Fighter Command or specific Groups or Sectors. They also had to be structured in a way that ensured there was no confusion with real raids by German aircraft. All the reporting procedures for the ROC were spelt out in HQROC Operations Instruction No. 5 from August 1942.

- 3 - SECRET

Z	Hostile Fighters	-	All Hostile aircraft definitely recognised or identified as Fighters without Bombers.
X	Unidentified	-	All unidentified aircraft.
M	Mix-up	-	All aircraft tracks which, resulting from the merging of Friendly Fighters and Hostile aircraft, cannot be recognised or identified as one or the other.
A	Friendly	-	All friendly aircraft whose Command is not known.
B	Bomber	-	All aircraft known to belong to Bomber Command.
C	Civil	-	All aircraft known to be employed on Civil Flying duties.
D	Dummy	-	Simulated tracks told for the training of ground personnel.
F	Fighter	-	All aircraft known to belong to Fighter Command.
G	Balloon	-	All drifting balloons.
I	Neutral	-	All aircraft known to belong to the Irish Free State Air Force.
K	Coastal	-	All aircraft (other than P.R.U. a/c) known to belong to Coastal Command.
R	Reconnaissance	-	All aircraft known to belong to P.R.U.
T	Test	-	All aircraft known to be operating on Exercises and Test Flights in connection with ground defences or raid reporting systems.

HQ ROC Instruction No. 5 specified how plots were to be identified by type on Group Centre tables. (HQ ROC Operating Instruction No. 5, p.3, via Alistair Mc Cann)

RAF Bomber Command Lancasters and Manchesters preparing to depart for a long range 'Bullseye' night training mission. (Crown Copyright)

Tip-and-Run

The series of Luftwaffe daylight tip-and-run raids began at the very start of 1942. Persisting throughout the year, relatively small numbers of mainly fighter aircraft, often Me 109s and FW 190s, carrying a single bomb in raids of one to four aircraft. They would attempt to hit selected targets, such as gas works and railway infrastructure, along the south coast as far as Cornwall. In the autumn, against Hastings and Canterbury, the Luftwaffe employed larger formations of around 20 aircraft with additional fighter cover.[24] The relative effectiveness of these operations, causing damage and significant disruption with few losses, meant they became a persistent feature of enemy operations.

For the British air defences, these raids posed significant challenges. The extremely low altitude of most of these attacks made existing RDF cover ineffective. The poor RDF coverage meant that anti-aircraft guns were regularly not warned of the raids' approach, and even so, most of the medium- and heavy-calibre guns were really optimised for medium-altitude attacks.

Totter

Measures taken in the Observer Corps to counter these tip-and-run raiders included the introduction of 'Snowflake' illuminating rockets. They were to be used only during daylight, when Posts saw raiders below 1,000 feet, to give urgent warning to pairs of patrolling fighters. Totter rockets were also issued to some Coastguard stations.

They were fired from an 'electric projector', and descended by parachute. Operational from October 1942, 69 Posts were selected to be equipped with the rockets codenamed 'Totter'. Each selected Post was provided with eight 'snowflake' rockets, one projector, nine cartridges, a battery holder and two batteries. Initially issued to the Groups along the south coast at Horsham, Maidstone, Winchester, Truro, Exeter and Yeovil, their use was later extended to the Bury St Edmunds, Colchester, Norwich and Bromley Groups.[25]

These rockets found an additional use when anti-V-1 operations began. A large screen of barrage balloons was assembled to protect London against the flying bombs. The rockets were passed to 17 more Posts in the Bromley, Maidstone and Horsham Groups. They were intended to be fired when intercepting RAF fighters came within three miles of Posts close to the balloon screen, to warn them of the collision risk.[26]

Satellites and Rats

The establishment of new Satellite Posts was another element in countering these raids, further closing gaps in the aircraft reporting network's coverage. These were necessary because along the coastlines of the Maidstone, Horsham, Winchester and Bromley Groups, there were still gaps in low-level coverage where enemy aircraft could penetrate the defences unnoticed. There were also 'blind alleys' where the enemy could still approach at up to 500 feet and remain unnoticed by RDF; the Thames being cited as one of these routes.[27]

Satellite Posts were created, linked to the nearest 'parent' Post. Most were only manned during daylight hours to report the movements of low-flying hostile or 'doubtful' aircraft to the parent Post. Having carefully surveyed a large number of potential locations, approximately 150 Satellites were created that formed a belt, approximately 30 miles deep, all along the south coast and up the east coast as far as Dundee and along the coasts of Cheshire and Lancashire. Locations for individual Satellite Posts included RAF stations, searchlight detachments and Coastguard stations.[28]

A new reporting procedure, codenamed 'Rats', was developed to try and speed up the reporting of low-flying enemy aircraft by Posts and Centres. From 24 February 1943:

> when a Post saw a low-flying enemy aircraft, it was to immediately pass the codeword 'Rats' and its own grid square to the Centre without further plot details. The highest-priority warning was to be passed immediately by the Sector Controller, with fighters scrambled or, if already airborne and on patrol, directed towards the reporting Post, using a map with all ROC Posts marked. The procedure was used by all the coastal Groups from Norwich to Truro.[29]

Combined, faster reporting procedures, standing fighter patrols, and the use of faster aircraft like the Typhoon and Spitfire IXs, these measures pushed up the cost of the Luftwaffe's incursions to the Germans and caused them to gradually decrease during 1943.

At Beachy Head, a Snowflake rocket is being prepared for use, intended to warn fighters about 'Tip-and-Run' raiders and later the V-1 flying bombs. (Crown Copyright)

10
HELPING THEM HOME

The large number of Observer Corps Posts and their widespread distribution across the country meant many Posts witnessed Allied aircraft losses throughout the war, whether due to enemy action, mechanical failure, poor weather, or other causes. However, isolating reliable figures on these losses proves extremely elusive. Some of the more carefully researched figures suggest that there were around 52,000 British and Commonwealth aircrew casualties between 1939 and 1947 in the UK. USAAF losses are estimated at over 30,000 personnel.

How many aircrew the Observer Corps assisted and successfully guided home can never be substantiated, but the numbers were certainly considerable. Some of the best indications we have come from Derek Wood. He suggests a 1945 figure given of more than 7,000 is almost certainly a large underestimation. As an indication, he states that among the RAFs five Fighter Groups between January and October 1944 they logged 338 instances where ROC information assisted distressed aircraft to a safe landing. Within that 12 Group aircraft ROC information was said to have assisted in 1,800 cases in the same period. Within 10 Group one case of assistance was said to have helped 85 USAAF C-47 Dakotas alone.[1]

Plotting lost aircraft and assisting them had gone on since the very start of the war. One early example comes from 26 January 1940. An unidentified 'coastal group' was advised that five Ansons were returning from a patrol in very bad weather, with some Posts reporting nil visibility. Three returned to their base safely. One was plotted by a coastal post and was almost to its home station when it became lost again and headed back out to sea. The other was detected already heading back out to sea. Using sound plots alone, these were passed to their home stations which coaxed one back to its home airfield and the other to a safe landing at an emergency landing ground.[2] Files from 1940–41 contain several suggested methods for assisting lost aircraft. The RAF supported some, such as laying out large white arrows, or cutting them into the ground and filling them with chalk, pointing them towards the nearest airfield when required, or firing very pistols. Still, most of the ideas were considered impractical or of little value in poor weather.[3]

An Avro Lancaster waits at Elsham Wolds, Lincolnshire, before taking off for a raid on Duisburg. The Sandra lights, intended to help guide aircraft home, could also be pointed upwards to detect the cloud base height for departing aircraft. 107 sets were installed at ROC Posts. (Crown Copyright)

Not all the 'homing' events always used standard operating procedures. In another incident at 16 Group's V1 Post, near RAF Coltishall, in Norfolk, a Stirling bomber was heard circling overhead, after midnight, at around 2,000 feet. Passing the message via Centre to Fighter Command, and assuring them it was a Stirling, Coltishall briefly turned on its airfield perimeter lights, and the station light illuminated its 'CS' identification letter. A short time later, Fighter Command notified the Post that it had received a message from the bomber saying, 'Thanks CS, can now set course for home'.[4]

Post Observers became familiar with the regular inbound and outbound routes used by bombers. Sometimes Observers recognised lost aircraft because they were circling or just simply 'out of place'. A Post would report it to their Centre; the Centre Controller would contact the ROC Liaison Officer (ROCLO) at the Fighter Group Operations Room, who would try to identify the aircraft. However, there was little real coordination, so the system failed more often than not.

By 1941, the procedure was for the lost bomber to circle for at least two minutes and to show the approved coloured lights of the time, or to switch on their downward recognition lights. When searchlight units saw the aircraft, they would point their beams towards an airfield for the plane to land, guiding it along the beam.[5] At certain stations, a 'canopy' of searchlights could be pointed skywards to guide the aircraft to a safe landing. The RAF managed to acquire 1,200 surplus searchlights from Anti Aircraft Command to improve their 'canopy' system. To further enhance coverage and fill some gaps, 107 searchlights were installed at ROC Posts, where they became known as 'Sandra' lights. At Sandra equipped Posts, it was necessary to have two extra Observers on duty.[6]

RAF Bomber Command had been undertaking night attacks on continental targets since the start of the war. In 1943, as the Combined Bomber Offensive ramped up, the number of British and US bombers rapidly grew. Groups and Posts from Yorkshire down to the South coast became familiar with the streams of RAF bombers departing each night and those of the USAAF heading for their targets each day. As the missions grew in size and complexity, new techniques were developed and spelt out in Operating Instruction No. 40 from October 1943, to plot 'mass raids' on Group tables and to prevent them from becoming overwhelmed with information.

Helping lost aircraft find their way home, or, in the event of an urgent emergency, any airfield became an increasingly important element of Observer Corps work as the war progressed. As the US Army Air Forces' buildup began across Britain, the number of aircraft requiring assistance, both day and night, grew. In the early stages of the war, the various flare systems had proved largely ineffective. As early as April and May 1943 this had become such a significant part of Corps operations that it became the subject of ROC Operating Instructions Nos. 25 and 29 detailing procedures to deal with suspected lost or damaged aircraft that were spotted. By 1944, a more effective range of measures had been developed, using visual observation, radio calls, and radar to get lost or damaged aircraft home, with the Observer Corps involved in all of them.

However, not all the assistance provided by Posts was to aircraft in trouble. Local, unofficial arrangements were often made between

Returning from a raid, a formation of 91st Bombardment Group B-17s arrives back at Eye Airfield in Norfolk. ROC Posts were often important for helping lost or damaged bombers get back to their home bases. (William D Pulliam)

Posts and their 'neighbours' in the area. As an example, 17/M3 Post at Ongar would phone the local airfield at RAF Fairlop, where Spitfire squadrons were usually based, to warn them 'if there were "hostiles" on the board'. They would also shout information to the nearby ARP when they knew where bombs had fallen and flash an Aldis lamp to the Americans at the nearby rail yards during 'Diver' alerts.[7] There were many similar examples of local cooperation spread across all of Britain.

Miss Poisonality

Many incidents occurred around the coast, near the shore, when aircrews abandoned their aircraft, waiting for rescue by RAF launches and RNLI Lifeboats. The 16 Group, Norwich, history records one such incident from early USAAF bombing operations.

On 13 May 1943, ROC Posts in the N, O and P Clusters, on the Norfolk coast, witnessed and assisted with a tragic incident that unfolded to a US B-17 42-29752, 'Miss Poisonality', of the 96th Bombardment Group. It took off from the USAAF airfield at Grafton Underwood, on the crew's first scheduled mission, their intended target the German airfield at St Omer in occupied France.

Second Lieutenant Norville Gorse, the copilot of the aircraft, later reported that soon after the plane took off, as it was passing 500 feet, 'A big bump jarred us against our safety belts and the nose of the plane reached for the sky'. The two pilots instinctively pushed the controls forward, and for some minutes struggled to get the Flying Fortress under control as it 'mushed along, still climbing, on the edge of a power stall'. They had to constantly battle to keep the aircraft in the air. They ascertained that the damage was caused when the right waist gunner had lost control of his weapon, it had gone off with some rounds shooting off the B-17's stabiliser root and damaged the right aileron. The tail gunner was seriously wounded, and the two waist gunners were injured by flying metal inside the aircraft.

Authorised to break radio silence, the wireless operator contacted the Grafton Underwood control tower. They were instructed to drop the wounded men over the airfield, then the rest of the crew were to bale out overland and abandon the aircraft at sea. This they duly did, pushing the injured tail gunner out of the aircraft and pulling his ripcord as they did so. Two more crew baled out of the stricken bomber as it approached the coastline.

Meanwhile, in the fields below, 'At 14.19 hrs, the first ROC Post reported a B-17 Fortress in distress with its engines running badly. Two of the crew baled out inland, and two more baled out near King Lynn'.

> At 15.10, the USAAF First Bomber Wing passed information to the effect that Fortress was still carrying a bomb load and its stabiliser had gone. The aircraft was instructed to fly over the Wash, jettison its bombs, and return to Wittering if possible. The Fortress was contacted, and it proceeded towards the Wash, steering a very erratic course.

The B-17's bomb doors could not be opened hydraulically, so they had to be manually opened and the bombload jettisoned. The aircraft contacted the RAF Air Sea Rescue by radio.

The Observers could see 'The aircraft was still orbiting over The Wash, and at 15.45 hours another member of the crew was reported to have baled out over the sea. The ROC had warned Wells Coastguards, and lifeboats were on the way to the rescue'.

Gorse wrote that the B-17's engines 'had been labouring for some time and the plane had been losing altitude despite running at full throttle. We were very low as we crossed the shoreline'. 'Then at 15.46, the aircraft was reported by the ROC to be down to 100 feet and circling a few miles north of Wells. The track finally faded about 16.00 hours in this position'.

Ordered by the pilot, Captain Derrol Rogers, to abandon the aircraft, Gorse jumped at less than 400 feet into the water, managing to release his parachute harness before hitting the water and inflating his life vest. About an hour later, he was spotted by an air-sea rescue RAF Stirling, which also dropped a smoke flare marker, and Gorse was pulled out of the water by an RAF rescue launch. The Sherringham Lifeboat put to sea and found the pilot, Captain Rogers, but he died of exposure.

As the 16 Group history recorded, 'Air-Sea Rescue was laid on, and nine of the crew were saved, one presumed to have gone down with the aircraft, one picked up at sea by boat, alive. First Wing was very grateful for this assistance rendered and the quick action taken by rescue crews'. 'This was a splendid display of co-operation given by the ROC, and great credit goes to them for the successful air-sea rescue'.[8]

Damaged aircraft ditching in the North Sea became a regular occurrence. B-17 42-29981 'Hell Lena' of the 92nd Bombardment Group had taken off from Alconbury on 26 July 1943, headed for Hannover. On its way home, badly damaged, the aircraft ditched, and an RAF Walrus seaplane picked up the crew from their dinghy. The image was taken from an RAF Coastal Command aircraft. (Via Picryl)

'Darky'

Darky was a radio system designed to assist lost aircraft. From 1941, TR9D high-frequency radio sets were installed at RAF airfields across the country and at other key locations, including approximately 50 ROC Posts. The system had to deliberately limit its signal power output to roughly 10 miles; otherwise, there was a high probability that the signal would be received by multiple ground sets, which might all respond and override each other. A formal procedure was developed for aircraft to contact ground stations and receive headings to reach nearby airfields.

In 1943, the selected ROC Posts were supplied with their 'Darky' radio transmitter sets. These Posts were chosen because of their location in areas where coverage from other RAF Darky transmitters was sparse. A listening watch was maintained during the hours of darkness and, at some Posts, also during the daytime. On receiving a call for assistance, the aircraft would be given its position and a course to steer to the nearest suitable airfield.[9]

One selected Darky Post was T3 at Loddon in Norfolk, approximately 10 miles from the coast. It was close to many airfields and the bomber routes to and from the Continent. Two wireless transmitter sets were installed: one operating on a Bomber Command frequency and the other on a Coastal Command wavelength.

T3's Head Observer, AS Chittock, said of the equipment that:

> It greatly increased the interest in being on duty. Although the sets were operational every night, the actual calls on them were not numerous, but on several occasions, we were able to provide direct assistance to aircraft in trouble. We remember one case when we were instructed to contact and provide homing details for a four-engined bomber that had been shot up and had lost its bearings. The instructions were repeated again and again to the bomber, but we could get no reply, and we assumed that, owing to some mechanical or other mishap, we had failed. But we hadn't. We were to learn later that the plane had been hopelessly lost but had picked up our message and had landed safely at an aerodrome in northern England. Later, Obs Off [Observer Officer] Reeve was at the RAF School of Recognition, where he met a member of the bomber's crew, who expressed appreciation for the great assistance we had given to his aircraft.[10]

GL Radar

The original GL Mk 1 (Gun Laying) radar system was developed by Metropolitan Vickers Limited and the staff of Bawdsey Research Station, in 1938–39, to detect the range and elevation of enemy aircraft to aid more accurate anti-aircraft gunnery. Still, it was soon redundant when improved models came along. The system was developed and improved during the war to interrogate aircraft rather than just track them.[11]

At night, once aircraft passed in over the coast, there was no way to positively identify them except by sight, and that was rarely possible. Despite the weaknesses of the GL Mk 1 system, it was capable of electronically interrogating the Mark II and Mark IIG Identification, Friend or Foe (IFF) sets then carried by many RAF bombers and other aircraft. For Bomber Command, their aircraft were told to turn the system on as they headed outbound until they were 50 miles out from the coast, and also when heading back, when 100 miles out, until they landed.[12] One intention was to prevent the Luftwaffe night-fighters from infiltrating the returning bomber

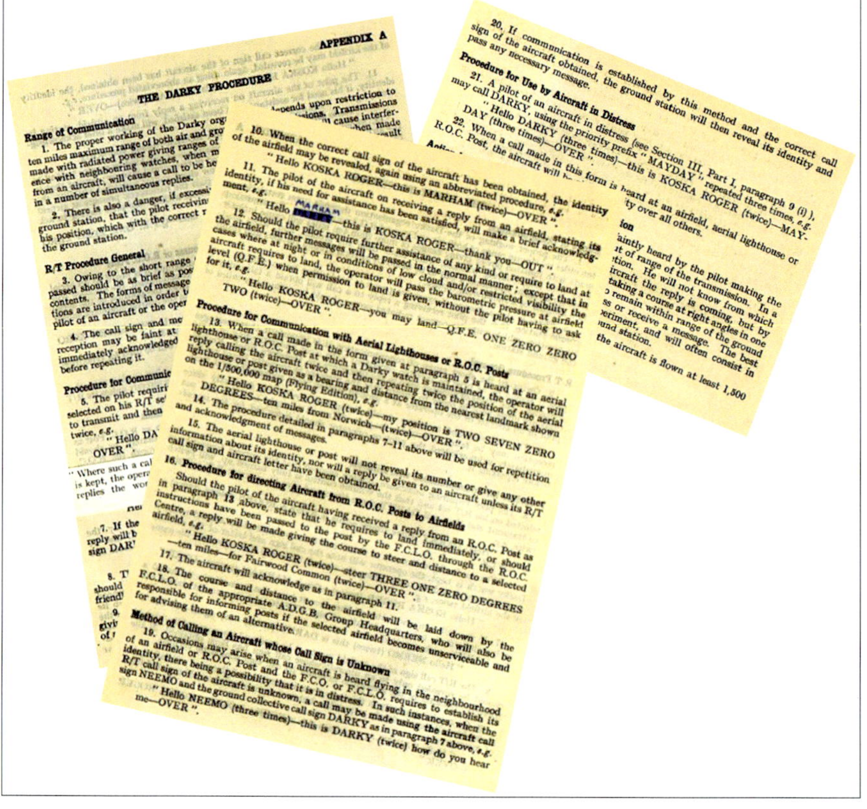

APPENDIX A

THE DARKY PROCEDURE

10. When the correct call sign of the aircraft has been obtained, the identity of the airfield may be revealed, again using an abbreviated procedure, *e.g.*
" Hello KOSKA ROGER—this is MARHAM (twice)—OVER ".

11. The pilot of the aircraft on receiving a reply from an airfield, stating its identity, if his need for assistance has been satisfied, will make a brief acknowledgment, *e.g.*
" Hello MARHAM—this is KOSKA ROGER—thank you—OUT ".

12. Should the pilot require further assistance of any kind or require to land at the airfield, further messages will be passed in the normal manner; except that in cases where at night or in conditions of low cloud and/or restricted visibility the aircraft requires to land, the operator will pass the barometric pressure at airfield level (Q.F.E.) when permission to land is given, without the pilot having to ask for it, *e.g.*
" Hello KOSKA ROGER—you may land—Q.F.E. ONE ZERO ZERO TWO (twice)—OVER ".

Procedure for Communication with Aerial Lighthouses or R.O.C. Posts

13. When a call made in the form given at paragraph 5 is heard at an aerial lighthouse or R.O.C. Post at which a Darky watch is maintained, the operator will reply calling the aircraft twice and then repeating twice the position of the aerial lighthouse or post given as a bearing and distance from the nearest landmark shown on the 1/500,000 map (Flying Edition), *e.g.*
" Hello KOSKA ROGER (twice)—my position is TWO SEVEN ZERO DEGREES—ten miles from Norwich—(twice)—OVER ".

14. The procedure detailed in paragraphs 7–11 above will be used for repetition and acknowledgment of messages.

15. The aerial lighthouse or post will not reveal its number or give any other information about its identity, nor will a reply be given to an aircraft unless its R/T call sign and aircraft letter have been obtained.

16. **Procedure for directing Aircraft from R.O.C. Posts to Airfields**

Should the pilot of the aircraft having received a reply from an R.O.C. Post as in paragraph 13 above, state that he requires to land immediately, or should instructions have been passed to the post by the F.C.L.O. through the R.O.C. Centre, a reply will be made giving the course to steer and distance to a selected airfield, *e.g.*
" Hello KOSKA ROGER (twice)—steer THREE ONE ZERO DEGREES—ten miles—for Fairwood Common (twice)—OVER ".

17. The aircraft will acknowledge as in paragraph 11.

18. The course and distance to the airfield will be laid down by the F.C.L.O. of the appropriate A.D.G.B. Group Headquarters, who will also be responsible for informing posts if the selected airfield becomes unserviceable and for advising them of an alternative.

Method of Calling an Aircraft whose Call Sign is Unknown

19. Occasions may arise when an aircraft is heard flying in the neighbourhood of an airfield or R.O.C. Post and the F.C.O. or F.C.L.O. requires to establish its identity, there being a possibility that it is in distress. In such instances, when the R/T call sign of the aircraft is unknown, a call may be made using the aircraft call sign NEEMO and the ground collective call sign DARKY as in paragraph 7 above, *e.g.*
" Hello NEEMO (three times)—this is DARKY (twice) how do you hear me—OVER ".

Copy of the Darky system manual issued to aircrews. (Crown Copyright)

stream to shoot aircraft down. The system was critical because the IFF Mk II carried by aircraft was not triggered by the many Chain Home Low radar stations operating along the coast.[13]

Following a conference at Fighter Command on 6 August 1942, it was agreed that AA Command should arrange for the provision of 10 GL Mk 1 sets to be allocated to ROC Posts along the east coast from Flamborough Head to Shoeburyness. Two sets were assigned to 10 Group (York), three to Norwich, two each to Lincoln and Colchester and one to Bury St Edmunds.[14] Because of difficulties in installing extra telephone lines, the sets were used during the hours of darkness, when GL operators took over the Post line to the Centre.

By far the most detailed description of the GL sets comes from the Norwich Group. Details arrived there in a 'Most Secret' letter from the Midland Area dated 1 October 1942:

> The sets will be maintained and serviced by the RAF, and a mechanic will be on-site during the operating hours. In the first instance, operators will also be supplied by the RAF, but it is proposed that these operators shall train the ROC personnel…with a view to this commitment being taken over permanently by the ROC.

The letter indicated that it was:

> An entirely new development as far as the ROC is concerned, and after due consideration and discussion, it is not considered that there will be any difficulty in training efficient ROC Operators. The work will be most interesting, and it is believed that Observers will be delighted to undertake it.

Secrecy was considered vital and emphasised in the letter:

> The Head Observer of the Post may be told of this development, but it must be emphasised that this is not to be discussed, and the actual provision of the sets is a matter for secrecy, as well as their function.
>
> Observers will be required to sign an undertaking in regard to secrecy, and it will be fully appreciated that in allowing ROC personnel to operate radio-location apparatus, it necessitates entrusting Observers with most secret information; gossiping, therefore, must not take place.[15]

At each GL Post, the No. 1 Observer would operate the 'range Tube' (and have the Head and Breast set), No. 2 would operate the Bearing Tube and No. 3 the transmitter. The working range of the GL set was said to be 12 to 15 miles.

At the selected ROC Centres, a member of personnel known as the 'Interrogator' would pass details of unidentified plots to the GL operators. They would check whether any of the plots showed an IFF signal and, if so, reclassify them as friendly. That information could then be passed up the chain to RAF Fighter Command Operations and Filter Rooms.[16]

When a track approached within 15 miles of a GL Post, the Centre Interrogator would tell the Post the latest plot. They would try to detect the aircraft and report it as 'not seen', 'friendly', 'hostile' or 'unidentified'. It also allowed the identification of aircraft in distress by use of an 'SOS' option on the airborne set.

Initially, the systems were manned by five RAF or Army personnel, but ROC members later replaced them once they became proficient in operating the equipment. Two RAF maintenance technicians were responsible for first-line maintenance.[17]

The GL Mk1 was not well-suited to its original gun-laying purpose. Newer versions soon replaced it, but 10 Mk1s were passed to the ROC and repurposed to interrogate aircraft IFF systems. (Hamilton, p.99)

A report produced in February 1943 indicated that 8,500 aircraft had been challenged by the GL radars, resulting in 85 raid tracks being reclassified as friendly, reducing double-tracking on 14 occasions and picking up 10 aircraft emitting 'SOS' messages. Later, dedicated phone lines were authorised for the sets.

Not all the work was bomber-related. Just as often, it was fighters in difficulty. USAAF Brig Gen FH Griswold, Chief of Staff of 8th Fighter Command, praised the ROC on his own account in a letter to 17 Group HQ:

> On my first flight in a Thunderbolt in this country, I became unsure of my location and the station I was looking for (Bovingdon), as I had no homing facilities. I called Bovingdon on RT, told them I was lost and waited. In a few minutes, I was told to fly a course of 340 degrees for nine minutes and soon found Bovingdon. The control people there had called the Royal Observer Corps and asked them to locate a Thunderbolt wandering around the vicinity of London. This they immediately did, informed Bovingdon of my location, and a course home came to me by RT.[18]

Crash Reporting

Often, the first official information about the crash of an aircraft, friendly or hostile, was based on a report from the local police or

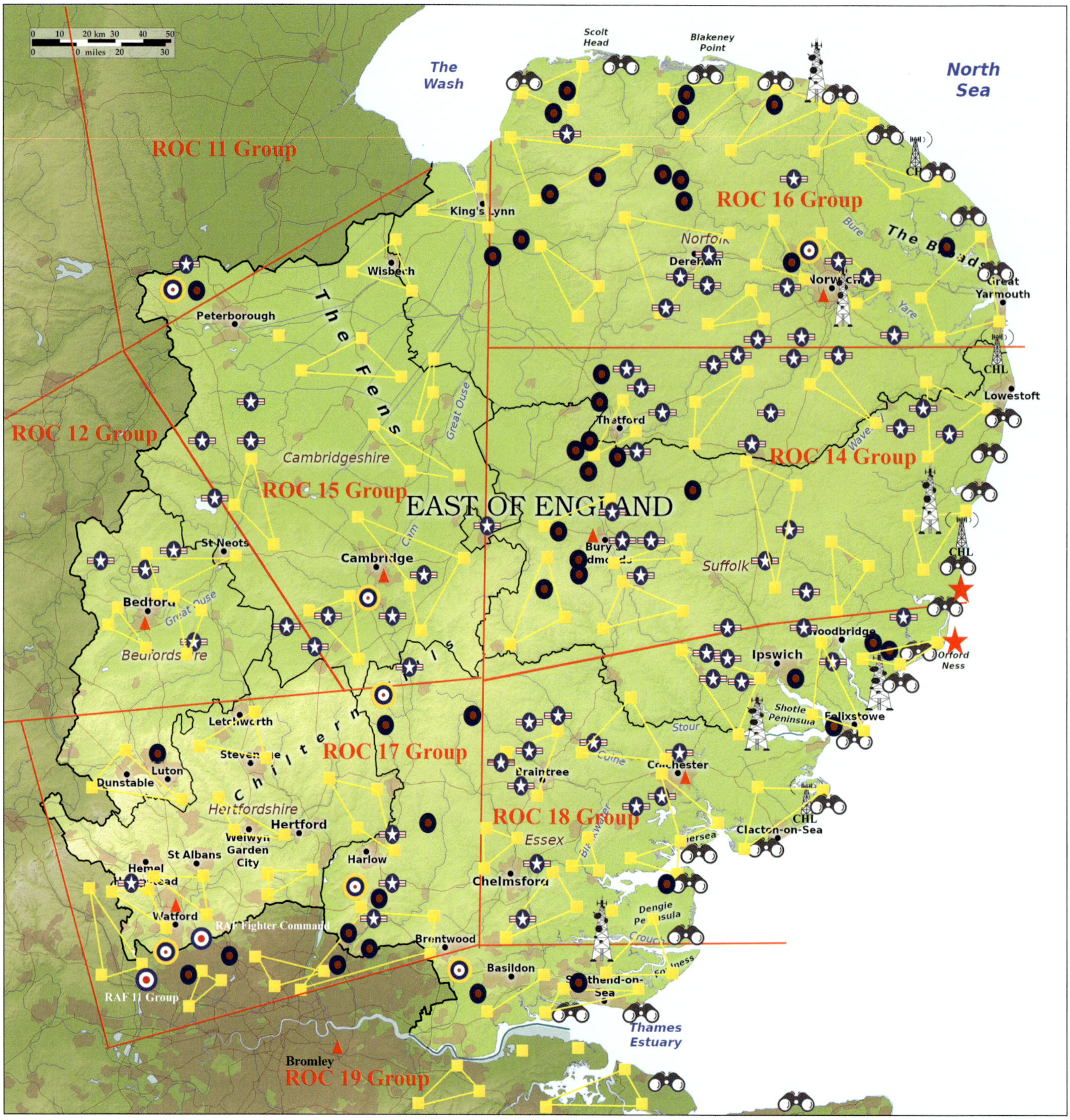

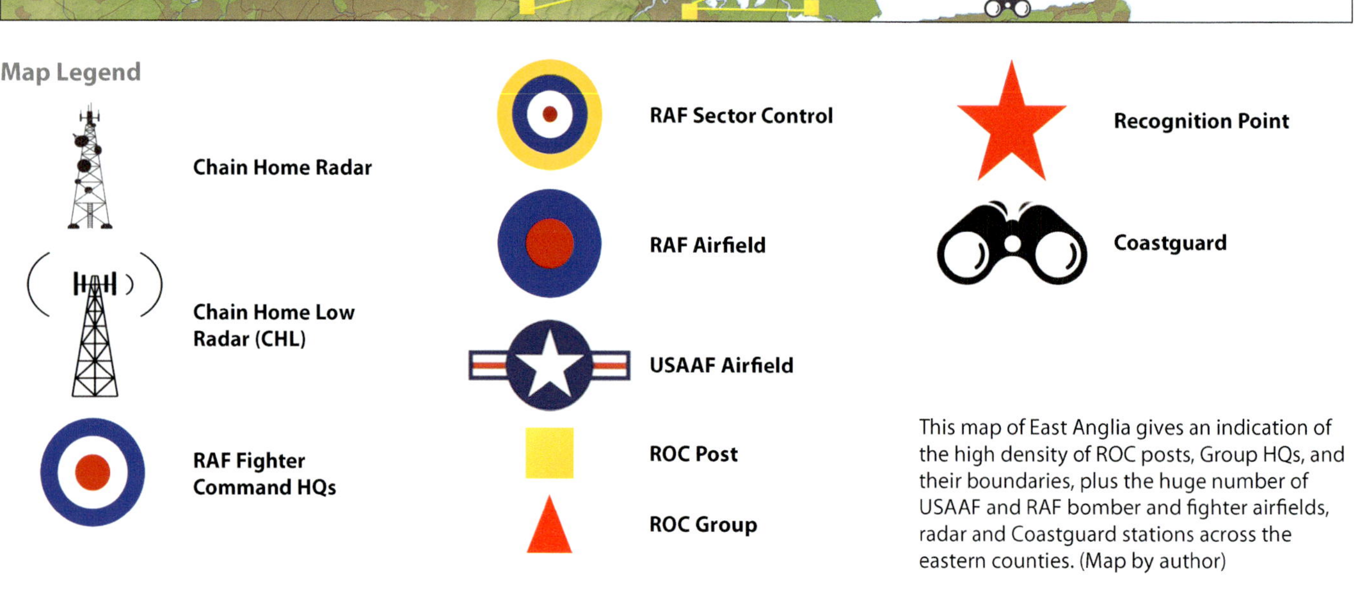

This map of East Anglia gives an indication of the high density of ROC posts, Group HQs, and their boundaries, plus the huge number of USAAF and RAF bomber and fighter airfields, radar and Coastguard stations across the eastern counties. (Map by author)

B-17 42-87855 from the 601st BS, 398th Bomb Group, based at Nuthampstead in Hertfordshire, despite being battle-damaged, just managed to reach the beach near Sandwich in Kent on 9 July 1944. It was returning from a mission on Humieres, roughly 40 miles south of Calais.

an Observer Corps Post. Especially in the early years of the war, the two worked well together, given that many pre-war Observers were Special Constables. In rural areas, individuals often knew the local constable personally, and the telephone numbers of stations, so during the war's early stages, at least some information was passed freely and quickly between the two. As the war escalated, the RAF designated 'Crash Officers' responsible for recovering all crashed aircraft (and any unspent munitions) for intelligence purposes, spares or just scrap.

The Allied bomber offensive grew from 1943 as the USAAF arrived in force. There were increased numbers of crashes as damaged bombers and fighters failed to make it back to their home bases.

Coastal Posts and the Coastguard played a vital role in quickly reporting crashes so that rescue efforts could be launched. Many aircrews owed their survival to the quick response of air and seaborne rescue crews, aircraft and boats.

Too Close for Comfort

With so many Posts, crashes were sometimes dangerously close. In the early hours of 17 August 1941, things got uncomfortably close for Q3 Post of 16 Group at Melton Constable in Norfolk.

Wellington MkII W5444, from 12 Squadron based at Binbrook, was returning from a mission over Cologne. Over the city, the aircraft's starboard engine was damaged by anti-aircraft fire. Crossing back over the North Sea, flying on one engine, the Wellington gradually lost height. It made landfall, and searchlights were pointing the way to the nearest airfield. In the last moments, the pilot mistook some railway signals for airfield signal lights, and the aircraft crashed into a railway bridge.

From the history of 16 Group ROC, we have the following account:

> In the early hours of August 17th, Observers G Parnell and A Wiseman were on duty at Q3. At 01.25 hrs, they plotted a Wellington at 90 degrees flying north, very low, and a bright light flashing from its interior. It turned West, then East, and whilst they were actually still reporting it to the Centre, it struck their telephone wires and crashed into the railway bridge close to the post.
>
> In the hut, Observers H A Swithson and A R Oxborough were sleeping prior to going on duty at 03.00. They were awakened by the plane passing overhead, then, upon hearing the crash, rushed outside. An emergency such as this needs cool heads and prompt action. One is liable to do the wrong thing in the excitement of the moment, but these four Observers did exactly what was right.

Obs Wiseman stayed to guard the Post, while Parnell fetched flex and tools from the Post hut to try and repair the damaged phone lines and re-establish contact with Norwich Centre. Smitheon cycled off to Melton Constable Police Station to warn the police and phone the Centre, whilst AR Oxborough ran to the crashed plane. Due to an electrical fault, one of the aircraft's 2,000lb bombs was still 'hung up' in the bomb bay.

When Oxborough got to the wreck, he said in his report:

> I shouted, 'Is there anybody about?' and was answered by one of the crew, 'Yes, mate'. I extricated him from the wreckage, some of which was burning. I asked him if there were any bombs. He said there was and plenty of petrol. I could hear this running out somewhere. I shouted, 'Is there anybody else?' and the rear gunner answered. I was endeavouring to get him out when Observer Smithson and two Home Guard members arrived. We got him out, found the pilot, and released him. More help arrived, and we rescued the remaining crew, but they were dead.
>
> By 03.00, Obs Oxborough and Smithson went on duty just as they would have done if nothing had happened; two typical Observers – and two brave men.

Later, Observers Smithson and Oxborough received personal letters of congratulations and thanks from the Commandant, Air Commodore Warrington-Morris.[19]

When 12 Squadron Wellington W5444 crashed near 16 Group Q3 (Melton Constable) in Norfolk, two Post members helped pull injured crewmen from the wreckage. (Picryl)

In February 1945, L/Obs Orum and Obs Butcher were on duty at 16 Group, Z2 (Swaffam) Post. They had been warned that the Navigator of an approaching Mosquito might bale out. He did so and landed close to the post. They took him up into their Post hut and made him warm and comfortable. Norwich Centre had informed nearby RAF West Raynham of what had happened and, within 30 minutes, an RAF truck arrived to collect him.[20]

EVERY POST WAS UNIQUE

Above: A very neat looking A1 Post at Great Offley.

Left: Fox 1 Post, Rickmansworth, made from an upended large diameter sewer pipe and then protected by a mound.

C1 Post at Kings Langley, occupies quite a large site, with an elevated observation platform and what looks like sizeable domestic accommodation.

C2 Post was at Elstree set on a hillside, protected by camouflaged corrugated iron.

Observers in their wet weather clothing at a very wet 17 Group Post with Obs Off EH Heath in attendance.

(All images: *Observers' Tale*)

Enemy Action

Post Observers saw much of the enemy's aerial action over the country during the war. During the Battle of Britain, it was the intense actions over the south-east of England; in later years, it was often the much smaller, low-level 'tip-and-run' raids the enemy engaged in across much of England and Scotland. On other occasions, Posts were machine-gunned or struck by enemy bombs, sometimes with fatal consequences.

For example, on 29 June 1942, a sneak German raider dropped four bombs on Cromer and the Q1 Post there was struck by one, which killed Observer Robert Bowditch and Fred Dugdale, who died a few days later.[21]

As well as dealing with Allied aircraft making forced landings, sometimes enemy aircraft crews would pay unscheduled visits to the Posts. On 24 July 1942, at Holbeach (D2 Post), their logbook recorded the following incident.

> **24-7-42 00.30hrs**
> A German airman surrendered to the Post and was handed over to the Police at 00.40.
>
> **00.50hrs**
> Another prisoner reported. Taken up to town in Mr E Bowser's car. Arrested by S Bayston. As a matter of interest, I log the following: "During intense air activity, I went to the Post to see if I could help. On nearing the Post, I saw two parachutes descending. I got a rifle and ammo and went in search of them. I found and arrested a German Officer.
>
> He had hurt his foot and was very much afraid I was going to shoot him. I took him to the hospital and handed him over to the Police".[22]
>
> (Signed) A S Bayston

Operation Granite

Significant numbers of aircraft each year were lost when they flew into high ground. 'Granite' was an initiative to prevent this from happening. The idea was to ignite powerful red flares on the ground to warn passing aircraft that they were too low. Begun in 1944, by April 1945, over 300 ROC Posts were taking part in Granite across 25 Groups. Together they covered north and west Wales, each side of the Pennines, the Lake District, south-west Scotland, the Isle of Arran, and the north and west of Montrose and the Ochill Hills.

Table 7: Granite Posts by Group[23]

Number of Posts	Group
	Southern Area
7	No. 2 (Horsham)
2	No. 4 (Oxford)
5	No. 19 (Bromley)
	Midland Area
19	No. 6 (Derby)
7	No. 5 (Coventry)
18	No. 8 (Leeds)
12	No. 9 (York)
5	No. 12 (Bedford)
20	No. 30 (Durham)
	Scottish Area
14	No. 31 (Galashiels)
20	No. 33 (Ayr)
7	No. 34 (Glasgow)
13	No. 36 (Dunfermline)
17	No. 37 (Dundee)
12	No. 38 (Aberdeen)
12	No. 39 (Inverness)
	Western Area
24	No. 21 (Exeter)
12	No. 22 (Yeovil)
13	No. 24 (Gloucester)
	North Western Area
11	No. 7 (Manchester)
19	No. 26 (Wrexham)
14	No. 27 (Shrewsbury)
14	No. 22 (Caernarvon)
17	No. 29 (Lancaster)
21	No. 32 (Carlisle)

Winslow recorded an incident on 17 January 1945, in which a C-47 Dakota overshot Turnhouse airfield due to a snowstorm and became lost. Picked up by 31 Group by sound, it passed to 36 Group, where it was visually identified. On the order of the ROCLO, at Group HQ, the Falkirk and Bannockburn Posts Granite was activated at 16.09 hrs. The aircraft climbed, and a few minutes later, on the instruction of the Flying Control Officer at the Fighter Group HQ, who was tracking the plane on the Operations Room table, the Blackford Post used its Granite flares. The Dakota turned south at around 4,000 feet to head south through the Galashiels Group, then into the Durham Group area, landing safely at Usworth at 16.53.[24]

In 1947, The ROC Gazette published a detailed description of the wartime programme written by Sqn Ldr D West.[25] As he described, the selected Posts were near hills on the 300-metre (1,000-foot) contour. Posts would light the flares when an aircraft was expected to pass near them, close to high ground and believed not to be landing at a local airfield. Flares were lit 10 miles in front of the aircraft and 10 miles each side of its expected track. At night, a single flare was lit; during the day, four were used to achieve the same level of illumination. As well as the description, West provided accounts of individual instances of aircraft climbing on seeing the flares or turning back on themselves to head for safety.

In some places, the system was complemented by high-frequency transmitters broadcasting on the Darky frequency. Operation of Granite resulted in a marked decrease in high-ground accidents.

SECRET

APPENDIX 'B'

TO HEADQUARTERS, ROYAL OBSERVER CORPS

OPERATION INSTRUCTION No.34

HANDLING OF "GRANITE" PYROTECHNICS.

(1) 20 flares and 20 porte-fires will be issued to each R.O.C. Post. They will be supplied in metal lined boxes or each flare will be enclosed in a metal case. Each is fitted with a 6 inch nail which is to be stuck in the ground or, if this is too hard, a sandbag should be used.

(ii) When the flare is touched by the porte-fire it lights immediately and burns with an intense red flame about 1ft. in length. The Observer should stand upwind of the flare and hold the porte-fire at the full extent of the arm. Care must be taken not to lean over the flare.

(111) The metal lined boxes or metal cases in which the flares are delivered are to be stored at the post for collection by the appropriate authority.

Details from the Operating Instruction on how the pyrotechnics for the Granite system were to be handled by Posts. (HQROC Operation Instruction No. 34, Appendix D, 20 January 1945, via Alistair McCann)

HOW PILOTS REACTED TO "GRANITE" WARNING

This table gives an analysis of the action taken by pilots as a result of the lighting of 521 red flares at Royal Observer Corps posts up to the 31st of March, 1945. It is a progressive table, and it will be seen that the greatest number of flares were lit in the dangerous winter months.

	Total Flares Lit	Aircraft Took No Action	Aircraft Changed Course	Aircraft Gained Height	Changed Course and Climbed
To 30th April, 1944	92	24	31	22	15
To 31st May, 1944	100	27	34	24	15
To 30th June, 1944	116	31	37	30	18
To 31st July, 1944	132	35	44	32	21
To 31st August, 1944	143	38	47	37	21
To 30th Sept., 1944	170	46	54	43	27
To 31st October, 1944	235	54	63	59	30
To 30th Nov., 1944	250	56	64	65	32
To 31st Dec., 1944	289	64	65	75	36
To 31st Jan., 1945	336	71	69	92	42
To 28th Feb., 1945	450	149	90	104	45
To 31st March, 1945	521	176	99	115	47

This table, published in the ROC Gazette by Sqn Ldr D West, indicates the value of the Granite system. (ROC Gazette, July 1947, p.24)

11
SEABORNE ON D-DAY

1944 was a landmark year in the war, and most definitely for the ROC, as several momentous events unfolded over a few weeks. To help naval anti-aircraft gunners accurately identify aircraft, D-Day would see selected volunteers onboard ships taking part in the Normandy landings. Within a few days of D-Day, the appearance of the first of Hitler's *Vergeltungswaffe* (Vengeance Weapon), the V-1, in the skies over south-east England brought a very serious new challenge to Britain's air defences.

Among the preparations for the long-planned retaking of Western Europe, massive Allied air armadas were assembled and dispatched each day and night to rain bombs on the enemy. Amid all the details of planning the landings, there was the realisation that on the many hundreds of ships that would be needed, very few had crews or anti-aircraft gunners trained in aircraft recognition, able to satisfactorily identify friend from foe. In addition, there was the disturbing intelligence that the enemy was preparing to launch large numbers of revolutionary 'pilotless aircraft' against the south-east of England, and somehow that threat would have to be countered. Meanwhile, daily life at ROC Centres and Posts continued.

Aircraft Identifiers

Whilst most Observers at Centres and Posts pursued their regular duties, another group were preparing to go to sea. Air Ministry and ROC files show that early in 1944, a decision was made to use ROC members as 'Aircraft identifiers' on Defensively Equipped Merchant Ships (DEMS) intended to take part in the Operation Overlord D-Day landings.

The initial Allied discussions were very secret, and settled on a requirement for a total of 500 Observers. Three hundred for US vessels and 200 for British manned ships.[1] The next stage was to decide who should be recruited, how they should be trained, billeted, and eventually employed during the landings.

The administration for the operation was convoluted. It involved the selected Observers being given 'leave' from the ROC to take part in the 'Seaborne' operation. Still in ROC uniform, with naval rank armbands, they were temporarily appointed as Royal Navy Petty Officers, or Chief Petty Officers and paid on that basis for the duration of their participation.

The first step in recruiting volunteers was contained in Air Ministry Confidential Order (AMCO) A.63/1944. From 28 April, this was distributed so that all male Corps members could decide if they wished to apply for the duty. Those who wanted to volunteer submitted a completed application form, accompanied by a recommendation from their Group Commandant. The terms, conditions, requirements and expected duties were all spelt out very clearly for everyone.[2] Applicants ranged in age from 17 to 70, with 1,376 applications from Observers (701 'A' and 646 'B'), plus 29 Officers, most of whom were assigned to instructional duties. 1,094 Observers reported for duty. Subsequently, 81 were rejected on medical grounds, 209 failed the 'very tough' aircraft recognition test, and eight withdrew at their own request. The remaining 796 were enrolled in the Royal Navy. Other individuals accepted temporary attachments to Posts on the south-east coast to backfill the gaps in the region left by others accepted for Seaborne.[3]

From 7 May onwards, those accepted began to arrive at the 'Depot' (the Bath Hotel,

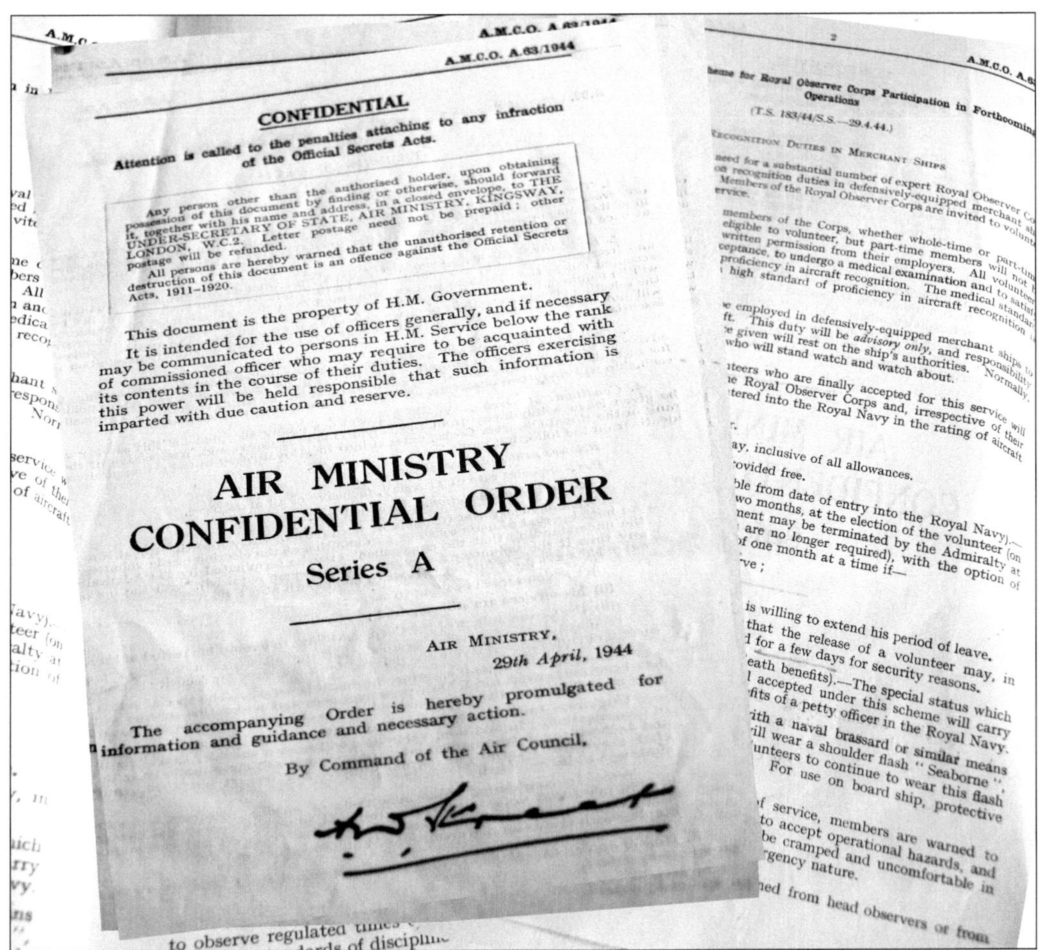

A.M.C.O. A.63/1944

CONFIDENTIAL

Attention is called to the penalties attaching to any infraction of the Official Secrets Acts.

Any person other than the authorised holder, upon obtaining possession of this document by finding or otherwise, should forward it, together with his name and address, in a closed envelope, to THE UNDER-SECRETARY OF STATE, AIR MINISTRY, KINGSWAY, LONDON, W.C.2. Letter postage need not be prepaid; other postage will be refunded.

All persons are hereby warned that the unauthorised retention or destruction of this document is an offence against the Official Secrets Acts, 1911–1920.

This document is the property of H.M. Government.

It is intended for the use of officers generally, and if necessary may be communicated to persons in H.M. Service below the rank of commissioned officer who may require to be acquainted with its contents in the course of their duties. The officers exercising this power will be held responsible that such information is imparted with due caution and reserve.

AIR MINISTRY
CONFIDENTIAL ORDER

Series A

AIR MINISTRY,
29th April, 1944

The accompanying Order is hereby promulgated for information and guidance and necessary action.

By Command of the Air Council.

2

A.M.C.O. A.6

heme for Royal Observer Corps Participation in Forthcoming
Operations

(T.S. 183/44/S.S.—29.4.44.)

RECOGNITION DUTIES IN MERCHANT SHIPS

need for a substantial number of expert Royal Observer Co
on recognition duties in defensively-equipped merchant sh
Members of the Royal Observer Corps are invited to volunt
ervice.

members of the Corps, whether whole-time or part-tim
eligible to volunteer, but part-time members will not
written permission from their employers. All voluntee
ceptance, to undergo a medical examination and to satisf
proficiency in aircraft recognition. The medical standar
high standard of proficiency in aircraft recognition

e employed in defensively-equipped merchant ships to
ft. This duty will be *advisory only*, and responsibility
e given will rest on the ship's authorities. Normally,
who will stand watch and watch about.

nteers who are finally accepted for this service will
e Royal Observer Corps and, irrespective of their
tered into the Royal Navy in the rating of aircraft

ay, inclusive of all allowances.
ovided free.

ble from date of entry into the Royal Navy).—
wo months, at the election of the volunteer (on
nent may be terminated by the Admiralty at
are no longer required), with the option of
of one month at a time if—
ve;

is willing to extend his period of leave.
that the release of a volunteer may, in
d for a few days for security reasons.
eath benefits).—The special status which
l accepted under this scheme will carry
fits of a petty officer in the Royal Navy.
ith a naval brassard or similar means
ill wear a shoulder flash "Seaborne"
unteers to continue to wear this flash
For use on board ship, protective

f service, members are warned to
to accept operational hazards, and
be cramped and uncomfortable in
gency nature.

ed from head observers or from

Air Ministry Confidential Order (AMCO) A.63/1944 was distributed to all male members of the ROC, seeking recruits to work as 'Aircraft Identifiers' on merchant ships during the approaching invasion of Europe. (TNA, AIR 16/994)

Bourne and Acklam had sailed on the *Empire Broadsword* as Aircraft Identifiers, stationed on each wing of the bridge. The ship made nine trips to Normandy. During the tenth trip, on 2 July 1944, it struck a mine close to Omaha Beach. Among the casualties that day was Obs WJ Salter, also from Acklam's Stroud Post. (Skylighters.org)

Bournemouth), where a permanent staff of ROC, RAF and Royal Navy personnel were to process them and act as instructors. There, and at a base in the New Forest, they were trained and equipped for the approaching task. As Derek Wood pointed out, most Observers were used to interacting in small units, whether at their Posts or within the larger Centre crews. To suddenly be brought together in a much larger concentration from all over the country to eat, train and relax together must have been a bit of a shock for some. By 15 May, the first had been allocated to their ships, just 16 days after the scheme was initially made known to them.

On D-Day itself, 6 June, almost 500 Aircraft Identifiers were onboard ships, usually working in pairs. By the following week, this had risen to 700. Some served for one month, but most served for two.

On board the Infantry Landing Liberty Ship SS *Empire Broadsword* were Obs Lt George AD Bourne from Watford Group and Obs Bill Acklam from 24 Group K1 Post at Stroud. Having been delayed for 24 hours because of bad weather, the *Broadsword* and other landing ships were silently joined by naval escorts as they headed towards France.

A Norwegian destroyer (the *Svenna*) was slowly overtaking them. Bourne was watching the ship when there was 'a flash, followed by a deafening explosion and a cloud of black smoke. More explosions follow, and the ship begins to sink'. In the vanguard of the assault ships, they could not stop to assist survivors and continued on to Normandy.

Dropping anchor a few miles offshore, at 05.55, 10 assault landing craft packed with Royal Marines began heading ashore from *Empire Broadsword*, part of the first wave of troops to hit the Normandy beaches. Constantly circling overhead were Spitfires and American P-38 Lightnings to provide fighter cover. As Bourne said:

> The gunners are 'itchy-fingered', each being keen to be the first to open fire. They are particularly suspicious of B-26 Marauders coming in low over the sea at zero feet to strafe the beach defences, especially as some of the big shells bursting in the water look suspiciously like bombs; but the system works, all are reported 'friendly', and the gunners hold their fire.
>
> A Douglas Boston flying in-shore, not more than 10 feet above the water's edge, lays a smoke screen which affords a brief respite for the men storming the beaches.[4]

Empire Broadsword, having unloaded its cargo, prepared to head for home, just before midday, it took on board casualties and a small number of prisoners. Part of a small returning flotilla, they slowed briefly to bury at sea a Norwegian officer, attended by a small group of his surviving shipmates, the ship's company and a Guard of Marines. Four hours later, as they approached the English coast, they saw more than 200 pairs of aircraft towing Horsa and Hadrian gliders heading towards the Continent. What they saw was most of the 256 gliders launched that night as Operation Mallard to strike inland on the Normandy peninsula.

Norfolk's Seaborne Observers

An account from the 16 Group (Norwich) wartime history provides a little more detail on training and preparations. Twenty-one members of the Group were selected for training and reported to Bournemouth.

Observers Gerry Mantripp and R Houchin, both from X2 Post, described the arrangements, 'The first test was, to many, a stiffish hurdle, and we wondered when it was over if we were really up to the task for which we had volunteered. But we must have done better than we had dared to hope, and we passed, and five days of continuous training gave us confidence in ourselves'.

L/Obs Adams of N2 (Docking Post) also had fears about the test:

> What a test – film shots, with little specks flitting one way or the other, interspersed with clearer views, but these of such brief duration. Everyone's certain that he was a 'failer', then the line up the same afternoon for the individual results, and the looks of relief, blended with unbelief, from the successful, and dejection on the faces of the unfortunates.

After more training and testing, they reported to their ship. Two were posted to each vessel and, as far as possible, the Observers were given the opportunity of choosing their partners.

Gerry Mantripp continued:

> In the charge of a Navy Petty Officer, twelve of us proceeded to London Docks through roads packed with military traffic. Owing to our boat having changed berth during

At RAF Tarrant Rushton on the afternoon of 6 June 1944, gliders and their Halifax tugs were prepared for Operation Mallard. Later, the massed formation overflew Obs Lt Bourne and Obs Bill Acklam on the SS *Empire Broadsword* as they headed home to port. (Crown Copyright)

the night, and being somewhat elusive, Ted Houchin and I were the last pair to leave the tender. Eventually, we found the SS *Fort Esperance* in the dock we had first visited. Our kit is tumbled out, and up the gangway we go to meet at the top the Officer i/c Troops, who bids us welcome, and assures us that he and his men are only too pleased we have 'come along to look after them' – it sounds little, but it helped a lot.

Then it was 'sailing orders' for D-Day. Obs AJ Adams explained:

> After joining the convoy off Southend, and slipping down the south-east coast, we were prepared for the sight of swarms of Jerry aircraft, but nothing happened in this line, although some, to their cost, got long-range shelling from the French coast round 'Hell-fire Corner.' An ear-splitting crash would thunder out, intimating that a missile had landed close, then lumps of shrapnel would zoom around, and it was noticeable that the old hands ducked quite as low, and as quickly, as the novices.
>
> After some hours, gunfire could be heard getting louder, and we gradually came in sight of a far-flung mass of shipping, with the coast of Normandy behind it.
>
> Each merchantman was directed to its anchorage and prepared to discharge its cargo of men and material. Landing craft of all sizes, up to the large 'Rhinos', came alongside, and lorries, jeeps and whatnot were slung over the ships' sides by the derricks. The sky was full of aircraft all the time, but during daylight, Jerries were conspicuous by their absence.
>
> Our mass of shipping was attacked by aircraft quite a bit at night, but although bombs fell all around, and ack-ack was heavy, this bombing was haphazard, and hits seemed few and far between.

Over the following few weeks, the two men were on the same vessel several times as it sailed between England and Normandy, carrying supplies to Allied troops ashore:

> On our last visit, we arrived and anchored off the beachhead in the early evening of Friday, July 7th, and were soon to see the sort of spectacle we had so often audibly yearned for in those night watches on the post – an RAF strafing. A low drone was followed by the appearance of a thick, broad stream of Lancasters and Halifaxes. There were still two hours of daylight, and, up on the monkey-island with our powerful binoculars, we saw Caen get it. The stuff that went down – cascades of multi-coloured incendiary leaves, followed by the HE's [sic] which throbbed in the ship after the vibration had traversed a few miles of land and a little sea: and the stuff that went up – flaming onions, ack-ack, and then luridly tinted dust and fragments. It made a never-to-be-forgotten sight; we missed nothing, not even the solitary aircraft that came down burning into the sea, although it seemed impossible for more than three out of 10 to survive that holocaust. Next morning, we heard on the ship's wireless that Caen had fallen following an attack by 400 to 500 heavies, of which one failed to return, and we remembered that, hearing such a bulletin at home, we would think – 'Ah, they daren't tell us the true losses.' But now we knew.

While most 16 Group Observers survived Overlord without a scratch, Obs SC Cranmer's (Y2 Post at East Dereham) experience was far tougher.

He boarded the SS *Cap Tourane* at Tilbury, joined a convoy at Southend, and headed to Normandy. Corvettes escorted them as motor torpedo boats and Albatrosses laid smoke screens as they passed Dover. They received a few shells from the Calais guns. The crossing was uneventful, and they reached the Normandy coast at 07.00 hours the next day. He explained:

> We were a depot and supply ship to the tiny LCVPs, and our complement was around 1,500 men. Our anchorage was one mile from shore opposite Ouistreham at the mouth of the Orne, the left flank of our whole landing assault. Jerry left us alone that day except for one FW190, which dropped two bombs fairly close, but we were attacked by Ju 88s that night.

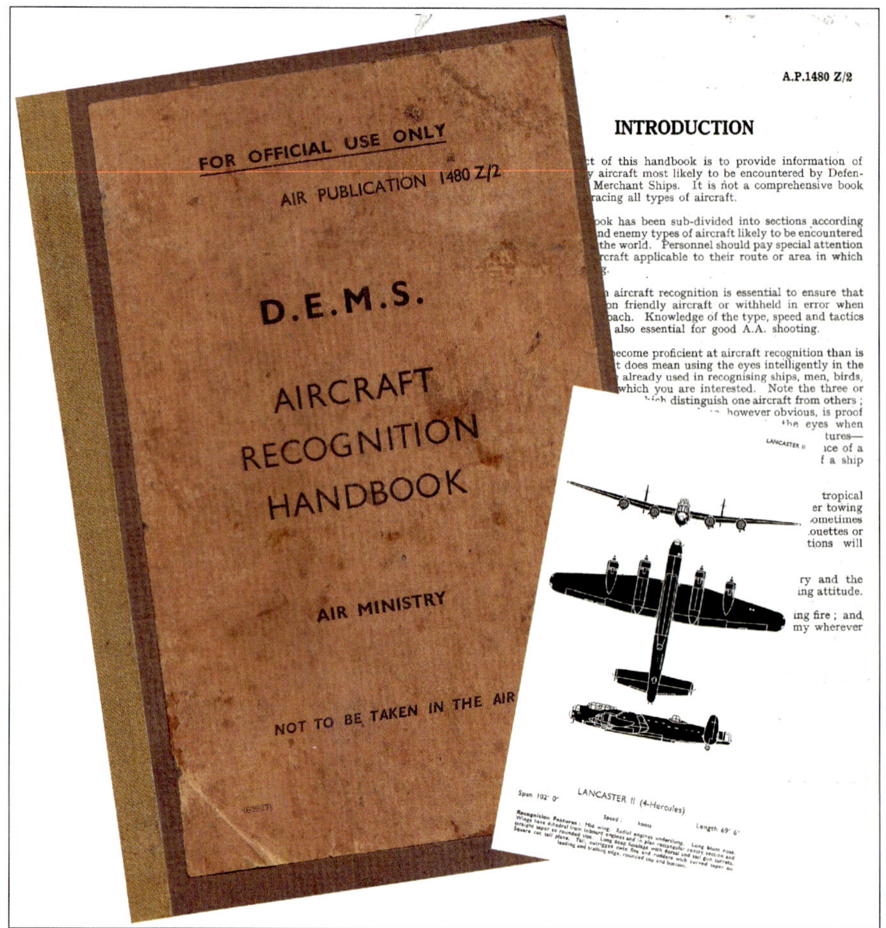

Containing silhouettes of aircraft they might well encounter, as early as March 1943, a special edition of the official aircraft recognition guide, AP1480 Z/2, was prepared for the Aircraft Identifiers planned to be on board the Defensively Equipped Merchant Ships (DEMS) that would take part in D-Day. (Crown Copyright)

The following day, he counted 15 enemy aircraft shot down and described how:

> The AA fire was a sight to remember, especially at night. Our balloon caught fire twice leaving, us beautifully illuminated as a target, but Jerry missed both times. Eventually, he hit our ship. There were 40 casualties. I was feeling seedy later, and went down with meningitis, and was shipped back to England.

Obs Cranmer was taken to a hospital in Leeds, having lost his kit. He was later transferred to hospitals in Harrogate and then Knaresborough, and did not leave hospital care until 13 October. As he said of the experience, 'We were dead scared at times…but, taking it all in, I wouldn't have missed it'.[5]

Obs Percy Heading was wounded during his Seaborne service when a shell struck the ship he was embarked on. In the hospital, he was visited by Obs Cdr WG Moore DSC, the No 2 Group Commandant in 1944. (Picryl)

Obs Heading, from 15 Group (Cambridge), J1 Post at March in Cambridgeshire, was on board the US lend-lease Liberty Ship SS *Sambut*. On D-Day, as it was heading towards Normandy, the vessel was hit by a shell from a Calais battery off Dover at 12.15. Some of the lorries and petrol cans on her deck caught fire, followed by a gelignite explosion in the hold. Troops tried to jettison some of the munitions. Within 15 minutes, the order to abandon ship was given, and by 12.45, the ship was completely abandoned and later sunk by the Royal Navy. Of 625 crew and military personnel, 136 were lost.[6]

Two Observers were killed during D-Day-related operations. In addition to Obs WJ Salter on the SS *Empire Broadsword*, Obs JBB Bancroft, of P2 Post (Blakeney) in Gloucestershire, was on the MV *Derrycunihy* when it hit a mine in the area off Sword Beach, breaking the ship in two, with the loss of 183 troops and 25 ship's crew, including Bancroft. A further 22 Seaborne Observers survived their ships being sunk, another was later injured by shell splinters and another by a V-1 which hit his ship whilst it was docked in England.[7]

Recognition

By every account, the Seaborne Observers performed their task excellently, a fact widely recognised by the RAF, the Royal Navy, the US Navy, Merchant Navy captains, senior ROC officers, and the Air Ministry. In addition to public praise, there were more comments in private about how well the DEMS ships on which most Observers served were much better disciplined and accurate in their aircraft recognition skills than those of many Royal Navy and US Navy vessels.

The most tangible recognition for the 'Aircraft Identifiers' was authorisation to wear a special 'Seaborne' flash on their uniforms. In October 1944, 10 members were singled out for a 'Mention in Dispatches', their names appearing in the *London Gazette*.[8] The Group was received at HQ ROC by Corps Commandant, Air Cde Finlay Carerar and afterwards paraded at HQ Fighter Command for ACM Sir Trafford Leigh-Mallory, who was CinC of the Allied Expeditionary Air Force for the Normandy invasion.[9]

Tragically, it was Leigh-Mallory's final official engagement before departing for a new position in the Far East. The aircraft carrying him and his wife to the Far East crashed in the French Alps on 14 November 1944, killing all 10 on board.

ACM Leigh-Mallory congratulates Obs Lt GAD Bourne on the award of his Mention in Dispatches at HQ Fighter Command with Air Cde Carerar behind. Bourne was also the officer responsible for the Windsor Post. (Whitty, p.63)

For good services as aircraft identifiers in Merchant Ships during the Invasion of France:

Mention in Despatches

Aircraft Identifier Thomas Henry Bodill, P/JS.2787 (Hucknall).
Aircraft Identifier George Alfred Donovan Bourne, P/JS.2453 (Barnet).
Aircraft Identifier Anthony William Priestley Dearden, P/JS.2360 (West Hoathley).
Aircraft Identifier John Hughes, P/JS.2394 (Mostyn).
Aircraft Identifier Derek Norman James, P/JS.2272 (Gloucester).
Aircraft Identifier Edward Jones, P/JS.2255 (Bodsari).
Aircraft Identifier Albert Edward Llewellyn, P/JS.2282 (Hirwann).
Aircraft Identifier George McAllan, P/JS.2829 (Bridge of Earn).
Aircraft Identifier John Wiston Reynolds, P/JS.2599 (Leamington Spa.).
Aircraft Identifier Joseph Douglas Whitham, P/JS.2407 (Forth).

(These awards are made as a token of the good work of those members of the Royal Observer Corps who temporarily joined the Royal Navy for this service).

The award of the 'Mention in Dispatches' to 10 representative members of the ROC for service as Aircraft Identifiers during the invasion of France was posted in the *London Gazette* of 6 October 1944.

New Recruit EJ Rudsdale

While some Observers were in training to take part in the invasion of Europe, just before D-Day in 1944, EJ Rudsdale was about to join an ROC Post in Essex. He would soon get to witness the D-Day preparations and 'flying bombs', sometimes too closely for comfort. Born in 1910, Rudsdale was a curator at Colchester Castle Museum when war broke out in 1939. Suffering from bouts of ill health, he was not conscripted for regular service but engaged in other war work. In 1944, he volunteered to become a B Class Observer and his personal journals give a detailed description of what life was like on an ROC Post as D-Day approached.

In April 1944, he phoned a contact at the local Labour Exchange to arrange his introduction to the Corps. On 19 April Rudsdale visited the new Colchester Centre on Lexden Road in the town. Waiting to be interviewed by an officer, he recorded, 'The whole place was very much in the RAF tradition. Endless girls rushing about, all in ROC uniform, obviously enjoying the nature of it'. Completing the necessary forms, he expressed his first misgivings: 'Suddenly felt very dreary about the whole affair, and I know I can't possibly make a success of it'.[10]

On 1 June 1944, Rudsdale had his first introduction to ROC Post life when he cycled to the nearby Boxted Post. Home to the P-47s of the USAAF's 56th Fighter Group, it was less than a mile and a half from Boxted airfield. Activities there produced a constant stream of movements during the daytime. Rudsdale described the Post:

> It is a small brick-built platform, about 4ft from the ground, surrounded by a brick parapet about 5ft high. On the west side is a roofed extension, making a tiny room not more than 8ft by 3ft, with a fireplace, an old desk, the seat out of a motor bus, two rifles, some shelves holding boxes of ammunition and official books, a noticeboard with a rota and the 'Post procedure' and notices about rations and clothing coupons.
>
> In the centre of the Post is the 'instrument' and the plotting table, marked off in numbered squares. The instrument is a curious thing of brass, showing heights in hundreds of feet,

Before D-Day, USAAF B-26 Marauders from the 397th Bombardment Wing at Rivenhall, just south of Colchester. All of East Anglia was covered by British and US airfields. These included the heartland of RAF Bomber Command in Lincolnshire, USAAF heavy bombers in Norfolk, Suffolk and Cambridgeshire and their light bombers and fighters in Essex. (Picryl)

> fitted with a sighting piece and various adjusting screws. The place had something of the appearance of a block-house on some remote frontier, the short drain-pipe chimney smoking and the telephone wires on little makeshift poles running away towards civilisation.
>
> I had to explain my presence, as the Centre had quite forgotten to tell anybody I was coming. However, I made myself known to the men on duty. They were very kind and explained the whole business very lucidly, although I had not been there five minutes before I realised that I was quite out of my depth. I had no idea how much depended on the ability of the individual Observer, as I had always believed there was some sort of instrument that automatically located enemy aircraft and registered their height. On the contrary, all this has to be done by the Observer himself, and I have not the slightest idea how high a plane may be.
>
> However, I stayed an hour and heard them plotting a good many planes. This Post is 'F 1', spoken as 'Fox One' (just as 'C' posts are 'Charlie', 'E' posts 'Easy' etc). The three 'Foxes' are linked together and can hear each other speaking. 'Fox 2' is near Earls Colne and can see the aerodromes at Colne and Wormingford, while 'Fox 3' is south of Sudbury and reports on Acton aerodrome, where the Flying Fortresses are stationed.

Colchester Centre members on a visit to the USAAF airfield at Boxted, close by the village, also the location for an ROC Post. The RAF and USAAF sometimes hosted visits of ROC members, an always popular move among Observers. The young man at the back in RAF uniform, wearing a forage cap, is local lad Douglas Carter. After the war, he returned and later became the Chief Observer at the Boxted Post, serving up to the mid-1980s before retiring. (American Air Museum)

Such was the density of USAAF and RAF fighter and bomber airfields in the region that virtually every Post was close to one or even several airfields. At that stage, there were plenty of rumours that the invasion of the Continent was about to begin, and on 5 June, local movements were effectively closed down as roadblocks were put in place.

Living between the USAAF's Boxted airfield with its P-47s and the 55th Fighter Group's P-38 Lightnings at nearby Wormingford, the two airfields less than five miles apart, Rudsdale heard part of the massive Allied air armada when they launched on their D-Day missions.

> **June 6 Tuesday**
>
> About 2 AM, I heard the sound of many planes warming up at Wormingford, but soon went to sleep. Woke soon after 3 AM to a tremendous roar and looked out to see the whole sky filled with 'planes, all carrying their navigation lights, dropping red and green flares in every direction. Just before four, the Boxted aerodrome lights came on, and all the Thunderbolts

took off in pairs in a series of shattering roars, coming up over the house and flashing away to the south-west. The sky was just a mass of gleaming lights of all colours, and the house trembled with the vibration of thousands of engines. Have never known the Americans to take off before dawn, so guessed this must be something big and was not surprised to hear on the 8 o'clock news that there had been heavy raids on Calais and Dunkirk and that British naval forces were off Le Havre, while the Germans had announced that landings were being attempted both by sea and air.

And so comes what we were promised was to be the great climax of the whole war, when the great Allied armies are to storm 'Hitler's fortress' and 'liberate starving Europe.'

Further up the east coast, the view was slightly different. In the runup to D-Day, the Posts belonging to 16 Group (Norwich) had witnessed firsthand the growing might of the United States Army Air Force:

Liberators and Fortresses, supported by Mustangs, Thunderbolts and Lightnings, were now going out daily in hundreds. It is a fact that posts have been known to plot 1,000 aircraft in a single four-hour watch.

These huge formations created difficulties for the ROC. There were two distinct limitations to be borne in mind: the number of tracks that could be reported by Posts and displayed on the Centre table, and the number of confirmed tracks that could be told to their customers. To overcome this, mass plotting and telling was constantly under review, and new methods were adopted.

How times have changed. To quote Reggie Ray 'Once, if 12 Spitfires were expected to enter our area, and proceed to Coltishall, all the crew were mustered, and when the planes were picked up, they felt they had done a worthwhile job. Now, with perhaps 1,500 American planes over Norfolk, and mass plotting in force, a new member were heard to observe in the Rest Room, 'Oh, there's nothing doing, only the usual Mass Raid.'

However, even at this stage, sometimes the enemy would put in an unexpected appearance:

One Saturday evening, the Luftwaffe really did get one in on us. The Americans went out at tea-time, rather later than usual, and by the time they returned, it was getting dusk. Somebody at a high level in the Luftwaffe thought quickly, realised that the Americans were not used to night flying and would be forced to land at their bases in the dark, and sent his Ju88s and other fighter-bombers back with the stream. The situation that developed when the Liberators and Fortresses switched on their lights to come in, and land could be described as almost chaotic. The Huns pounced on the Americans, and when other planes, which had not been attacked, realised the position, they were still in a quandary as to how to get down. We can perhaps count ourselves lucky that the casualties were not greater that night.[11]

On D-Day, the USAAF's P-47 Thunderbolts of the 56th Fighter Group were based at Boxted Airfield. (American Air Museum)

P-51D Mustangs of the 361st Fighter Group, line up for take off on D-Day at Bottisham. (Picryl)

Air Armada over Watford

Back in the Centre at Cassiobury Drive, Watford:

> On the eve of June 6th, 1944, the Southern Area was advised that a big 'show' was impending and that it could expect to be dealing with aircraft in very great numbers. A few hours later, 'everything but the kitchen sink' was airborne, and never before had anything been seen approaching the scale of the formation. Long Range Boards and Tables in every Centre in the South of England displayed hundreds, and in many cases, thousands of aircraft. Bombers, fighters, gliders and their tugs covered the skies until both Centre and Post Observers felt that there was no end to them. Many of the planes had navigation lights on, and this gave the impression that the RAF was certain that interception by the enemy would be negligible. It seemed to be an impertinent gesture, a nose-thumbing, expressive of defiance, and backed by the menace of sure strength.
>
> Though no official word had been given, the inclusion of gliders and tugs in the huge formations provided food for thought, and Observers guessed that the invasion of Europe had commenced. The pressure at Centre was terrific. As it happened, a crew consisting almost entirely of women was on duty at Watford, and they handled this invasion eve air traffic superbly, the plotting on the Long Range Board being especially efficient. If justification of the LRB, Mass Raid and Filter procedure were required, this D-Day traffic provided it. It would, of course, have been quite impossible to deal with such vast numbers of aircraft under the old system. The elimination of aircraft that did not need to be 'told' saved an enormous amount of work, and the Centre was able to present a clear, filtered picture to the RAF Ops Rooms.
>
> At Watford Centre, it was actually well into the early hours of D-Day before pressure became heavy. The Table was virtually empty from midnight until about 02.00 hours, when an immense force of RAF heavies swept down from the Bedford and Cambridge areas, crossed No. 17 Group, and disappeared to the south-west. There was a lull until 04.30 hours, when the USAAF staged a repeat performance using Fortresses and Liberators.
>
> Then the party really started, for while the Americans were on the way out, the RAF heavies were returning, and at one period, there were almost 2,000 bombers being plotted simultaneously. The Ops Room was in a buzz of activity, and this state of affairs continued until 07.40 hrs, when a new peak was reached. The Fortresses and Liberators returning crossed tracks with countless flights of Marauders and Bostons of the 9th Tactical Air Force, winging their way to the battle. There was no longer any doubt that the invasion of Europe had commenced. The Plotters, already close to exhaustion but stimulated by the wonderful events in which they were participating, felt that if this terrific pace was to be kept up, they would need ice water and wet towels.
>
> But at eight o'clock the relief crew took over, and then they streamed outside into the gorgeous morning sunshine and the invigorating fresh air, and above their heads and before their eyes the great formations of aircraft which they had been plotting were crossing the skies. Some mere silver specks, others skimming the rooftops, whilst the great mass were sandwiched in between. The Plotters, their eyes still dazed with fatigue, gazed with admiration and awe, and as they trudged their weary way homewards, paused constantly to view the mighty air armada. Truly, the job had been worthwhile.

However, the fear and thrill of D-Day were soon to be countered by a sudden and ominous new danger.

12
THEN CAME THE DIVERS

Historian Rick Atkinson records that 10,492 V-1s were launched at Britain between June 1944 and the war's end, most at targets in south-east England.[1] Better known to the ROC by the codeword 'Diver', it is estimated that around 2,500 of them hit in and around London. The first landed in Kent on 13 June 1944, just a week after the Normandy landings. Not widely appreciated, the detection and tracking of these 'flying bombs' was perhaps the Royal Observer Corps' greatest achievement.

From intelligence collected by agents, resistance members, and aerial photographic imagery, a considerable amount was already known about the distinctive V-1, its flight and performance characteristics. High-level preparations for the expected launch of V-1 attacks had been ongoing for some time. With many of the expected launch sites located in north-west France, discussions of them became intricately linked with the plans for Operation Overlord.[2] By December 1943, extensive preparations were underway for the arrival of these pilotless aircraft in the skies of Britain.

Early on in communications classified 'Most Secret', many questions were being posed on how to detect, monitor and deal with these new weapons. Coastal radars, Type 16 radar stations for directing RAF fighters, and ROC Centres were all to play a key role in initially identifying the pilotless aircraft as they approached the coast.[3] On detection of a 'Diver', the report was to be immediately passed to the RAF Filter Rooms. If they were first detected by the ROC, this was to be done through the ROC Liaison Officer or Plotter and to their linked RAF Sector Control. Diver warnings were to be spread across the RAF command and control system, to the Home Office War Room and to the Air Ministry. This required installing some additional communication links from ROC Groups to HQ 12 Group at Uxbridge.[4] The Operation 'Diver' warning was to remain in place until cancelled by the Duty Group Captain at HQ Air Defence Great Britain (ADGB).

Once radars were able to pick up the launch of V-1s over the French coast, their characteristic flightpath distinguished them from manned aircraft. Once reported to the RAF Filter Room, the ROC Group Sea Plotter would broadcast the DIVER-DIVER-DIVER warning to alert the Corps to go into action. (Whitty)

In late April 1944, ROC Groups across south-east England received a secret Operation Instruction, 'Detection and reporting of hostile pilotless aircraft', which was distributed to Centres and Posts on the south coast. It soon had to be spread much more widely.[5]

Operation Instruction No. 51, provided details on how Posts were to report a Diver sighting and Centres were to display them on the plotting table and the Long Range Board using a distinctive 'red circling counter before the raid designation on the raid plaque'.[6]

The account in 17 Group's *Observers' Tale* gives a good description of Operation Instruction No. 51:

> This stated that the enemy might launch pilotless aircraft against Southern England from sites in the Pas-de-Calais and Cherbourg areas, and it proceeded to outline the measures to be adopted to combat this peculiar form of attack. This amazing document provided information concerning the size, shape, performance and general characteristics of the pilotless aircraft, but so engrossed were most Observers in the matter of the impending attempt to land forces on the Continent, and so high ran the feeling of optimism generally, that the warning as to the use of this new and revolutionary weapon caused but a mild and temporary flutter. Some, indeed, were of the opinion that this weird and doubtful aircraft was a thing of imagination, deliberately conjured up for the express purpose of counteracting undue optimism regarding the probable date of the end of hostilities, and with the special intent of keeping all Observers on their toes.
>
> The code word 'Diver' had been given to cover the procedure to be employed should the strange aircraft be used, but the whole project appeared to be fantastic, and very few Observers could bring themselves seriously to contemplate such an event. Still less did they appreciate the timeliness of the warning, and it was not until two months later when the shattering impact of the first 'Diver' crashing brought a realisation of the patience and foresight which had been expended in providing such accurate information, that they fully understood how the defence authorities had worked in order to be in a position to cope with the menace.
>
> It is, of course, easy to be wise after the event, but in the spring of 1944, when the terrific Allied air assault was virtually reducing whole German cities to rubble, and the Luftwaffe's only response was feeble and infrequent, it seemed that danger of any further bombing of England, by any means, was almost out of the question. Week succeeded week, and the bogey plane did not appear, and in these circumstances, it is perhaps not surprising that although Observers assimilated the instructions for plotting the 'Divers', they doubted whether they would ever be called upon to put them into effect.

First 'Diver'

After the months of expectation, the first Divers arrived over south-east England on 13 June 1944. On duty were Observers EE Woodland and AM Wraight at the Dymchurch (M2) Post, 1 Group at Maidstone. Their Post Log read as follows:

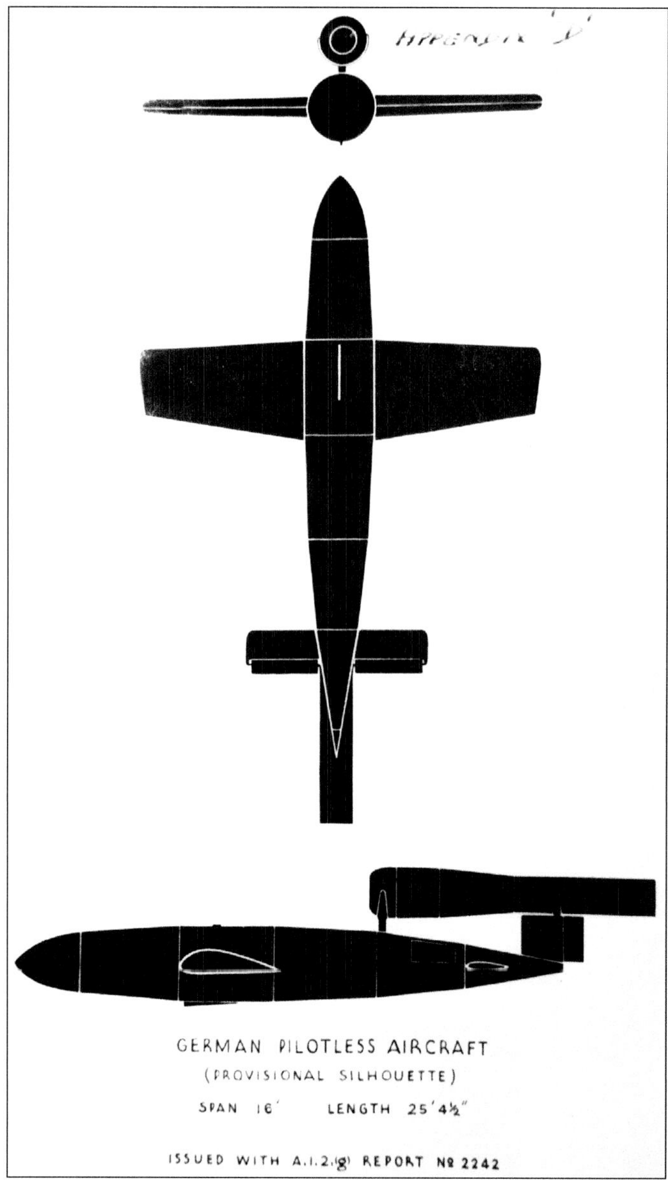

A provisional silhouette of a V-1, together with very accurate estimated dimensions, was issued to the ROC as part of Operation Instruction No. 51 in April 1944, prior to their first use in an attack on Britain. (TNA, AIR 16/449)

> 00.35 Special Vigilance off
> 00.50 Force of heavy bombers flying south
> 02.00 Local alert tested
> 03.42 Air Raid Warning. Raiders passed 04.00
> 04.05 First light 04.28, last light 23.18
> 04.08 A Diver was seen, heard and identified. N West at 1,000 feet. Plotted until lost
> 04.10 Air Raid Warning. Raiders passed 04.40
> 04.15 The Divers as seen through the binoculars show a long red rocket shape with a yellow flare and sparks leaving the tail end; the speed seemed to be that of a fighter plane. We were lucky enough to be the first Post to identify these as Divers.[7]

By the time it was five miles out from the coast, both Observers were quite certain that it was a Diver:

> Woodland reported to Maidstone Centre 'Mike Two, Diver — Diver — Diver, one four, north-west, one at one'. The plotter at Maidstone Centre was momentarily stunned, but reacted instinctively, bellowing 'Diver — Diver' across the operations room. The tellers on the balcony called 'Diver' down every line, including that to the headquarters of 11 Fighter Group, and in seconds, a further call was on its way to Bentley Priory.

As they tended to arrive in significant numbers over several hours once a 'Diver' alert was declared, it would remain in force until cancelled by the Duty Group Captain at HQ ADGB. (Whitty, p.48)

On the Maidstone Group balcony was the Air-raid Warning Officer, and within two minutes, he had set the sirens wailing. Other Posts in the Group soon plotted the Diver as did Posts in 19 Group at Bromley tracking it until the bomb suddenly dived to earth and detonated at Swanscombe, between Dartford and Gravesend.

Dymchurch plotted more Divers at 04.15 and 05.00. One V-1 went off course and was reported by Horsham Posts until it landed near a viaduct on the main London-Brighton railway line north of Cuckfield. At 07.07, the Diver alert was cancelled.[8]

The distribution of the first Diver report across the Observer Corps system was incredibly speedy. Just four minutes after the initial Diver call, at 04.12, the message was logged by C2 Watch at Colchester Group in their Centre Log.[9]

The best contemporary summary of the Corps' experiences during the use of the V-1 against Britain comes from *Observers' Tale*:

> It normally travelled below 3,000 feet and followed a straight course, with the peculiar wobbling roar of its propulsion unit and, at night, the exhaust flames from its tail clearly indicating its course. It was thus quite easy for the Corps to plot the bomb, and in fact, it was child's play compared

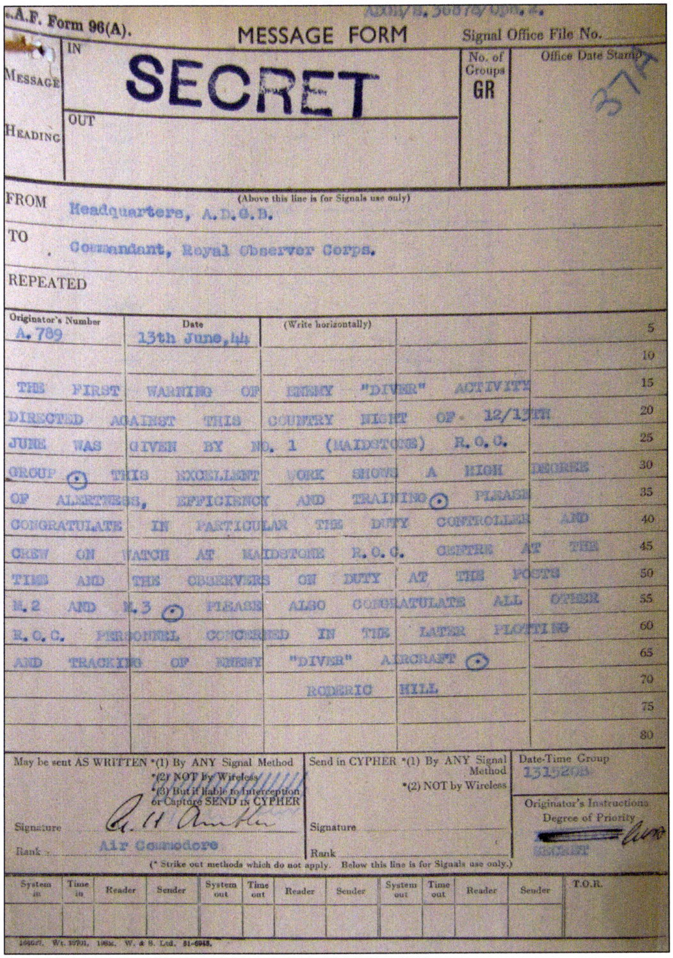

A.F. Form 96(A). MESSAGE FORM Signal Office File No.

SECRET

IN / OUT MESSAGE HEADING — No. of Groups: GR — Office Date Stamp

(Above this line is for Signals use only)

FROM Headquarters, A.D.G.B.

TO Commandant, Royal Observer Corps.

REPEATED

Originator's Number: A.789 — Date: 13th June,44 — (Write horizontally)

THE FIRST WARNING OF ENEMY "DIVER" ACTIVITY DIRECTED AGAINST THIS COUNTRY NIGHT OF 12/13TH JUNE WAS GIVEN BY NO. 1 (MAIDSTONE) R.O.C. GROUP ⊙ THIS EXCELLENT WORK SHOWS A HIGH DEGREE OF ALERTNESS, EFFICIENCY AND TRAINING ⊙ PLEASE CONGRATULATE IN PARTICULAR THE DUTY CONTROLLER AND CREW ON WATCH AT MAIDSTONE R.O.C. CENTRE AT THE TIME AND THE OBSERVERS ON DUTY AT THE POSTS M.2 AND M.3 ⊙ PLEASE ALSO CONGRATULATE ALL OTHER R.O.C. PERSONNEL CONCERNED IN THE LATER PLOTTING AND TRACKING OF ENEMY "DIVER" AIRCRAFT ⊙

RODERIC HILL

May be sent AS WRITTEN *(1) By ANY Signal Method *(2) NOT by Wireless *(3) But if liable to interception or Capture SEND IN CYPHER

Signature [signature]

Rank Air Commodore

Send in CYPHER *(1) By ANY Signal Method *(2) NOT by Wireless

Signature

Rank

Date-Time Group 131520B

Originator's Instructions Degree of Priority SECRET

(* Strike out methods which do not apply. Below this line is for Signals use only.)

System in	Time in	Reader	Sender	System out	Time out	Reader	Sender	System out	Time out	Reader	Sender	T.O.R.

The ROC Commandant received a congratulatory message from HQ ADGB, later that day, on the Corps' handling and reporting of the first Diver arrival. (TNA, AIR 16/449)

to the usual work of tracking fast fighters operating at 20,000 feet.

London was the target for the flying bombs, and though less than one in three reached the capital, a great deal of damage was done. Many tributes have been paid to the work of the Royal Observer Corps, but it is probably true to say that in the plotting and tracking of the flying bombs, it performed one of its most useful functions. At the time, it was difficult for some Post Observers in the London area to feel that they were making any useful contribution, but from every point of view, it is apparent that the Corps rendered most valuable service.[10]

Issued the day before D-Day, Operating Instruction No. 54 from HQROC detailed the special circuits that were then in the process of being installed between designated RAF Ground Control Intercept radar stations and paired ROC Centres to speed communication and provide the GCI stations with indications and clarifications of aircraft flying within their coverage area.

The Corps' accurate and careful reporting was very important during the early phase of the V-1 offensive, the RDF system were far less effective than expected for the first few weeks. Both by their distinctive shape and noise, Posts were able to accurately detect the V-1s day and night. To speed the interception response, the RAF quickly placed Forward Controllers at both the Maidstone and Horsham Centres and, using VHF radios, spoke directly to the fighters that accounted for the destruction of more than 200 V-1s alone.[11]

The wisdom of distributing Operations Instruction No. 51 more widely than originally thought necessary became apparent just a few days later. On 16 June 1944, L2 Post at Woolverstone in Suffolk, further north, reported the first sighting of a Diver in that Group's area.[12]

In addition to ROC warnings, RAF fighters, anti-aircraft guns a huge number of barrage balloons were concentrated around London, as another line of defence against V-1s aimed at the city. (Via Picryl)

The Chain Home and Chain Home Low systems had difficulty in recognising the V-1s, often failing to detect those launched from the Dieppe area until they were well over the sea.[13] It took the next few weeks to reposition radar and anti-aircraft guns, and to establish fighter patrol lines to make the defences far more effective as the V-1 offensive ramped up.

Back in Colchester, EJ Rudsdale's journals give a feel for what it was like at an ROC Post during a 'Diver' attack. Once it had been detected, usually, but not always, by a coastal Post, the Group Controller could give a rough pre-warning to other Posts of their approach. However, that could not compare to hearing and seeing V1s as they neared, and hopefully, passed by before their engines cut off and they dived, exploding as they struck the ground.

Rudsdale was a member of 'Fox 1' Post at Langham/Great Horkesley, less than two miles from the US Army Air Force airfield at adjoining Boxted and home of the 56th Fighter Group, equipped with P-47 Thunderbolts. Being new to the Corps and inexperienced, he was always paired with a much longer-serving colleague. Being a 'B' Class man and having to work during the day, he often drew shifts in the early hours, from 1 to 5 AM. Until the advent of the V1s, these would generally have been considered 'quieter' shifts, hearing the return of RAF bombers from their night missions. From Rudsdale's journal:

July 23 Sunday

Got to the Post before one AM. A few minutes later, a huge mass of bombers came in, back from a raid. After the planes had gone, all was quiet for more than three hours, hardly a thing about. The Centre shut off and went to supper. We had our tea and sandwiches, and old Diaper (who was on with me) had just gone out to wash up. I had the phones on when suddenly Centre came through to say that two Divers were crossing the coast at Bradwell. The Controller said, 'Fox One and Two, you may be able to see them. They're going west'. I called Diaper, and we looked through the glasses and saw two little golden balls, far away to the south, as if they were crawling along the ground. Suddenly heard a voice say: "My God, look! There's another one there, heading straight at us!" And another voice said: "No, it's turning – it's over Jig Three now, more towards Horkesley". Then a third voice: "That's the one that came in over Walton: A pause, then the first voice called: Look out! Fox One! There's a Diver coming up to the east of you!' I said: 'OK, Centre".

Looked east and saw a big light, like a comet, leap over a tree, apparently half a mile away. I said into the microphone: 'Christ, here it comes, Centre, south of the Post, on 47, about 500 feet, going west'. It sailed by us, slightly south-west now, with a steady glow and a deep, low roar, which seemed to follow some little way behind the light. I logged it across our circle. It did not seem to be moving very fast; in fact, dear old Diaper remarked: 'That don't seem to move no quicker'n a fast trot', and passed out of sight towards Fordham. I stood on the coping of the Post, with a slight feeling of bewilderment and a sort of wonder that we were still all there.

Heard no explosion, but Centre said it had crashed about 35 miles away, somewhere in the direction of Brentwood. Although it sailed right over Langham and Wormingford aerodromes, not a shot was fired at it. Perhaps the Americans were too surprised to move.[14]

September 23 Saturday

To Post at 9pm. A clear, starlit night and not very cold. Thought the quiet too good to last, and Diver came on before 10pm, before we had had any tea.

A few Mosquitoes came around, and then we saw a Diver to the north-east, over Dedham way, in a cone of searchlights. It seemed to track along the river, over Stoke Church, at great speed but not very high, its light huge and flickering. One of the Mosquitoes suddenly dived from about 3,000ft, with lights on, tracer squirting. We both cheered. Nothing happened. The plane did it again and had another shot. Still, the Diver went on steadily until it suddenly flared up into a great ball of fire, tongues of flame shooting out all around. It seemed hours before the flame finally went out, and then another few seconds passed before the Diver crashed on the marshes, a wave of scarlet flame flecked with silver flowing up behind the trees. There was a tremendous explosion, and the Post shook so that the flame of the lamp ducked down. 'Well', said old Diaper,

A V-1 drops on a city. The V-1 was unguided, its range determined simply by the fuel load on board, it would simply cut out when all the fuel was gone and drop on whatever was below. (NARA)

'That was a piece, I must say!' Then he reported the thing out – 'Fox One, Diver crashed on 3547, about 3 miles north-west of the Post'. We were breathing again until Diaper heard over the phones that another Diver was coming up on the same line as the first. We saw it, a third behind it. Both rushed by, about a mile north of us and disappeared from view like twin comets.

Diaper, still on the phones, suddenly said, 'Christ! They've got Easy One!' and told me he had heard Easy One say the third Diver had cut out to his east, almost above him and then his voice shouting, 'We're baling out, Centre!' after which his line was silent and did not answer to repeated calls from Centre and the other two Easys. We were both very shaken and saw, in imagination, two little figures dropping over the wall of the Post and running away across the wet fields, lit by the flame of the explosion. 'Ah well', said Diaper, 'maybe they're alright. P'raps it's just brought the wires down, so they can't talk'. We said nothing more about it, but we were both thinking, 'it might have been us'.

There were two more flashes far away, beyond Hadleigh, and then Diver was off, and the first 'all clears' came through. 'Good', I said, 'now we can have a cupper char. Reckon we deserve some', and old Diaper replied, 'Kettle's on the boil'. So we sat drinking out of the big mugs (tea too strong as usual), staring at the notices on the brick wall in front of us, about Gas and Recognition tests and so forth, both still thinking about that shout of 'We're baling out, Centre'.[15]

We have no record of what happened to the crew at Easy One, because Rudsdale departed for Yorkshire the next day, although no casualty records for the locality on that day can be located.

The Corps were not immune to casualties from the V-1 with members killed when they were off duty when their homes were struck. The Chigwell Post members experienced some of the worst of the Diver attacks. 'During 1944-45 every member's house received some enemy damage. Nine had to leave their houses because they were destroyed or made uninhabitable'. Five members were killed and two more seriously injured. The last was Obs S Bostock who was killed by a flying bomb.[16]

It was only in early September that the V-1 offensive began to slow, as Allied forces overran launch sites across France, Belgium and into the Netherlands. Then a new twist emerged with the air-launched V-1s from He 111s. Over 1,200 V-1s would be launched this way between September 1944 and January 1945 targeting London, Southampton, and Gloucester. The air-launched V-1s sometime gave radar little time to warn of their approach, especially against Norfolk and Suffolk.[17]

On Christmas Eve 1944, 50 He 111s launched weapons at Manchester, although only one reached the city. Many of the V-1s fired during this period fell in the Colchester Group's area.

One extraordinary escape was reported on 5 November 1944, when at 20.24, a somewhat shaken Observer from H1 Post on the coast at Aldeburgh reported to Colchester that 'Diver 286' had passed 'within zero feet of the Post, with the motor still running', and torn through the adjacent AA battery, crashing into their tents and setting them alight. Fortunately the ammunition heaped near the Post nor the V-1 warhead detonated. 'Permission was given to evacuate the Post, but the crew decided to stay put'. Later, it was discovered that the V-I had hit one of the guns and the warhead had split apart without exploding. The fire was caused by fuel from the V-1 tanks.

The last air-launched V-1 to strike Britain came down at Hornsey in North London, during the early hours of 14 January 1945. The last land-based-launched V-1 to reach Britain came from a site in Holland on 3 March 1945, hitting Bermondsey in London.[18]

To air-launch V-1s, the Luftwaffe modified a number of He 111s to carry them under one wing. Launches began on a small scale from mid-June 1944 and the tempo gradually increased. The missions against Britain were flown over the North Sea at low level, at night. They would fly a designated heading aimed towards their target, climb to around 1,500 to 2,000 feet, start the ramjet and release the V-1 on its way. (NARA)

13
WAR'S END AND STAND DOWN

While the Allies were pushing through Europe and even as 'Divers' were striking across the south-east during the rest of 1944, thoughts in Whitehall began turning to what would follow the defeat of Germany. What that future would be like was incredibly uncertain. However, before that, there were more immediate challenges.

Codename Big Ben

In addition to the hunt for the V-1 through Operation Crossbow, intelligence began to be received about a new missile, codenamed 'Big Ben', that became better known as the V-2. When it became operational, its performance made it way beyond anything that existing defences could hope to deal with. A 2,200lb warhead, able to travel 55 miles skyward and at a max speed of over 3,500 mph, meant no existing defences could counter it. Its only limiting factor was its comparatively short range of just over 200 miles. As the Allies pushed into Europe, they quickly overran many launch sites, but it took much longer than hoped before they finally pushed the missiles out of range of England. The first V-2 landed at Chiswick on 8 September 1944, to the surprise of most. In total, some 517 would hit London, and another 537 would strike 11 other English counties. They caused considerable destruction, killing 2,754 people and injuring over 6,500. More would fall on Belgian cities.

Although they could do nothing to counter V-2s, ROC Posts did sometimes see evidence of their rocket trails as they were launched from the Continent. They took a bearing and elevation on the missile if they could, and reported the points of impact if missiles landed nearby. They could be seen over incredible distances. Some Posts in the Manchester area reported V-2 rocket trails over London, around 200 miles away, during a night attack on 29 November 1944.[1]

Being pushed out of range of London, 43 V-2s were aimed at Norwich between September and mid-October 1944. We have a slightly more detailed account of how they affected the ROC from Norwich Group. The city was first targeted on 25 September 1944, followed by one on the next day, and three on 27 September.

The Norwich Group's Centre had this description of V-2 explosions in its wartime history:

> After hearing the first few posts' reports, they realised what they were and did not like them. One minute all would be peace and quiet, and the next minute would come a tremendous double explosion, which would be so unexpected and shattering that your heart would jump into your mouth, and a cold sweat would come out on your forehead.
>
> It was rotten for the chaps on the posts, but it was far worse for the girls in the Centre. There might be nothing on the table, then one post would report an explosion, the plotter would put down an explosion counter, then another post would give the same report, then another, and the rash of explosion counters would gradually work outwards, like the ripples when a stone is thrown into a pond, until half the table was covered with them, all pointing to one spot. This might happen several times in a day, and it must be remembered that these girls knew all there was to know about the rockets by now, and they realised that they were right in the middle of the target, and that at any minute, without warning, one might land on top of them. We had heard it said that, when girls were first introduced into the Ops Room, that they would panic and be useless in a blitz; these critics were completely confounded by the girls' behaviour during the rocket period. They were grand.[2]

Despite their supposed limited range, the last V-2 to strike British soil was at Orpington in Kent on 27 March 1945.

The Luftwaffe's Last Gasps

Whilst air attacks on Britain were certainly reducing, it was still too early for the air defences to relax totally. In Lincolnshire, as late as

The launch of V-2s could be seen at huge distances. This remarkable shot captures two V-2s heading towards London, launched from a site near The Hague, in the Netherlands. They were photographed from the Noorderlaan in Antwerp, nearly 50 miles away. (https://www.v2rocket.com/start/chapters/antwerp.html)

3–4 March 1945, the Luftwaffe launched a mass night operation of low-level penetrations of the British air defences between Northumberland and Oxfordshire. They hit some 14 RAF bomber airfields and intended to shoot down RAF bombers at their most vulnerable as they prepared to land at their home airfields. As Obs Jack Perotti Kelway was driving to 11 Group's L1 Post (Hackthorn), very close to RAF Scampton, his car was hit by a Ju 88 as the German bomber struck telegraph poles in an apparent misjudged strafing attack on the vehicle, killing Kelway and the aircraft's four crew.[3]

On the same night in Norfolk, between 30 and 40 hostile aircraft appeared over the Group. Their purpose was, in part, propaganda and to surprise and shoot down returning RAF bombers:

> Not dropping any weight of bombs, but mostly concerned with the shooting up of any likely objective. Obs Lt Flack, driving along the Market Road into Swaffham, was startled to see a stream of tracer fire hit a truck just ahead of him. The traffic all pulled up, and an ATC boy was killed. Another hostile swept low over R1, firing its cannon.[4]

The next evening, some of the German bombers returned.

To ensure that Bomber Command received immediate warning of intruder activity, the Observers used the 'Bugs' procedure. As soon as a Post believed German intruder activity was taking place, they would pass the codeword to Centre, which would then send it to Bomber Command, and that warning would be immediately passed to the threatened airfields.

The last bombs were dropped on Norfolk on 20 March 1945, at RAF Swanton Morley. Afterwards, C/Obs Shoesmith of W3 (Guist) Post reported that:

> A hostile approached from the north, passing over the post at about 1,500 ft. The lights in an empty hangar on the aerodrome were full on, and the western doors were wide open. We reported this to the Centre, but they were not extinguished; in fact, they were not put out till the raid was nearly over.

The Ju 88 returned, passed over the Post at 500ft and made three more runs over the airfield before dropping its bombs, but it did not aim for the lit-up hangar. That was the last the Group saw of the Luftwaffe.[5]

From July 1944, some parts of the Group ROC network began to scale back activities slowly, although 10 and 11 Groups maintained full operations. It was not until April 1945 that nine ROC Groups in the north were released and 'stood down'.

Whilst everyone looked forward to VE Day, the Observer Corps was warned that it might be necessary for it to remain in operation in order to 'defend the country against possible air incursions by uncontrolled elements of the German Air Forces'. In those last few days, the most important work done by many Posts, including those at Watford's Toddington Post, was plotting the many Dakotas returning to Britain with released prisoners of war on board.[6]

It was not until 17.00 hours on 12 May 1945, four days after VE Day, that the telephone lines and the teleprinters of the Royal Observer Corps finally went silent as the organisation finally stood down after the last signal 'CEASE PLOTTING'.[7]

MESSAGE FROM THE COMMANDANT

TO ALL MEMBERS BEING STOOD DOWN.

We shall all view the demobilisation of the Corps with mixed feelings, feelings of pride and feelings of regret: regret that post and centre are shortly to be empty and silent: regret that our slowly acquired skills must be laid aside: regret that many friendships and associations will be broken. Everyone of you may take pride, however, in the knowledge that the Corps has fulfilled the great responsibility laid on it in 1939, and fulfilled it successfully.

For very many of you it has been a long hard task, especially to those already sorely-tried who willingly gave hard-earned hours to the Corps and so to the Royal Air Force. For all of you it has been a task demanding qualities of courage and patience, self-sacrifice and loyalty, a sense of responsibility and, above all, a determination to see the job through. Especially during these last few days have these qualities shown their worth. Fighter Command's call to stand-by at readiness with them has been answered and you have not let them down.

The Observer Corps mobilised in 1939 quietly and almost unknown. Through these six years it has grown and developed, adapting itself and its methods to the ever increasing needs of the Royal Air Force. And today the Royal Observer Corps can claim to have completed successfully its important and vital part in the Air Defence of the country. The proof of that lies in the fact that the Corps will go on.

To many of you the invitation to carry on will be more than welcome: to some it will be a challenge: and to others who are weary it is at least a compliment. To all of you I need say no more than that the name you have won is so high and that you are wanted as co-guarantors of an efficient peace-time system of defence.

The days of peace lie before us now and perhaps at first may be as difficult and trying as those of war. There must be a few of us to whom the Corps has not given something: a sense of comradeship, an opportunity for service, for devotion and for self-sacrifice, a common cause for which to strive. The problems of peace will demand these qualities no less than did war.

Go out and take the traditions and spirit of the Royal Observer Corps with you. You may well be proud of them.

Good luck to you all!

Finlay Crerar

Air Commodore,
COMMANDANT.

Headquarters,
Royal Observer Corps,
Bentley Priory,
Stanmore, Middx.

11th May, 1945.

With the German surrender a few days before and many services already stood down, much of the ROC had remained on duty 'just in case'. On 11 May 1945, the eve of stand down, Commandant ROC, Air Cde Finlay Crerar sent a carefully crafted message of thanks to all the Observer Corps members recognising their wartime service and sacrifices and already hinting at an uncertain future. (Via Alistair McCann)

ROC 'Ensign'

In the summer of 1945, there was a discussion about presenting an 'ensign' to the ROC. Even using the term became caught in officialdom and the College of Arms, given the organisation's status as a civilian body, rather than a military one. By 4 June 1945, the design of the 'ensign', incorporating the Elizabethan beacon lighter, was submitted to the Palace for approval, which was soon granted.[8]

As the ensign was to be presented at a ceremonial parade, it was to be handmade in silk by Hobson and Sons of London for the sum of £75, plus £4 10 Shillings for the case.[9] There was considerable pressure to get it finished in time for the parade planned for 24 June 1945, and Hobson's put in considerable effort to meet the urgent deadline.

As the beacon lighter design for the ensign had never been approved by the King, it was also submitted to King George VI for royal approval at the same time as the flag design. A now rather dog-eared black and white copy of those designs, signed by the King, remains in the ROC's official files. (TNA, AIR 2/6874)

DEDICATION AND PARADE

The ROC got to formally parade its new ensign just once, before entering stand down. In recognition of its wartime service, the Air Ministry held a massed ROC rally at RAF North Weald from Saturday, 23 to 25 June 1945. Over 1,800 personnel from all Groups across the country were invited. On Saturday, over 40 British, US and German aircraft were parked around the airfield for the Observers to look over, with Dakotas providing joy rides over London. On Sunday, 24 June, there was a large airshow and at 18.00 hours a parade. The gathered Observers formed into a large open square and the new ROC ensign was presented by Lord Beatty, Under-Secretary of State for Air, and dedicated at this special service. The ensign was carried by Obs Lt James Pollock VC, accompanied by C/Obs BJ Phillips and Obs CE Farrow.[10]

Taking the salute during a march past, Lord Beatty paid tribute to the unfailing devotion to duty which the Corps had shown during the war before members marched past, accompanied by the band of the RAF.

The dedication of the ROC 'ensign' at RAF North Weald on 24 June 1945, as part of a national stand down parade. (AHB)

A Gloster meteor runs in during the Airshow at RAF North Weald for members of the Royal Observer Corps on 24 June 1945. (Picryl)

The Way Ahead?

In September 1944, plans were put forward for the demobilisation of the ROC upon the end of hostilities. It was to be done in such a way as 'not to involve any disintegration of the Corps, and to ensure it could, if necessary, be brought into full operation again at short notice in the event of another emergency'. As the stand down took place, nearly 32,000 Observers were on strength in May 1945, of whom just over 24,500 expressed a willingness to serve again in a post-war organisation.[11]

Within parts of the RAF, especially at ADGB, there was the view that radar would not make any great technical leap forward to justify permanently doing away with the Corps. There were also concerns about radar's vulnerability to emerging electronic warfare. An immediate post-war analysis of German air defences by the RAF showed that, as the war progressed, the Germans had become increasingly reliant on their own, much simpler observer system for information because of the success of Allied electronic warfare. This potential vulnerability to electronic warfare would be an important argument for retaining the Observer Corps within the British peacetime air defence network.[12]

Thus, the Corps entered a period of 'care and maintenance' that was a form of limbo. Whilst this saw the retention of some 230 full-time staff, there were a few cluster meetings and some participation in public events, including airshows, at a sort of 'semi-official' level, but there was no operational training or exercises.[13] By the end of December 1945, it was becoming clearer that the ROC would be retained in some form, and staffing arrangements began to be put in place more suited to peacetime, with a reduction in the number of full-time officers and a shift toward part-time senior staff.

Even a year later, during May 1946, the big decisions about air defence remained undecided. However, the Air Council was very aware that until those decisions were made, efforts needed to be made to prevent the Corps from completely 'disintegrating'. Because it was relatively inexpensive, the ROC was to be retained until the fundamental policy decisions were taken.[14] There were suggestions that the Corps be disbanded as a civilian organisation and instead incorporated into an element of the RAF's reserves.

The move towards reactivation came on 15 November 1946, when the recently appointed Corps Commandant, Air Commodore Lord Bandon, wrote to the former Observers who had previously expressed a willingness to re-enrol. With it went a pamphlet on the new terms and conditions of service including a three-year commitment to serve and 36 hours of training per year. The following day, Government minister Herbert Morrison made a BBC broadcast encouraging new recruits for the Corps.[15]

As 1947 began, the ROC was to be gradually resuscitated; premises were dusted down and essential repairs carried out, and training arrangements put in place. There was even a brief period of alert when, in early 1947, there was intelligence that the 'Stern gang', a violent element of the Israeli independence movement, was thought to be planning to drop explosives from light aircraft over London. On the afternoon of 5 September 1947, the Horsham and Maidstone Groups were called out, and some 267 ROC personnel were on duty within four hours. Connected again to the 11 Group Fighter Command Filter Room, they reported aircraft movements whilst fighters maintained standing air patrols. Just after midnight, the alert was called off when the gang members were captured by the Paris police.[16]

Whilst there were domestic agonies about the future of British air defences and the shape of the ROC, far away, there were more fundamental forces at work. In Eastern Europe, there was the imposition of communist governments, the souring of relations with the USSR, and soon, the Berlin blockade and airlift. Combined, these would see the Soviet Union quickly emerge as the primary security threat to Britain and Europe. That fear was exacerbated with the Soviets' first atomic weapon test in August 1949. It ushered in a new climate of fear, in which the Soviet air threat became existential to the nation's survival.

To properly defend Britain, there was again a need for highly effective air defences, one in which the Royal Observer Corps would still have a role. As the Cold War developed, and the Soviet nuclear spectre grew, the Royal Observer Corps would adapt too. It would become a modest but significant role, part of the UK's plans to address this new horrific dimension to total war.

BIBLIOGRAPHY

Galland, A, *The Battle of Britain*, translation by RAF AHB, https://www.raf.mod.uk/what-we-do/our-history/air-historical-branch/ahb-translations-from-captured-german-documents/the-battle-of-britain-by-general-adolf-galland/

Grehan, J, *Royal Observer Corps: The 'Eyes and Ears' of the RAF in WWII, An Official History* (Frontline Books: Barnsley, 2017)

Hamilton, T, *Identification Friend or Foe: The story of aircraft recognition* (HMSO: London, 1994)

House of Commons Library, *Summary of the Decisions reached by the SoS Air after review of certain questions relating to the status and conditions of service*, April 9, 1941, (HoC)

Jones, I, *Tiger Squadron, The story of 74 Squadron, RAF* (WH Allen: London, 1954)

Kinsey, G, *Seaplanes – Felixstowe* (Terence Dalton: Lavenham, 1978)

Pearson, C, *EJ Rudsdales Journals of Wartime Colchester* (History Press: Cheltenham, 2010)

RAF Air Historical Branch, *The Royal Observer Corps* (Military Library Research Service, Buxton: undated)

Weinberg, GL, *The Foreign Policy of Hitler's Germany: Starting World War II, 1937-1939* (Chicago: Chicago University Press: 1980)

West, D, 'Operation Granite', *The ROC Gazette*, Vol 2, No 1, July 1947, pp.21–24

Whitty, HR, *Observers' Tale: The Story of Group 17 of the ROC* (Roland Brothers, London: 1950)

Winslow, TE, *Forewarned is Forearmed* (William Hodge & Co, London: 1948)

Wood, D, *Attack Warning Red: The Royal Observer Corps and the Defence of Britain 1925 to 1992* (Carmichael and Sweet, Portsmouth: 1992)

Further Reading

For those interested in reading in a lot more details about the ROC's part in the Second World War, the Whitty, Winslow and Wood books listed above are by far the most detailed.

ENDNOTES

Chapter 1

1 TNA, AIR 2/3492, Encl 2A, Major and Minor Exercises, 1939.
2 TNA, AIR 2/3492, 26th June, 1939, HQ Fighter Command, Instruction No 1 for No 11 (F) Group Home Defence Air Exercise, Ref: FC/S.16770/Ops, 8/9 July 1939.
3 https://www.britishpathe.com/asset/151450/ (Accessed 6 August 2025).
4 TNA, AIR 2/3492, 'Minutes of Conference held at HQ Fighter Command, on Monday, 24th July, 1939 to discuss the Group Air Exercises', Ref: FC/S.17051/Ops, 2nd August, 1939.
5 Derek Wood, *Attack Warning Red: The Royal Observer Corps and the Defence of Britain 1925 to 1992*, (Carmichael and Sweet, Portsmouth: 1992), p.57.
6 TNA, AIR 2/3492, FC/S.17183/Ops. 29th July, 1939. 'Report on Home Defence Air Exercise, 11 Group Area. 8/9 July, 1939'.
7 TNA, AIR 2/3492, 'Report on Home Defence Air Exercise, 12 Group Area. 13/14 July, 1939', August 2nd, 1939.
8 RAF Air Historical Branch, *The Royal Observer Corps*, (Military Library Research Service, Buxton: undated). Also available online at https://www.raf.mod.uk/what-we-do/our-history/air-historical-branch/second-world-war-thematic-studies1/ (Accessed 11 August 2025).
9 Wood, pp.57–58.
10 *Auckland Star*, Volume LXX, Issue 181, 3 August 1939, p.11.
11 https://asn.flightsafety.org/wikibase/179353 (Accessed 4 August 2025).
12 *Evening Post*, Volume CXXVIII, Issue 37, 12 August 1939, p.9. References from, Dave Homewood, https://www.key.aero/forum/historic-aviation/127554-battle-of-britain-in-august-1939?page=0 (Accessed 6 August 2025).
13 TNA, AIR 16/995, No 19 Centre, Bromley, Kent, Log Book No 1.

Chapter 2

1 Cabinet Minutes March 18, 1939, quoted in Weinberg, Gerhard L, *The Foreign Policy of Hitler's Germany: Starting World War II, 1937-1939*, (Chicago: Chicago University Press: 1980), p.542.
2 TNA, CAB 24/288/28, p.9.
3 TNA, CAB 24/288/29.
4 18 Group, Colchester, Centre Log 24-25 August, 1939. Hampshire County Archive, ref: 36M96/C18/1/1. Exactly the same message is recorded in the 19 Group, Centre Log. TNA, AIR 16/995, No 19 Centre Bromley Kent, Log Book No 1.
5 TNA, AIR 16/1018, p.10.
6 TNA, AIR 16/1018, p.3.
7 TNA, AIR 16/1018, p.10.
8 TNA, AIR 16/1018, pp.12–13.
9 Winslow, p.57.
10 Tim Hamilton, *Identification Friend or Foe: The story of aircraft recognition*, (HMSO: London, 1994), p.57.
11 TNA, AIR 27/527/3, p.2. and TNA AIR 27/527/2
12 TNA, AIR 27/1018/2, p.8.
13 Hamilton, p.79.
14 18 Group, Colchester, Centre Log, 6 September 1939, 36M96/C18/1/1.
15 Nick Black, 'The Battle of Barking Creek', *Epoch Magazine*, No. 1, September 2020. https://www.epoch-magazine.com/blackbattleofbarkingcreek. (Accessed 26 August 2025)
16 TNA, AIR 16/995, Bromley Log entry, September 26, 1939.
17 18 Group, Colchester, Centre Log, 7 November 1939, 36M96/C18/1/2.
18 Derek Wood, pp.64–65.
19 Wood, p.67.

Chapter 3

1 These images are now held by the National Council of Aerial Photography and have been digitised and can be viewed via their website: at www.ncap.org and https://www.raf.mod.uk/what-we-do/our-history/air-historical-branch/second-world-war-thematic-studies/photographic-reconnaissance-vol-i-1914-april-1941/ p.335
2 Gordon Kinsey, *Seaplanes – Felixstowe*, (Terence Dalton: Lavenham, 1978), pp.25–27.
3 Wood, pp.66–67.
4 TNA, AIR 16/1018, pp.10–11.
5 TNA, AIR 16/1018, p.15. Centre Log, 18 Group Colchester, May 18, 1940, Hampshire County Archive, 36M96/C18/1/08.
6 TNA, AIR 16/980, documents relating to the 'Status of the Observer Corps'.
7 TNA, AIR 16/980, Brassards, Ref: OC/S.18, 19 May, 1940.
8 TNA, AIR 16/980, Commandant OC to Ops 2, SASO, file OC/S18, 20 May, 1940.
9 TNA, AIR 16/980, S.2838/S.5.E, Air Ministry to Commandant, Observer Corps, June 4, 1940. Ref: OC/S.18 Commandant OC to Under Sec State Air Ministry (S5E), August 1940.
10 TNA, AIR 16/1018, p.16.
11 HR Whitty, *Observers' Tale: The Story of Group 17 of the ROC*, (Roland Brothers, London: 1950), p.17.
12 TNA, AIR 16/980, PWD24/2/3 MP Murray, Air Ministry, Draft Circular, 14 August, 1940.
13 Wood, p.88.
14 TNA, AIR 16/1018, p.14. Centre Log, 18 Group Colchester, May 10, 1940, Hampshire County Archive, 36M96/C18/1/08.
15 Centre Log, 18 Group Colchester, May 10, 1940, Hampshire County Archive, 36M96/C18/1/22, rear cover.
16 Rear inside cover, Centre Log, 18 Group Colchester, June 1, 1940, Hampshire County Archive, 36M96 C18 1 23.
17 For example in Centre Log, 18 Group Colchester, June 1, 1940, Hampshire County Archive, 36M96/C18/1/09.
18 TNA, AIR 16/1018, p.14.
19 Winslow p.61
20 TNA AIR 16/1000, June 19, 1940
21 TNA, AIR 16/1018, p.17.
22 TNA, AIR 16/1000, June 19, 1940.
23 Winslow, p.266.
24 TNA, AIR 16/1000, June 19, 1940.
25 Ira Jones, *Tiger Squadron, The Story of 74 Squadron, RAF*, (WH Allen: London, 1954), p.220.
26 TNA, AIR 16/49, Air Ministry to AOC Fighter Command, Ref: S.61453/04, May 4, 1940.

Chapter 4

1 RAF Air Historical Branch, *The Royal Observer Corps*, (AHB1(RAF)S259, 1973), pp.50–51.
2 TNA, AIR 16/50, AOC Fighter Command to USoS AM, Ref: FC/S.15111/Ops.2(b), August 18, 1940.
3 RAF Air Historical Branch, *The Royal Observer Corps*, (AHB1(RAF)S259, 1973), pp.50–51.
4 Adolf Galland, *The Battle of Britain*, translation by RAF AHB, p.19, https://www.raf.mod.uk/what-we-do/our-history/air-historical-branch/ahb-translations-from-captured-german-

documents/the-battle-of-britain-by-general-adolf-galland/ (Accessed 26 October 2025).

5 Galland, *The Battle of Britain*, p.13.

6 RAF Air Historical Branch, *The Royal Observer Corps*, (Military Library Research Service, Buxton: undated), pp.50–51.

7 TNA, AIR16/218, *Success of 'Observer Corps Spitfire'*, November 24, 1940, Ref: 11G/s.456/Ops.

8 Wood, pp.121–122.

9 TNA, AIR 27/1680/31 310 Squadron ORB, November 19, 1941.

10 This extended account of the Corps part in the Battle of Britain draws heavily on HR Whitty, *Observers' Tale: The Story of Group 17 of the ROC*, (Roland Brothers, London: 1950), pp.10–11, edited lightly for continuity.

11 Whitty, *Observers' Tale*, pp.9–11.

12 Centre Log, 18 Group Colchester, July 15, 1940, Hampshire County Archive, 36M96/C18/1/10.

13 Detailed in *London Gazette*, January 9, 1946. He was awarded his ROC Medal in 1950 and clasp in 1962.

14 TNA, AIR 16/218, Southern Area Commandant, Ref: SA/551.

15 A more thorough account of the action that day can be found at https://battleofbritain1940.com/entry/sunday-18-august-1940/ (Accessed 28 October 2025)

16 Grehan, p.43.

17 Whitty, pp.11–12, edited lightly for continuity.

18 Whitty, pp.49–50.

19 The National Archive, https://www.nationalarchives.gov.uk/education/resources/british-response-v1-and-v2/ (Accessed 1 September 2025).

20 Wood, p.105, Whitty, pp.49–50. https://focus52.blogspot.com/2011/08/aldwych-aftermath-of-v1-attack-world.html (Accessed 8 December 2025).

21 18 Group, Colchester, Centre Log 15 June, 1940. Hampshire County Archive, ref: 36M96/C18/1/09.

22 TNA, AIR 16/1018, p.25.

23 Wood, p.94.

24 TNA, AIR 20/3537, Battle of Britain, ROC.

25 TNA, AIR 20/3537, Battle of Britain, ROC.

Chapter 5

1 RAF Air Historical Branch, *The Royal Observer Corps* (Military Library Research Service, Buxton: undated), pp.50–51.

2 RAF Air Historical Branch, *The Royal Observer Corps*, Appendix IV.

3 TNA, AIR 16/1018, p.25.

4 Winslow, p.62.

5 TNA, AIR 16/1018, p.16.

6 Grehan, p.39.

7 T Hamilton, *Identification Friend or Foe: The story of aircraft recognition*, (HMSO: London, 1994), pp.80–84.

8 Wood, p.115.

9 Hamilton, p.96.

10 Wood, pp.1–6.

11 Wood, p.263.

12 TNA, AIR 16/219, *To Sqn Ldr McNeil, GIO, No 11 Group*, December 12, 1940.

Chapter 6

1 Pearson, C, *EJ Rudsdales Journals of Wartime Colchester*, (History Press: Cheltenham, 2010), p.47.

2 TNA, AIR 16/1018, pp.11–12.

3 TNA, AIR 16/1018, p.25.

4 HR Whitty, *Observers' Tale: Post Stories*, p.19.

5 TNA, AIR 2/19920, *Wigram to Hamilton, Ref: SA/144/1/AIR*, April 30, 1943.

6 TNA, AIR 2/19920.

7 Mosquito PR Mk IX, MM249, of 140 Squadron crashed on 15 July 1944. Having completed its photo reconnaissance mission over France, the aircraft was returning to base when one of its engines failed. During the forced landing in bad visibility at Windsor Great Park both crew were killed.

8 HR Whitty, p.31.

9 TNA, AIR 2/19920, *HQ ROC to HQ Southern Area, ROC*, ROC/420/17E.4, December 5, 1945.

10 TNA, AIR 2/19920, *Gowrie to HQ Southern Area ROC, SA/17/E.4*, December 21, 1945.

11 TNA, Air 16/1018, p.28.

12 Royal Observer Corps, Hansard, HC Deb 9 April 1941, vol 370, cc1549–50.

Chapter 7

1 Wood, p.124.

2 TNA, AIR 8/713, *Sholto Douglas to CAS*, Ref: ROC/S500/3/Org, September 10, 1942.

3 RAF AHB, *The Royal Observer Corps*, Appendix IX, pp.2–3.

4 RAF AHB, *The Royal Observer Corps*, Memorandum No. 5, Paras 2 and 3.

5 RAF AHB, *The Royal Observer Corps*, Memorandum No. 5, Para 15.

6 TNA, AIR 2/9304, *IVH Campbell, S5 Air Ministry to CROC*, October 8, 1943.

7 TNA, AIR 2/9304, *CROC to US of S (S5 E)*, REF: ROC/1103/2/P3, October 20, 1943.

8 TNA, AIR 2/9304, *WA Davey to CROC*, REF: ROC/1103/2/P3, February 10, 1944.

9 Whitty, pp.16–17.

10 TNA, AIR 16/1018, p.56.

11 TNA, AIR 16/1018, p.58.

12 Whitty, p.24.

Chapter 8

1 TNA, AIR 16/990, *ROC Committee, Notes on 1st Meeting held on Wednesday, 29 January, 1941.*

2 TNA, AIR 16/990, *Report of the Committee on the Observer Corps (Revised Draft)*, February 19, 1941.

3 TNA, AIR 16/991, *Notes on Some Observer Corps Complaints*, Minute No. M.14, Ref: IG/329, February 9, 1941.

4 TNA, AIR 2/9304, *Minute J Whitworth Jones for PS to PUS*, March 10, 1942.

5 TNA, AIR 2/9304, *Secret, Note on Reorganisation of the ROC*, Enc 7A.

6 *Hansard*, Observers (Uniform), August 21, 1940, Vol 364.

7 Copy of: *ROC, Summary of the Decisions reached by the SoS Air after review of certain questions relating to the status and conditions of service*, April 9, 1941. Supplied by House of Commons Library.

8 *Hansard*, HC Deb December 10, 1941, Vol 376, C1505.

9 TNA, AIR 2/9304, *AM Sholto Douglas to CAS*, WSD/C.71, April 22, 1942.

10 TNA, AIR 2/9304, *AM Sholto Douglas to CAS*, WSD/C.71, April 22, 1942.

11 TNA, AIR 2/9304, *Memo on ROC Centre Policy, Appendix A*, p.1.

12 TNA, AIR 2/9304, *AM Sholto Douglas to CAS*, WSD/C.71, April 22, 1942.

13 TNA, AIR 2/9304, *Ambler, CROC to Air Ministry US of S*, Ref: ROC/S.500/ORG, July 20, 1942.

14 TNA, AIR 8713, CAS to CinC Fighter Command, September 18, 1942.

15 TNA, AIR 2/9304, *ACM Douglas to Air Ministry US of S*, Ref: FC/S.27788, 10 July, 1942.

16 TNA, AIR 2/9304, *ACM Douglas to Air Ministry US of S*, Ref: ROC/S.500/ORG, October 21, 1942.

17 RAF AHB, *The Royal Observer Corps*, p.129.
18 RAF AHB, *The Royal Observer Corps*, pp.130–131.
19 Hansard, HC Deb, 25 November 1942, vol 385 cc 698–701.
20 ROC Manual 1943
21 Wood, p.129.
22 RAF AHB, *The Royal Observer Corps*, p.190.
23 Wood, p.155.
24 TNA, AIR 2/9304, *Minute PS to PUS*, June 8, 1943, Enc 9A.
25 TNA, AIR 2/9304, CROC *Finlay Crerar to IVH Campbell, Air Ministry S5*, Ref: CROC/DO/ROC, August 27, 1943.
26 TNA, AIR 2/9304, *Robertson to Air Cde Crerar*, August 23, 1943.

Chapter 9

1 Wood, pp.102–103.
2 Wood, p.104.
3 TNA, AIR 16/984, *Minutes of a Meeting at the Air Ministry Whitehall on 27th May 1941 to Discuss Plans for the Establishment of an Air Raid Reporting System in Northern Ireland.*
4 The Republic established the 'Marine and Coast Watching Service' in 1939. A network of 83 Look Out Posts (LOPs) were built around the coast of Ireland, manned by members of the Local Defence Force. The Coastwatchers were responsible for identifying and reporting on shipping and aircraft movements and any communications between ship and shore.
5 TNA, AIR 16/984, *Formation of Observer Corps in Northern Ireland*, Ref OC/S.59, April 1, 1941.
6 TNA, AIR 16/984, *CROC to S H Knight, Communications Dept, GPO London*, Ref: OC/S.59, April 2, 1941.
7 TNA, AIR 16/984, *Minutes of the Second Meeting of the Planning Sub-Committee to Consider the Air Defence of Northern Ireland held on the 30 June 1941 at the Air Ministry, Whitehall*, p.1.
8 RAF AHB, *The Royal Observer Corps*, p.110.
9 RAF AHB, *The Royal Observer Corps*, p.116.
10 Whitty, pp.45–46.
11 RAF AHB, *The Royal Observer Corps*, pp.118–120.
12 Winslow, p.155.
13 Wood, p.125.
14 *Supplement to the London Gazette, 9 January 1946*, p.318. http://eastlothianatwar.co.uk/Radio%20Security%20Services.html (Accessed 18 November 2025).
15 TNA, AIR 16/5357, *DF Ops*, Ref: S.75272, January 14, 1942.
16 TNA, AIR 16/5357, *Minutes of Meeting held in the Air Ministry, Whitehall on February 17, 1942, to decide ROC Centre Policy.*
17 TNA, AIR 16/5358, AIR 16/5359.
18 Winslow, pp.101–102.
19 Wood, p.136.
20 Whitty, p.25.
21 TNA, AIR 16/5357, *Report 257, Visit to 9 & 10 Observer Corps Centres at York on May 7, 1942, by the Inspector General.*
22 TNA, AIR 16/1018, pp.35–37. These pages from the Norwich Group history, contain excellent firsthand accounts of events at the Centre during the Baedeker raids in 1942.
23 RAF AHB, *The Royal Observer Corps*, pp.81–84, Grehan, pp.66–71.
24 RAF AHB, *The Royal Observer Corps*, p.85.
25 Wood, pp.141–42, RAF AHB, *The Royal Observer Corps*, p.86.
26 Grehan, pp.125–126.
27 Winslow, p.108.
28 RAF AHB, *The Royal Observer Corps*, pp.87–89.
29 Wood, pp.143–144.

Chapter 10

1 Wood, p.152.
2 Wood, p.78.
3 TNA, AIR 16/248, RAF Kenley to HQ 11 Group, March 13, 1941, Ref: KEN/S/42/Air.
4 TNA, AIR 16/1018, p.32.
5 This is illustrated in the Air Ministry film on the 'Scope and Purpose of the Filter Room', https://www.youtube.com/watch?v=RGwUn07EHmg (Accessed 1 December 2025)
6 Wood, p.149.
7 Whitty, (Post Section), p.47.
8 TNA, AIR 16/1085, p.55. https://www.americanairmuseum.com/archive/media/media-19260pdf, https://www.norfolkwreckresearch.co.uk/project-page (Accessed 1 December 2025).
9 *RAF History of the ROC*, p.143.
10 TNA, AIR 16/1018, p.40.
11 Winslow, pp.102–103.
12 *The Second World War, 1939-1945, RAF, Signals: Vol 5, Fighter Control and Interception* (RAF AHB: 1952), p.81. https://www.raf.mod.uk/what-we-do/our-history/air-historical-branch/second-world-war-thematic-studies/signals-vol-v-fighter-control-and-interception/ (Accessed 19 November 2025).
13 *The Second World War, 1939-1945, RAF, Signals: Vol 5, Fighter Control and Interception*, p.82.
14 Wood, p.145. 10/L4 Keyingham and 10/G2 Driffield; 11/K3 Louth and 11/G1 Old Leake; 18/C3 Lexden and 18/H3 Orford; 16/V2 Brundall, 16/N2 Docking and 16/Q3 Melton Constable; 14/E1 Halesworth.
15 TNA, AIR 16/1018, p.41.
16 Grehan, pp.79–81.
17 TNA, AIR 16/1018, p.42.
18 Whitty, p.19.
19 TNA, AIR 16/1018, History of 16 Group, Norwich, p.30. https://aircrewremembered.com/mcveigh-charles.html (Accessed 18 November 2025).
20 TNA, AIR 16/1018, p.72.
21 TNA, AIR 16/1018, p.40.
22 Winslow, pp.231–232.
23 HQROC Operation Instruction No. 34, Appendix A, 20 January 1945- via Alistair McCann
24 Winslow, p.190.
25 D. West, 'Operation Granite', *The ROC Gazette*, Vol 2, No 1, July 1947, pp.21–24. https://thetimechamber.co.uk/beta/wp-content/uploads/2017/04/granite.pdf (Accessed December 2, 2025).

Chapter 11

1 TNA, AIR 16/994, Employment of ROC Personnel in Merchant Vessels During Operation 'Overlord.' Minutes, April 5, 1944, p.1.
2 TNA, AIR 16/994, AMCO A.63/1944, pp.1–4.
3 RAF Air Historical Branch, *The Royal Observer Corps*, pp.159–163.
4 Whitty, pp.54–57.
5 TNA, AIR 16/1018, pp.61–64.
6 English Heritage, https://thewreckoftheweek.com/2014/06/06/no-55-sambut/ (Accessed November, 2025)
7 Wood, p.163.
8 *London Gazette*, October 6, 1944, Supplement 36738, P.4639.
9 Whitty, p.60.
10 EJ Rudsdale, p.167.
11 TNA, AIR 16/1018, p.65.

Chapter 12

1 Rick Atkinson, *The Guns at Last Light: The War in Western Europe, 1944-1945*,(Abacus, London: 2013), Vol 3, pp.110–111.
2 TNA, AIR 16/449, *ADGB provisional and Concurrent Air Defence Plan for Operations 'Overlord' & 'Crossbow'*. Ref: ADGB/MS.36661/Ops 5B, February 18, 1944.

3 Codewords 'Pikestaff', and 'Crossbow' were provisionally employed during early discussions. 'Big Ben', was used as an early codename for 'enemy long range rockets' that became the V-2. TNA, AIR 16/449 ADGB/S.33834/Ops 2(b), March 11, 1944.
4 TNA, AIR 16/449 Appendix B, *ADGB provisional and Concurrent Air Defence Plan for Operations 'Overlord' & 'Crossbow'.*
5 TNA, AIR 16/449, *Detection and Recognition of Pilotless Aircraft*, Ref: *HQROC* Operations Instruction No. 51, ROC/S.501/OPS, April 22, 1944.
6 TNA, AIR 16/449, p.4.
7 Winslow, p.271.
8 Wood, p.8.
9 Centre Log, 18 Group Colchester, June 13, 1944, Hampshire County Archive, 36M96/C18/1/51.
10 Whitty, pp.26–27.
11 Wood, p.172.
12 Winslow, p.267.
13 TNA, AIR 16/449, *Inter-Departmental Radio Location Committee, Minutes June 20, 1944*, Ref: IDRC (44) 4th Meeting, p.2.
14 EJ Rudsdale, pp.179–180.
15 EJ Rudsdale, pp.189–190.
16 Whitty, p.29. (Post section), p.47.
17 Winslow, p.157.
18 Wood, pp.175–176.

Chapter 13

1 Wood, p.178.
2 TNA, AIR 16/1018, pp.69–70.
3 Winslow, pp.229–230. Wood, p.178, http://www.roc-heritage.co.uk/1940s-into-war.html (Accessed November 20, 2025).
4 TNA, AIR 16/1018, p.72.
5 TNA, AIR 16/1018, pp.72–73
6 Whitty, (Post Stories), p.44.
7 Wood, pp.180–181.
8 TNA, AIR 2/6874, AM to JD Heaton Armstrong, HM College of Arms, June 4, 1945.
9 TNA, AIR 2/6874, Hobson & sons to AM, June 30, 1945. Ref: CM 18/242.
10 https://www.eppingforestdc.gov.uk/app/uploads/2024/01/spirit-of-north-weald-booklet-7.pdf (Accessed, 16 December 2025). Whitty, pp.31–32.
11 TNA, AIR 2/5701, *ROC, Proposals in Regarded to Post War Organisation*, Ref G.114241, p.1.
12 Wood, pp.185–186.
13 Wood, p.189.
14 TNA, AIR 2/5701, *Conclusions of the Air Council*, May 2, 1946.
15 Wood, p.190.
16 Wood, p.191.

ABOUT THE AUTHOR

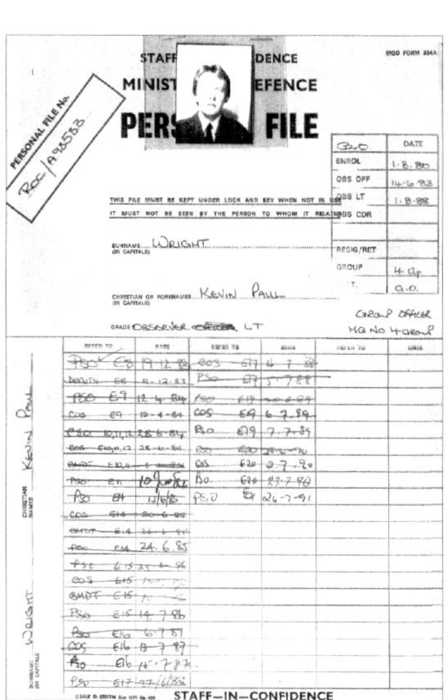

MOD FORM 334A

STAFF ... DENCE

MINIST ... EFENCE

PERS ... FILE

PERSONAL FILE No. ROC/A93583

THIS FILE MUST BE KEPT UNDER LOCK AND KEY WHEN NOT IN USE

IT MUST NOT BE SEEN BY THE PERSON TO WHOM IT RELATES

SURNAME (IN CAPITALS) WRIGHT

CHRISTIAN OR FORENAMES (IN CAPITALS) KEVIN PAUL

GRADE OBSERVER LT

	DATE
ENROL	1.8.80
OBS OFF	14.6.83
OBS LT	1.8.88
OBS CDR	
RESIG/RET	
GROUP	4 Gp
	G.O.

GROUP OFFICER HQ No 4 GROUP

STAFF—IN—CONFIDENCE

Kevin Wright joined the Royal Observer Corps in March 1980, initially as a member of Colchester 42 Post at Woolverstone in Suffolk. From 1983 until stand down in 1991, he was a Group Officer responsible for five underground monitoring posts in rural South Suffolk and North Essex.

Today, having taught Cold War history, international security and politics, he is now a regular contributor to several UK aviation magazines. Other Books for Helion have included *The Collectors*, two books on CIA, British and Taiwanese U-2 operations. Other publications have included books on Cold War aerial intelligence and contemporary military aviation.

His research interests include a special interest in CIA aerial operations, reconnaissance and 'spyflights'.